T0228643

MIND
CONTROL

BOOKS PREVIOUSLY PUBLISHED

by Dr. Haha Lung

The Ancient Art of Strangulation (1995)
Assassin! Secrets of the Cult of Assassins (1997)
The Ninja Craft (1997)
Knights of Darkness (1998)
Lost Fighting Arts of Vietnam (2006)

Written with Christopher B. Prowant

Shadowhand: Secrets of Ninja Taisavaki (2000)
*The Black Science: Ancient and Modern Techniques of Ninja
    Mind Manipulation* (2001)

Written as "Ralf Dean Omar"

Death on Your Doorstep: 101 Weapons in the Home (1993)
Prison Killing Techniques: Blade, Bludgeon & Bomb (2001)

Written as "Dirk Skinner"

Street Ninja: Ancient Secrets for Mastering Today's Mean Streets (1995)
X-Treme Boxing: Secrets of the Savage Street Boxer (2002)
    with Christopher B. Prowant

MIND CONTROL

Dr. Haha Lung

CITADEL PRESS
Kensington Publishing Corp.
www.kensingtonbooks.com

CITADEL PRESS BOOKS are published by

Kensington Publishing Corp.
119 West 40th Street
New York, NY 10018

Copyright © 2006 Haha Lung

All rights reserved. No part of this book may be reproduced in any form or by any means without the prior written consent of the publisher, excepting brief quotes used in reviews.

Neither the author nor the publisher assumes any responsibility for the use or misuse of the information contained in this book.

All Kensington titles, imprints, and distributed lines are available at special quantity discounts for bulk purchases for sales promotions, premiums, fund-raising, educational, or institutional use. Special book excerpts or customized printings can also be created to fit specific needs. For details, write or phone the office of the Kensington sales manager: Kensington Publishing Corp., 119 West 40th Street, New York, NY 10018, attn: Sales Department; phone 1-800-221-2647.

CITADEL PRESS and the Citadel logo are Reg. U.S. Pat. & TM Off.

First printing: August 2006

25 24 23 22 21 20 19 18 17

ISBN-13: 978-0-8065-4077-1
ISBN-10: 0-8065-4077-X

Printed in the United States of America

Library of Congress Control Number: 2005938610

Electronic edition:

ISBN-13: 978-0-8065-4078-8 (e-book)
ISBN-10: 0-8065-4078-8 (e-book)

To Agnes Shifferly and Shirley Marsee

To Charles and Carolyn Shumway

To Chaplain Bob Gibson and Attorney Norman Sirak

To Eric Tucker, Eddie Harris, and

The Warriors of the Zendokan

CONTENTS

INTRODUCTION:
"The More Things Change"

Approximately 2,500 years ago a certain prince of India named Siddhartha successfully deciphered the basic nature and fate of mankind. His conclusions: Life pretty much sucks and we cause our own problems because we either can't—or else refuse to—control our desires.

Around the same time a little farther north, a Chinese soldier named Sun Tzu, already a veteran of a dozen bloody military campaigns, was also busy collecting and cataloging observations and insights into the human condition.

Both these men were eventually able to peer into the collective mind of mankind, to successfully discern the facts, fancies, and foibles that motivated and manipulated their fellows.

That's where the similarity between these two early "psychologists" ends. Disappointed and depressed by his discoveries, Prince Siddhartha abandoned his kingdom to become a penniless wanderer. Sun Tzu, on the other hand, finally finished jotting down his astute observations on human strengths and weaknesses, compiled them into his *Ping Fa*, "The Art of War" and was soon offering his considerable insight and skill into human nature to the highest bidder.

Sun Tzu went on to become the greatest strategist China—and perhaps the world—ever produced. His *Art of War* is still considered the most insightful and applicable treatise on warfare ever written.

Two men, Sun Tzu and Siddhartha, both gave us invaluable information into the inner workings of the human mind; two men whose observations and conclusions about human behavior propelled them in radically different directions, leading them to completely different ends.

Sun Tzu's skill at manipulating not just individuals but entire armies—his own as well as the enemy's!—allowed him to rise from obscurity to become China's greatest general. Sun Tzu died peacefully in his sleep after a long and illustrious life during which he used his insights into human nature to win fame and fortune.

In case you're wondering, ex-Prince Siddhartha also did all right for himself. He eventually found peace of mind, changed his name to "the Buddha," and won worldwide acclaim as a great teacher of "enlightenment" . . . before eventually being poisoned to death by one of his many less "enlightened" enemies. Perhaps an enemy who had read Sun Tzu's *Ping Fa?*

So you see, it's not only *what you know,* it's *what you do* with what you know.

One man, an idiot, will accidentally cut himself if you hand him a sharp knife. Another man, desperate for food or driven by whisperings of some inner demon, might suddenly put that same knife to your throat. Still another man, perhaps schooled in medicine, might in an emergency adroitly wield that same knife as a makeshift scalpel to save your life.

As with the knife, so with knowledge.

Black Science (Lung and Prowant, 2001) made a convincing argument that "knowledge is power," that the more you know, the more "intelligence" you gather about yourself and your enemy, the better your chances of first *surviving* and then *prospering* in a world where increasingly the dish du jour is dog-eat-dog!

Black Science taught you how to size up a potential enemy by his "shadow-talk" (his body language, choice of words, etc.). You also learned how to discern and decipher what emotions, hopes, and fears dominate him. How to tell if he's being truthful . . . or just full of it. And, most important, what deep, dark personal secrets he is so desperate to keep hidden from the light of day.

Rest assured, you'll get your money's worth of more mind-bending tactics, techniques, and tricks in this volume. But our only giving you a keen knife of knowledge isn't enough. Learning *how* and *when* to wield such a "dangerous" weapon, *that* is the secret to dissecting the mysteries of the mind—both your own, as well as the mind-set and motivation of your enemy.

What's that you say? You don't *have* any "enemies"? That's what your enemies *want* you to think!

Do you know why psychology, hard-sell advertising, con games, cult-recruiters' spiels, police interrogation techniques, lovers' lies, and hypnosis all work?

Because every one of us—bar none—is 100 percent convinced these mind-manipulation "tricks" won't work on *us*!

And we're all 100 percent wrong. They will—and do—work on us every day.

So many shady characters, from used-car salesmen to enemies we don't even know we have, daily use such distractions, devices, and devious ploys to get their foot in your door, their hand in your pocket, and their you-know-what in your panties!

But, relax, all these techniques—and a score more—also work on your enemy. And like you, he's 100 percent certain they don't work on *him*. Heh-heh-heh.

Once having mastered these techniques, you'll be well prepared to "go to work" on your enemy. That is, if you master these techniques *before*, and *better* than, your enemy does!

By the way, if calling them your "enemy" offends your sensibilities, call them "competitors" instead. For in truth, we are all in competition, each of us with our fellows. Oft times it is to our advantage to work together for the common good. Sometimes there really is safety in numbers. Other times, you're on your own. Root hog or die. Hell take the hindmost!

Whatever our ultimate goal, altruistic or opportunistic, it behooves us to keep abreast of the latest findings in the field of "Black Science," from recently unearthed ancient Tibetan manuscripts teaching "forbidden" mind-control techniques, to modern computer microchips implanted in the heads of the unsuspecting.

And we learn from our enemy. Hopefully before he gets the upper hand by wresting *our* most closely guarded secrets away from us.

We also learn much from studying master "mind-slayers" of the past. Thus, in the present volume, we study and steal the tactics and techniques of not just accomplished Asian masters like Sun Tzu and Buddha, Yoritomo and Musashi of Japan, and various East Indian masterminds, but also from less well known, but no less accomplished Middle Eastern masters such as Jesus Sirach and Abdullah ibn Maymum—the sinister ninth-century "father" of modern Middle Eastern terrorism.

To balance out our study, to satiate our hunger for *useful* knowledge, we'll also prick the brains and pick clean the bones of Western master-minds—both the infamous and the only slightly less so; master mind-benders as diverse in method and motivation as Rasputin, billionaire J. Paul Getty, and that acknowledged Western master of ruthless strategy, Machiavelli.

But rather than nitpicking apart their differences, we will search for similarities in their methods, their motivations, and, yes, perhaps their madness.

Many of you will resent, resist, and ultimately reject the idea that over two millennia after Sun Tzu the lot and lusts, goals and gullibilities of collective man have changed so little, that plots and ploys in use 2,500 years ago on the other side of the world are just as effective today on this side of the world. Or that such "outdated" schemes and skulduggeries could still possibly work on *you*. Heh-heh-heh.

Ultimately the prize goes to the swift and the well studied. Of course, sometimes being *sneaky* helps!

And when the smoke finally clears, and the awards—and indictments!—are handed out, will you find yourself the *winner* . . . or only the *thinner*?

Part I

PERCEPTION AND POWER

"Man, your head is haunted!"

—Max Stirner, anarchist

 Introduction

Be realistic! How can you expect others to deal with you honestly, reasonably, or at least logically, when you can't even trust your own mind to faithfully serve you, to acquire information accurately, and to arrive at reasonable and logical conclusions as to the actual nature of the world around you?

Read the following sentence *out loud*:

FINISHED FILES ARE THE
RESULTS OF YEARS OF SCIENTIF-
IC STUDIES COMBINED
WITH YEARS OF EXPERIENCE.

How many "F's" are there in the sentence you just read? Count them. . . . Don't use your finger.

Now count them again, because *you're wrong*.

There aren't just three, there's actually *twice* that many. There are six, but everyone initially sees only three because our minds see (i.e., "hears") the word "OF" not as "O"–"F" but as "O"–"V," pronounced "UV."

So don't panic, "seeing" only three "F's" means your brain is functioning perfectly normal.

How often have you heard, "The hand is quicker than the eye," or "My eyes were playing tricks on me"? Any trip to a David Copperfield performance will validate both these statements.

Like a thirsty man stumbling across the desert, how many times have you mistaken a mirage for a miracle, optical illusions for opportunities?

Look at the three vertical, slightly slanted lines in Figure 1:

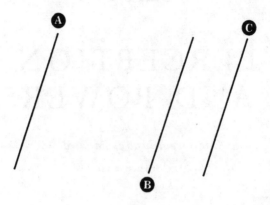

Figure 1.

Which is the greater distance, that between points A and B, or between points B and C? Your eyes (and your "common sense") tell you it's farther from A to B than from B to C. Your eyes lie. Measure the distance. It's the same.

What about the horizontal lines in Figure 2? Do they appear "slanted" to you?

They're not.

Now study the mandala meditation design in Figure 3 for a few seconds:

Does the mandala appear to be vibrating or oscillating?

Figure 2.

2

Figure 3. Mandala

Of course, you "know" it's not really moving. And this is an example where your logic ("higher reasoning") overpowers your (false) perception. All too often however, it's the other way around, with faulty perception (false impressions) winning out.

There's always a reason why we mis-perceive, why our senses sometimes "lie" to us. Sometimes Mother Nature is to blame, other times it's Father Nurture's fault.

Bet you'd say the white inner square is bigger than the black inner square in Figure 4?

That's because Nature designed us (our eyes, our brain) to give priority

3

Figure 4.

to perceiving lighter outlines and forms to help us better pick out lighter shapes against darker backgrounds, increasing our chances of surviving at night.

Thus the white square is "more important" to our brain and we "see" it as "bigger."

Now compare the two lines in Figure 5:

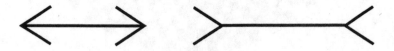

Figure 5.

Does the line on the right look longer than the line on the left?

Big surprise, they're the same length.

We see the line at the right in Figure 5 as longer because it resembles the angles of a room, growing "larger" (i.e., longer) as it expands toward us. (See Figure 6.)

Likewise, we see the left line in Figure 5 as "shorter" because it reminds us of lines (e.g., streets) moving away from us. (See Figure 7.) Our brain (common sense again!) tells us that when things recede into the distance they become "smaller."

Think your peepers are the only one of your senses you can't trust? Chemicals in food trick our taste buds all the time ("I can't believe it's not butter!").

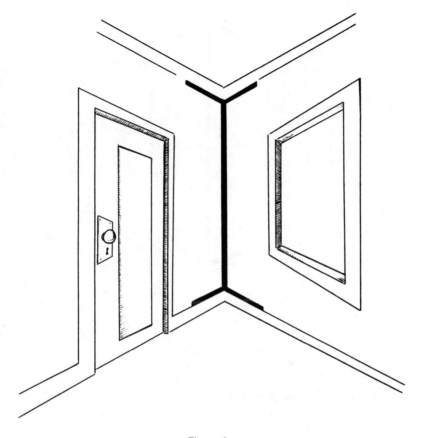

Figure 6.

Faux fur and fake fabrics confuse our sense of touch. And our ears? Can we really believe what we're hearing? How often do we actually notice the nuance that distinguishes sincerity from scheming?

The '60s trickster Abbie Hoffman tried to warn us, "Believe nothing you see and only half what you hear . . . and have your ears examined at least once a month!"

And it's not just your five senses, *your whole body betrays you*. For example, someone asks you to describe a spiral staircase and—before you can stop yourself—your index finger is dancing circles in the air. *Everyone* does it.

Your involuntary blush of embarrassment, that sudden lump of tension

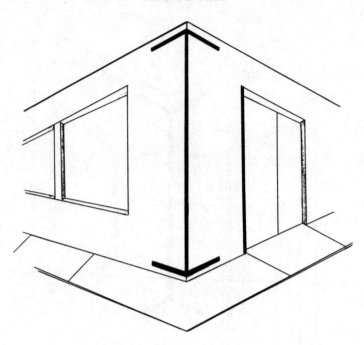

Figure 7.

in your throat you can't help but swallow, and a host of other "tells"—all give you away a dozen times a day and always at the worst of times. (See Shadow-Walkers, chapter 5.)

But not just Nature's to blame. How we're raised—what prides and prejudices, what fears and foul manners are instilled and drilled into us at an early age—all these contribute to how accurately we "see" the world as adults.

Even after we reach adulthood, sudden trauma or "drama" (i.e., repeated negative experiences) can tint and taint how we perceive the world.

Back in the '70s an experiment was done where a mix of black college students and white college students were shown a film of a white man and a black man fighting. A straight razor was clearly visible in the white man's hand.

Yet when asked afterward, the majority of the students—black and white—"remembered" the razor being in the black man's hand

Damn! Seems, just like our senses, we can't trust our memory half the time!

That's because our faulty memories—which *are* "us"!— are dependent upon our faulty senses. Like pure white light passing through a prism, pure *objective* information gathered in through our senses quickly becomes *subjective* and all too often skewed (with details lost, or deliberately deleted or added) as our perceptions pass through any number of "filters" pulled from our "personal file cabinet"—that place where we keep all our petty fears and major phobias, our prejudices, our hidden desires, and oh-so shameful secrets.

All these personal likes and dislikes "color" how we perceive, process, and ultimately "file away" for future use incoming information. (See Figure 8.)

Thus, where one man sees a harmless length of rope, another is startled by a coiled "snake."

You and an associate listen to the same proposal from the sharp-dressed

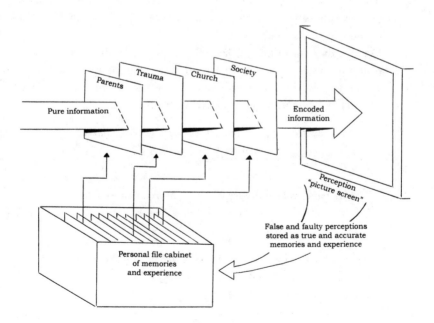

Figure 8. Faulty perceptions

Sicilian businessman. But where your associate hears "An offer you can't refuse," you feel the short hairs on the back of your neck begin to tingle.

In this instance, how you process information can spell the difference between your wearing patent-leather shoes or your being fitted for a pair of concrete galoshes!

In a less extreme scenario: What subtle "body language" signals or slips of the tongue pass between you and that job interviewer, or between you and that blonde sitting across the bar from you? Are you "receiving" the signals you think you are?

Is *your* body sabotaging you by sending out subconscious signals? Don't let the fact that your senses . . . and your body . . . and probably even your memories can't be trusted ruin your day. All this is not necessarily a bad thing.

It's bad for you, of course, if you're not aware of it . . . but now you are! And that gives you a decided advantage over your enemy who still doesn't have a clue how "screwed up" *he* is, how unreliable his information-gathering process really is!

The more aware we become of these inherent "weaknesses" that *all* human beings possess, the better our chances of arming ourselves against exploitation. Thus, we study to survive.

On the other side of the two-headed coin, we might, out of necessity or just plain nastiness, decide to try our hand at exploiting our enemies.

Either way, we begin arming ourselves by first learning the "Three Knows" and by then making allies of the Killer "B's."

> *"All we see depends on our senses: suppose they lie to us?"*
> —Aleister Crowley, 1920

> *"Our minds sometimes see what our hearts wish were true."*
> —Dan Brown, *Angels & Demons*

> *"Times have changed, but our eyes and the way our brains*
> *process information hasn't."*
> —Lung and Prowant,

1

The Three Knows

"Once we understand how the eye gets its information, it is a simple matter to confuse an enemy's eye into misinterpreting the incoming information."
—Lung, *Knights of Darkness*

There are three vital variables, three "knows," we must become aware of and then stay constantly aware of if we are to survive to earn our Ph.D. in Black Science. (Ph.D. = penetrate his defenses!)

Many of the great minds in history took a decidedly dim view of mankind as a whole, weighing in on the side of pessimism by declaring man's collective cranial capacity to be half empty, rather than half full.

We've already seen how Sun Tzu's astute observations into the motivations and manipulations of his fellow Chinese still easily apply to people anywhere in the world 2,500 years later. Thus, while technology has improved, people have remained just as petty, just as pliable.

Two thousand years after Sun Tzu, Japan's greatest swordsman Miyamoto Musashi came to pretty much the same dismal conclusions. Man can improve the temper of his sword steel a thousandfold, yet his own fragile temper will forever remain his deadliest foe.

Around the same time Musashi was literally hacking his way into history, on the other side of the world in Italy, Niccolo Machiavelli penned, "Men have and always have had, the same passions" (Discourses, III:3). Or, to put it even more bluntly, "Men are a sorry breed" (*The Prince*, XVII).

Mark Twain (1835–1910) was hardly less generous when he quipped: "Thank God for stupid people, they make the rest of us look good!"

After a lifetime of probing the collective psyche of man, the father of modern psychology, Sigmund Freud (1856–1939) concluded the mass of mankind is "lazy and unintelligent," and (literally) possessed of desires and passions we can't or won't control: "Among these instinctual wishes are those of incest, cannibalism and lust for killing" (Freud, 1927:12).

Freud's main disciple, Carl G. Jung (1875–1961), expressed similar dismay and disappointment in his fellow man. According to Jung (1964):

I have always been impressed by the fact that there are a surprising number of individuals who never use their minds if they can avoid it, and an equal number who do use their minds, but in an amazingly stupid way. I was also surprised to find many intelligent and wide-awake people who lived (as far as one could make out) as if they had never learned to use their sense organs: they did not see the things before their eyes, hear the words sounding in their ears, or notice the things they touched and tasted. Some lived without being aware of the state of their own bodies. There are others who seemed to live in the most curious condition of consciousness, as if the state they had arrived at today were final, with no possibility of change, or as if the world and the psyche were static and would remain so forever. They seemed devoid of all imagination, and they entirely and exclusively depended upon their sense-perception. Chances and possibilities did not exist in their world, and in "today" there was no real "tomorrow." The future was just the repetition of the past. (page 48)

Despite such dismal descriptions of the human condition, we can still generally count on our good points, our "bright side" to be self-evident. After all, our "bright side" is the face we take pains to paint on daily for an undeserving—and unappreciative!—world.

But other aspects of ourselves we keep hidden, under wraps. This is our shadow self. We must acknowledge—and accept—all aspects of ourselves, including this shadow self, our "night-side."

Don't fret, our enemy possesses a "night side" too, a shadow self that—even if he is aware exists—he doesn't want to talk about and wants desperately to keep hidden from the world at large.

But we have ways of making him talk.

In addition to learning more about ourselves and our enemy, we must also take the time to learn how to "read a room," to evaluate situations and circumstances in order to more quickly and easily turn "environmental considerations" to our advantage.

KNOW YOURSELF

"The unexamined life is not worth living."
—Socrates

In the same way we're all so 100 percent god-awful certain we can trust our senses (heh-heh-heh), we're all also 100 percent convinced we're "cool," "hip," "with it," that we've "got our fingers on the pulse," and that we're "keeping up on the latest."

But in our effort to keep up on what's coming—the next big thing—we all too often miss what's current, what's already right in front of our face; both ignoring immediate dangers around us, while at the same time missing out on opportunities that may not be here tomorrow.

Worse still, we look to others for our "salvation"; looking to politicians and cult leaders who already have their Ph.D. in Black Science.

In this case, Ph.D. means "perpetuate his delusions," which is exactly what these accomplished mind-slayers do: encouraging our least doubt, they perpetuate and pander to the delusions we have about life in general and ourselves in particular.

Ancient Chinese Taoist adage: What the fool seeks in others, the wiseman finds in himself.

Cicero's Six

By all accounts, Marcus Tullius Cicero (106–43 BCE) was an astute observer of human nature. However, being both a philosopher and a politician, Cicero already had two strikes against him when it came to keeping his mouth shut.

Cicero eventually succeeded in pissing off Marc Antony, who just happened to be ruling Rome at the time.

So, no more Cicero.

Lucky for us, before his untimely—though not wholly unpredictable death—Cicero took time to write down what he saw as the Six Mistakes Men Make:

1. Believing that one man can profit by crushing another.
2. The proclivity people have of worrying about things they can't change.
3. The tendency people have of insisting that something is "impossible" just because *they* can't do it, because *they* can't conceive how such a thing might be accomplished.
4. People holding fast to trivial pride, preference, and prejudice.
5. The fact that people stop learning and do not continue to hone their minds, particularly by acquiring the habit of reading and studying. And finally,
6. People's consistent and insistent attempts to compel others to believe and live as they do.

While we might do well to examine ourselves and exorcise Cicero's six failings from our own personality, as Black Science "majors" we rejoice in the fact that other human beings—our enemies in particular—possess these tendencies, false beliefs, and nasty habits, or rather, that these inner demons—and a score more!—possess them!

Over or Under?

It has been said we are "seen" in one of three ways: There's how we see ourselves. There's how others see us. And there's how we *really* are!

As already established, for the most part our senses lie to us, therefore, "The way we see ourselves" is "filtered" through our prides and prejudices, dreams and desires, fears and fouls.

Likewise, the way others see us is filtered through *their* prejudices and preferences . . . and *their* preferences and prejudices can be easily manipulated by anyone with a Ph.D. in Black Science. (Ph.D. = plot his downfall.)

Finally, there's the way we really are, with all our phobias and faults, but also with untold and untapped potential.

Mental health experts tell us that the closer we can bring these often widely differing perspectives into sync, the more we can "integrate" the three, the more realistic our grasp on reality.

From a Black Science perspective, however, the *farther apart* we can pull our enemy's image of himself from the way the world sees him, the easier it is for us to waylay his carefully laid plans.

The skill of correctly assessing our own abilities, assets, and allies, as well as those of our enemy, is the single most vital survival skill we can ever develop.

We must also examine the habits, hobbies, and hates of our enemy as well as ourselves, discovering new insights into our own minds, while simultaneously discovering the unguarded back door into our foe's mind!

> *"We use 10 percent of our brains. Imagine what we could accomplish if we used the other 60 percent."*
> —Ellen DeGeneres

Abilities, Assets, and Allies

What abilities, assets, and allies do you have? Make a list of them . . . now cross out half of them and you'll have a list that's closer to the truth, closer to your *real* assets and allies, the ones you can really count on when the chips are down.

Never overestimate the amount of "ammunition" you have for a fight. Conversely, never underestimate your own potential and possibilities to pull through in a pinch. We all have abilities, assets, and allies we don't know we have.

"Human beings only use 10 percent of their brain" is a misquote. It should read that most people only use their brain "10 percent efficiently."

Thus, you have within you abilities you've never used.

For example, you probably don't use your time efficiently. How often do you complain, "There just aren't enough hours in the day to get everything done"?

Yet consider how many times a day you stand in a queue (e.g., a grocery check-out line, a line at the bank) for fifteen minutes at a time, patiently waiting your turn. Or what about being stuck in traffic, just "doing nothing," for God knows how long?

Fifteen-minute "doing nothings" four times add up to a full *hour* of your life, an hour you could spend making yourself mentally sharper and physically stronger. Wasted hours add up to wasted days, wasted days . . . a wasted *life*.

So, you can waste your life . . . or you can waste your enemy's life by helping him waste *his* time.

One of the six mistakes Cicero points to is that we stop learning. Recall how Carl Jung also lamented that some people live "as if the state they had arrived at today were final, with no possibility of change."

But life changes every day. Every minute of every day new technological inventions threaten to give our enemies—our competition—the edge in business, the upper hand in life.

Likewise, every day the biological and psychological sciences gain new insights and make bold in-roads into understanding the human psyche.

Many of these "new discoveries" merely verify what accomplished mind-masters realized intuitively in centuries past.

In the East there is a saying that "There are no new answers, only new questions," meaning the "old ways" of dealing with problems—and problem people—are still valid.

The poet who penned "Music hath charms to soothe the savage breast" didn't live long enough to see science verify that specific sound frequencies indeed affect mood and influence attitude.

Like a professional soldier eagerly trading in his musket for an AK-47, so, too, mastery of the Black Science requires we not only learn the tried-and-true tools and techniques of past adepts, but also that we constantly upgrade our mind-manipulation skills by diligently seeking out new abilities, assets, and allies while eagerly embracing new insights and innovations.

The better we come to "know" ourselves, the easier it will be to "No!" our enemy.

"Know yourself" and all else follows.

"Nothing ought to keep us from directing our observation to our own selves or from applying our thought to criticism of itself."
—Freud, *The Future of an Illusion*

KNOW YOUR ENEMY

"There is nothing so disorienting as the loss of a good friend, except perhaps, the loss of a good enemy."
—Barash, *Beloved Enemies*

In his insightful *Beloved Enemies: Our Need for Opponents* (1994), David Barash convinces us that we *need* enemies.

On the plus side, enemies give us focus, provide a challenge, and keep us sharp and on our toes. When real enemies can't be found, it's sometimes necessary to create them.

Some people go so far as creating "anti-identities," taking their identity and feelings of self-worth, not from what they have accomplished in life, but from what and who they hate and by who they have convinced themselves hates them. For some people, having big and bad "important" enemies means that they too are "important."

External enemies are often a way of *not* dealing with "uncomfortable" inner turmoil. Barash said:

> In short, we see, and often create, the enemy outside as a way of denying the enemy that is within us, and also as a way of justifying that interior demon. (page 97)

Cults and wag-the-dog politicians are notorious for manufacturing "enemies" in order to attract and motivate followers.

So who's your enemy? Simple: Who's in your way? Who's keeping you from getting what you want? More important, who thinks—rightly or wrong—that *you* are in *their* way?

If you play your cards right, the former will never see you coming and will never know what hit them. The latter kind of enemy, on the other hand, may already be digging up dirt on you. But, dig up enough dirt on your enemy and you'll have a hole big enough to bury him in!

The more information and insight you can gather—by hook or by crook—on your enemy's habits, hates, and hobbies, the easier it will be for you to decipher what kind of thinker your enemy is.

It is of the utmost importance that, early on, you determine whether he is a patient, logical, and methodical planner or, like most people, bases 90 percent of his decisions on emotion (Lieberman, 1998:173).

The more he is led by his emotions, the easier it will be for *you* to lead him where you want him to go.

What are his motivations and goals? Can you identify with (or at least pretend to identify with) his motivations in order to win his ear?

Can you offer him a strategically placed stepping-stone (i.e., bribe) to help him reach his goals or is it in your best interest to throw a stumbling block in his way?

Habits, Hates, and Hobbies

It has been said that habits are first cobwebs, but soon become cables. So, too, our hates and hobbies help define who we are, often revealing more of us to the world than we realize.

Professional athletes always study their competition beforehand. And it is unheard of for a warrior to go into battle without first studying his enemy. Likewise, you must also study your enemy, even as he is right this minute studying *your* habits, hates, and hobbies.

Habits. Our routine quirks mark us. These habits are all-too-inviting chinks in our armor where an enemy can all-too-easily slip in a dagger of the mind.

Thus, we must brutally examine our own routines and habits to make sure they actually safeguard us better than they serve our foes.

Simultaneously, we must apply the same ruthless eye to our enemy's routine and habits in order to take full advantage of his lapse in concentration to trip him up and trap him.

Hobbies. What kind of hobbies does your enemy have? How does he spend his leisure time? Does he even have leisure time?

How people spend their leisure time tells more about them than does where they work. You might have no choice but to work a lousy job just to make ends meet, but your "free time" is your chance to do what you *want* to do. There's quite a difference between someone choosing cooking over taxidermy, gardening over gun collecting, as their hobby.

Any first-year psychology student can tell you an individual's choice of hobbies often has a symbolic and subconscious meaning to that person. In other words, there is often an underlying "night-side" reason a person chooses one hobby over another.

Does his choice of hobby inadvertently reveal a hidden desire for power? (See chapter 2, Power for the Taking.)

Does his hobby flirt with danger and taboo? Does collecting porn really qualify as a hobby?

Hates. In the same vein, what does your enemy "hate"? What does he vehemently rant and rave against? Conversely, what type of subjects does he hate talking about? More on this in a minute.

Getting to Know His "Night-Side"

"Light necessitates shadows."
—Masonic adage

Good psychiatrists don't need Hamlet's mother ("Me thinks the lady doth protest too much!") to remind them that when a patient expresses intense hatred, or rants and raves against any particular thing or person, it all too often indicates that the patient has a secret attraction for the very thing or person he claims to hate.

(Remember the little girl whose pigtails you always pulled in grade school? You pretended to hate her but you secretly had a crush on her, didn't you? Same principle. We only *think* we grew up.)

Thus, a priest, a politician, or a police officer with a subconscious "night-side" obsession for pornography finds "his calling" as an overzealous antiporn crusader. . . . Of course this position gives him plenty of opportunity to sit around all day looking at kiddie porn, with no one the wiser . . . including *himself*!

We all have subconscious "shadows" lurking within, ready to rear their ugly hydra-like heads at the most inopportune and dangerous times. Miller (1981) said:

> The shadow is like a foreign personality—a primitive, instinctive, animalistic kind of being. It is the collection of uncivilized desires and feelings that simply have no place in cultured society. The shadow is everything we would *like* to be but don't dare. The shadow is everything we don't even want to know about ourselves and have thus conveniently "forgotten" through denial and repression. (page 23)

Though this "shadow" hides well on our "night-side," we can often get a glimpse of our enemy's elusive shadow by studying his habits, hates, and hobbies.

A word of warning: Our own night-side is all too often also our "blind side."

Old Norse saying: "Test yourself with fire and ice before your enemies do!" In other words, shine light on your own night-side before your enemies do.

Conversely, digging up the dirt on your enemy, finding his flaws, expos-

17

ing his night-side to the glare of public inquiry (or at least threatening to do so) gives you a bludgeon with which to beat down your foe.

The Enemy of My Enemy

Other than you, who are your enemy's enemies?

Remember, "The enemy of my enemy is my friend" . . . or at least my temporary ally. (More of this in chapter 3, The Killer "B's.")

Sometimes these allies you don't know you have are actual physical people. . . . If only the people who hate your enemy/their enemy more than they hate you!

Other times these unexpected allies are psychological in nature.

Your enemy's physical enemies. They're real and easy to spot. They're people he's pissed off or else people that have pissed him off. They're out to get him, or at least he *thinks* they're out to get him . . . perhaps because *you* make him think this!

Your enemy's real—physical—enemies can be incited against him. This is known as the "get a dog to eat a dog" ploy. This is analogous to throwing a single bone to a pair of starving hounds and is especially effective (and gratifying!) when used to get one of your enemies to destroy the other (hopefully destroying himself in the process).

The winner in such a fight will be weakened, and thus more susceptible to your attack.

Other times you can neutralize an enemy by convincing him that joining you is the only way he can overcome his real or imagined enemies. This of course includes "shadow enemies" you conveniently create for him to quixotically tilt against, expending his limited resources, resources no longer at his disposal when the time comes for him to rally his forces against your "attack."

You gain his alliance by exaggerating the potential and plottings of his real—and imagined—enemies. (Cults are masters of this ploy.) If he remains unresponsive to your "peace" overtures, join his real enemies. Whenever possible, *secretly*.

The enemy of my enemy is my friend.

Your enemy's psychological enemies. Psychological enemies are a little harder to spot. They are literally "in his head," whether inherited weeds of worry and phantoms of paranoia he's dragged behind him like a shitty diaper since childhood, or the entangling vines of doubt and disappointment you adroitly plant in his mind via your Black Science.

Unlike actual physical enemies, these psychological enemies are less tangible, and often impossible to get a grasp on. Basically, what's good for your enemy is usually bad for you. On the flip side, what's bad for your enemy is probably good for you, or at least can be turned to your advantage.

Psychological disturbances like frustration, irrational fears, and debilitating stress, although your enemy, are also your enemy's enemy. Discovering that your enemy is plagued by one of these psychological enemies will not only give you insight into his thinking processes, but can also provide you with avenues of direct (*cheng*) or oblique (*ch'i*) attack.

Phobias. We're all afraid of something. Lord knows there's plenty out there to be frightened of!

Paralyzing phobias on the other hand are just that: *paralyzing*.

Such phobias can often be triggered by innocuous objects. For example, a phobia of rats might "accidentally" be triggered by a pair of furry house slippers or by that lucky rabbit's foot you "innocently" pull from your pocket.

Figure 9 illustrates some common phobias.

Allergies. In the same vein, discovering your enemy has an allergy of some kind can also provide you with an avenue of attack.

Some allergies are merely irritating, producing symptoms similar to a cold—yet irritating enough to make your rival miss an important meeting? Other allergies can induce suffocation, seizures, and even death (See Figure 10).

Drugs and medication. It is always a joy to find out your competition is hooked on illegal drugs. Life just got simpler! Other times you discover your enemy is using (and/or mis-using?) prescription drugs. What kind(s) of medication(s) is he using? Are these medications for potentially deadly—or at least debilitating—allergies? Or perhaps his medications are for psychological problems such as depression, OCD (obsessive–compulsive disorder), bi-polar disorder, or some form of major psychosis.

MOST COMMON ANIMAL PHOBIAS

1. Spiders (arachnephobia)
2. Bees and Wasps (bees: apiphobia; wasps: spheksuphobia)
3. Reptiles (batrachophobia)
4. Snakes (herpetophobia, ophidiophobia)
5. Mice (musophobia, muriphobia)
6. Dogs (cynophobia, kynophobia)
7. Birds (ornithophobia)
8. Frogs (batrachophobia, see "Reptiles")
9. Ants/horses/rats (ants: myrmecophobia); horses: eqinophobia; rats: no medical term) (Russell Ash, *The Top 10 of Everything*. A DK Book: 1997)

MOST COMMON PHOBIAS OVERALL

1. Spiders
2. Social situations/people (anthrophobia, sociophobia)
3. Flying (aerophobia) (marked increase afer 9/11!)
4. Open spaces (agoraphobia)
5. Confined spaces (claustrophobia)
6. Vomiting (emitophobia)
7. Heights (acrophobia)
8. Cancer (carcinophobia)
9. Thunderstoms (brontophobia)
10. Death (thanatophobia)

Figure 9. Most Common Phobias.

MOST COMMON FOOD ALLERGIES

1. Nuts
2. Seafood/shellfish
3. Milk (dairy)
4. Wheat
5. Eggs
6. Fresh fruit (strawberries, etc.)
7. Fresh vegetables
8. Cheese (dairy)
9. Yeast
10. Soy Protein

MOST COMMON ENVIRONMENTAL ALLERGIES

1. House dust mites
2. Grass pollen
3. Tree pollens
4. Cats
5. Dogs
6. Horses
7. Molds
8. Birch pollen (see tree pollen)
9. Weed pollen
10. Wasp/bee pollen

Figure 10. Most Common Allergies.

What possible (and potentially useful!) side effects are associated with his medication? What will happen when he thinks he's taking his medication but is really only taking a sugar pill? Will his boss mistake his sudden sweating and stumbling disorientation for his being drunk on the job? Conversely, what would happen if he accidentally took *too much* of his medication? (**Note**: How are we to come by this kind of personal information about our enemy, you ask?)

First, people love to talk about themselves. (It's called "bitching" and "whining.")

If they don't talk directly to you, they'll talk to one of your well-placed "operatives."

Second, people often inadvertently leave personal information just lying around for us to find in their desk drawers, in their trash cans (the poor man's Internet), their medicine cabinet, or their computer at work and at home (once we figure out that damn password!), and in that row of locked file cabinets in their psychiatrist's office.

And there's always the Internet.

In a perfect Gandhi world, you get rid of your enemies by turning them into your friends. (By the way, Gandhi was gunned down in 1948.)

In a slightly less-perfect Gandhi world, but one still ruled by a semblance of reason (and optimism), you threaten a dangerous foe with "deadly force" and they back down.

In the real world, it does little good to point a pistol at a suicide bomber and threaten, "Halt, or I'll shoot!"

We do have real enemies.

Black Science is not in the business of manufacturing enemies—quite the opposite.

Black Science offers a variety of means and methods (most non-violent) for getting rid of your enemies. Having "options" is always good.

Ask an adept at Black Science about his enemies and he'll wink, "*My enemies are an endangered species!*"

> ***"Hell is other people."***
> **—John-Paul Sartre**

KNOW YOUR ENVIRONMENT

"The universe is not some mechanical system, but a concept,
a perception."
—Pearsall, *Superimmunity*

Whatever the nature of the dramas played out between ourselves and those around us, those dramas play out against a background that we help create. This background, our environment, in turn, helps make us who we are.

We all contribute to, and thus help create, the world around us both through our actions and by our inaction.

In the ancient Hindu holy book *Bhagavad-Gita* ("The Song of God"), India's greatest warrior, Arjuna, finds himself standing in the middle of a great Indian civil war.

Seeing his brothers and cousins, uncles and teachers, ready to spill their blood on both sides, Arjuna is so suddenly overcome with sorrow he throws down his weapon and declares, "I will not fight!"

Krishna, Arjuna's chariot driver (who also just happens to be God in disguise), spends the rest of the Bhagavad-Gita explaining to Arjuna that it is Arjuna's karma that has brought him to this troubled point in life; it doesn't matter whether Arjuna actively participates in the coming battle or not, this battle is still going to take place.

Thus our environment contributes to us just as we contribute to it, both by our actions as well as by our inaction.

How we interact with any particular environment depends to a great extent on how we "see" the world—the universe—in general. And how we see the world tells others more about us than it does about the actual nature of the world:

"The universe around you is a sign of your focus."
—Linn, *What Your Face Reveals*

Some people see the universe as "unfair." The celestial deck is stacked against them. They swear the universe has singled them out for specific abuse. Others perceive a universe filled with possibilities. The fact that the most worthwhile of these possibilities are also the most challenging (i.e., dangerous) just helps to separate those with a sharp eye from those with a sharp stick in their eye!

In the same way, people interact and how they interact tells a lot about them. People react and interact differently depending on the particular environment.

I know what you're thinking: "Oh no, I'm the same person no matter who I'm talking to, no matter what situation I'm in!"

Heh-heh-heh.

Ever hear of the "bystander effect"?

Research has proven time and again that when we witness an accident or a crime, we are more likely to get involved and help if we are the only witness.

On the other hand, if we are in a crowd, it is less likely we will speak up or actively try to help because we expect that someone else in the crowd will be the one to step forward and help. Being "lost" in the faceless crowd makes us feel less personal responsibility (i.e., guilt), making us feel we will receive less ridicule for not helping then if we were the only person available to help.

Such studies prove that we do act differently depending on environment—in this instance, on how many other people are sharing that environment—situation—with us.

It's also important to realize people react differently when you speak to them privately, one on one, as opposed to approaching them in a crowded social situation.

For example, a businessman might feel more secure laughing off your proposal if you pitch it to him one morning while he's sitting behind his large, ornate desk in his big office than if you make him the same "offer you can't refuse" in a deserted, dimly lit underground parking garage late at night.

Whether back slapping or back stabbing, when dealing with others, be they family or friends, or dangerous foes, it's always important to take "when," "where," and "how many"—in other words, your environment—into consideration.

Our environment either provides us power or else sucks off our energy. To a great extent this depends on how the people in that environment positively or negatively relate to that environment.

Thus we all too often find ourselves cursed with myopic or well-meaning friends and family all too eager to strain our patience and drain our resources.

On the other hand, we find ourselves blessed with stupid enemies whose mistakes only open the door to new and endless possibilities for exercising our Black Science.

Family Environment

When the universe can't attack you directly, it comes at you through your loved ones. You can pick your friends, you can't pick your family. And unless you're Michael Corleone, you can't *ice-pick* your relatives. So you're stuck with them.

Speaking of *The Godfather*, remember how Corleone enemies set up Sonny by phoning to say his sister was being beaten again by her abusive husband who, in turn, had sold his duplicitous soul to the Corleone clan's enemies?

(Read the book, rent *The Godfather* DVD. Both are excellent studies in the Black Science. And, whatever you do, never ever piss off a Mario Puzo!)

From Sicilian culture, on to Asian culture, where the accomplishments and/or disgrace of a single family member reflects on the honor of the family as a whole.

Sometimes one bad apple really does spoil the whole bunch. Does the name Billy Carter ring a bell? Like it or not, we're intricately intertwined—or is that *chained*?—to our family.

For some, those links are golden, forged from love, trust, and devotion to family tradition—the kind of brotherly love that can inspire personal self-worth and even dreams of empire.

In the Indian *Mahabharata* (of which the *Bhagavad-Gita* is a part), Arjuna and his brothers succeed in winning a kingdom by sticking together through thick and thin. Hannibal and his brother had a good run, harassing the Romans for years until Hannibal's brother was killed. Genghis Khan and his sons did pretty well for themselves, as did Mattathius Maccabeus and his boys.

On the other hand, there's Shaka Zulu. Between 1816 and 1826 Shaka Zula ruthlessly carved himself an empire the size of France out of the wilds of southern Africa. He did so by first creating an army of professional warriors, the likes of which had never been seen before in southern Africa. From there it was then simply a matter of following *the conquerer's tried-and-true dictum*:[*]

---

[*]Not to be confused with Richard Nixon's "Dicked 'em"!

Reward all those wise enough to join you, utterly crush all who oppose you and do so in so savage a manner as to completely cower any others who might dream of resisting your will.

Armed with this two-edged spearhead of tactics and terror, in short order Shaka succeeded in uniting the many diverse tribes in the region under his standard.

It is speculated that Shaka Zulu, brilliant tactician that he was, might have eventually conquered the whole of Africa had he not overlooked one small fact: His half-brother and stepmother were even more ruthless than he was!

Shaka Zulu was literally stabbed in the back by his family.

So, don't fret if your family more resembles Norman Bates's than Norman Rockwell's. Even the Bible is full of fine examples of the kinds of family—and "family values"—you'd be better off without:

- Cain and Abel.
- Abraham offering wife Sarah to Pharaoh. (Genesis 12)
- Lot (Abraham's brother) offering his daughters to the strange men of Sodom . . . *really* strange men.
- Lot's daughters "thank" their father by getting him drunk and seducing him . . . *two nights in a row*? (Genesis 19)
- Judge Jephtnah using his daughter as a human sacrifice. (Judges 11)
- The love of Judge Samson's life, Delilah, sells him out to his enemies. (Judges 16)
- King Saul's son Jonathan betrays his own father because the prince's love for the rebel leader David was "passing the love of women" . . . hmmmm. (2 Samuel 2)
- Later, *King* David craftily arranges the death of his warrior Uriah in order to get in Uriah's wife Bathsheba's boudoir.
- Like father like son, King David's son Amnon rapes his sister Tamar and is, in turn, ambushed and murdered by his brother Absolom. (2 Samuel 13)

Recall from *Black Science* that everyone on Earth is connected to everyone else within "six degrees of separation." Thus one strategy for getting close to an elusive and reclusive enemy is by targeting the people around them (Lung and Prowant, 2001:45).

Thus, we must constantly guard ourselves—and those around us—to insure our enemy doesn't use this very ploy. Sadly, those closest to us are sometimes our biggest liability.

A loved one in trouble calls in a panic and we drop everything to come to their immediate aid. Of course, the "everything" we "drop" is exactly the thing our enemy is waiting to "pick up" . . . that is why he artfully crafted a crisis for our loved one in the first place!

Whether it's our birth family (parents, siblings, Kennedy cousins), or the family we create for ourselves as adults (i.e., our wife and kids), we must always be on the alert for our enemy trying to get at us through them.

No disrespect, but how far can you really trust those closest to you? What do you really know about your sister's new boyfriend? And just how deep in debt to his bookie is your knucklehead brother?

Remember that while "Blood is thicker than water" . . . *gold* is "thicker" than both. One word: *Fredo* Corleone.

Not that being close to your family isn't sometimes an asset. Can you say *nepotism*?

Of course, some might argue there's such a thing as being too close a family:

> The madam of a bordello finds a young boy standing at her door offering her a large jar full of coins. "I want a whore with V-D," the boy informs the astonished madam.
>
> "Why would you want a whore with V-D?" she sputters.
>
> "Because if I get V-D, *my little sister* will get V-D. If my little sister gets V-D, then *my dad*, will get V-D. If Dad gets V-D, then *my mom* will get V-D. If Mom gets V-D, then *the mailman* will get V-D . . . and he's the sonovabitch that ran over my dog!"

(**Beware**: "Family values" has become one of the most manipulative terms in the English language and, like all potentially manipulative terms, it can easily be twisted to mean entirely different things depending on the agenda of the particular word-wizard who's conjuring with it.)

For example, what's the chances your definition of family values is the same as some religious-minded Middle Eastern mother whose idea of family values includes raising *her* children to worship God by wearing C4-brand underwear?

So don't automatically assume when every self-serving politician, salivating priest, or sundry psychopath preaches family values that they are necessarily talking about your family or your values.

Didn't Charlie Manson also have something he called a "family"? (See Word Slavery in chapter 5.)

Speaking of "substitute families," your enemy can and will attack you through any surrogate families you might have. These families include your circle of friends, your religious group, as well as any fraternities and social clubs you belong to, everything from your Freemason lodge to your Friday-night poker buddies.

Our real family surrounds us, protects us, and insulates us from the cruel world. They give us hugs and make us feel better about ourselves. That's why purr words and phrases like "brother" and "We're family!" so easily penetrate past our paranoia straight to our pocketbook.

One of the biggest selling points cults and gangs have is that they offer us surrogate families, either offering to replace lost loved ones or else providing us the dream family we've always wanted. That's why cult leaders like to be called "Father" or "Mother" and your fellow converts "Brother" and "Sister." Cults are all just one big happy "family" . . . as long as the collection plate keeps getting filled.

Wily mind slayers (e.g., confidence men, cult recruiters.) are adept at anticipating our need for family, stepping forward at just the right time with just the right spiel to capture our attention and exploit our emotions.

For example, we are especially vulnerable to religious conmen consoling us immediately after the loss of a loved one. Old folks, having recently lost a spouse are specially targeted. But not just the elderly are susceptible. Young adults, faced with finally cutting the umbilical cord and moving out on their own into an intimidating world, are prime candidates for religious recruiters promising them a new family.

Of course, catching our enemy at such a vulnerable time (whether a naturally occurring loss or a crisis we've helped craft) means he is now susceptible to this approach, opening new possibilities for penetrating his defenses.

Social Environment

"Zen masters have known for thousands of years, the human
skin does not separate us from the rest of our environment;
it joins us to it."
—**Barash**, *Beloved Enemies*

From your neighbors, coworkers, peripheral friends, and associates, to that pimple-faced clerk down at the Kwik-Stop, any and all the people you interact with on any given day can be "co-opted" by your enemy.

Or any of these people could themselves harbor hidden grievances and agenda we don't suspect. Read Edgar Allan Poe's *The Cask of the Amontillado* (1846).

How well do you know your neighbors? Psychopathic personalities— serial killers and Middle Eastern terrorists—make perfect neighbors ("He was such a quiet person, always kept to himself . . ."). Is he religious? "Church-bingo-once-a-week" religious or "bomb-abortion-clinics" religious?

What about your coworkers? How well do you really know them? Do the words *postal, Prozac*, or *disgruntled* appear anywhere on their resume? Have any of your unstable coworkers recently been fired? What about that coworker who just broke up with her obsessively jealous crack-smoking gun-enthusiast boyfriend? Better hope her restraining order is written on Kevlar!

Does someone want your job? (**Hint**: *You* lose your job, *I* get promoted and *my* lazy brother-in-law finally gets a job—*your* job.)

How dependent are you on the job you have? Would suddenly and expectedly losing your job devastate you financially?

No chance of your getting fired? What if the job site itself got "fired" . . . literally! Would that leave you out in the cold? Could such an "accident" make you more likely to consider an offer tomorrow you wouldn't have given a second thought to yesterday?

What about the "little people"?

All too often we don't take time to really "look" at the other people around us—especially the little people, those faceless individuals who bag up our groceries, park our car, do our dry cleaning, and even watch over our children.

As a result, we fail to "see" their "tells"— subconscious sweatings and sputterings, verbal and nonverbal clues that would—should!—alert us to their treachery.

What do you really know about your new babysitter, nanny, or day care operator? You are trusting them with your greatest treasure, after all.

What about that valet you just handed your car keys to? Could he be bribed or threatened into planting a listening device, illegal drugs, or DNA evidence in your car? (Hey, if it could happen to poor O.J.!)

What about the teller at your bank? The secretary at your doctor's office? That foul-mouthed bi . . . *lady* down at the DMV?

What personal or financial information of yours could one of these little people pass along to your enemies? Either because they also hate you, or else because they have been forced to choose between your safety and the continued safety of their family?

What about your government? Can you trust "them"?

Whereas you may trust the abstract concept of "the government," how many of the millions of government workers do you know personally? Any of these could have you in their sights, targeted for personal revenge, their finger poised over the "delete" button of your identity and your financial security.

Worse still, you could be impersonally targeted for bulldozing by government bureaucracy only because you're in the wrong place (i.e., environment) at the wrong time.

Better the enemy you know than the enemy you don't know. Can you really trust the government to look out for your best interest?

2

Power for the Taking

Armageddon has come and gone and you're one of the "lucky" ones left alive. You're huddled in a bombed-out basement with your wife and your two little children, with one can of beans.

Who eats the beans?

You've probably been taught to do the noble thing, to do what a nice guy would do: Go hungry yourself and give that last can of beans to your starving wife and kids.

Well, there's a whole lot of ugly just the other side of that barricaded door hoping that's your answer, because now *you*—the would-be protector of your little tribe—will weaken, and once you are too weak to resist, the wolves will break in—both the four-footed and the two-footed varieties— and they will kill you, and they will rape your wife, and then they will *eat your children!*

All because you weren't strong enough—ruthless enough—to do what had to be done in the first place: *Feed yourself first, make yourself strong.* Only then will you be of use to others.

Of course, that's the worst-case scenario. Still it serves to illustrate how every day we make similar mistakes, doing what Society expects of us, doing what we've been taught a good person does, sacrificing our own needs and opportunities because we've been taught that sacrifice is noble.

This kind of false humility only weakens us. Worse still, it *endangers* others who are counting on us to make the hard decisions . . . to eat that last can of beans, to stay strong and keep the wolves from the door.

Mind slayers never tire of asking us to make sacrifices for God and country. Read *The Ego and Its Own* by Max Stirner.

All too often well-meaning friends, relatives, and lovers talk us out of doing things to improve ourselves, "selfish things" like losing weight, quitting our dead-end job, and going back to school. Is it any wonder these are called toxic relationships?

Taking care of number one, *self*-protection, is job one. We're not much good to anyone else unless we first get our own house in order. We can't help others unless we first make ourselves strong. It does no one any good if *you* drown while trying to save another drowning swimmer.

Read Joseph Wambaugh's *The Onion Field*.

GETTY'S FIVE

Billionaire J. Paul Getty (1892–1976), who made it his "business" to read men, identified five personality types that bubble to the surface whenever men are faced with challenge and adversity:

1. *The Helpless*, those who sit paralyzed, overwhelmed by the rush of unforeseen events.
2. *Cowards*, those ready to flee or surrender as soon as things start going sour.
3. *Flailers* who strike out blindly and ineffectively, flailing about, squandering precious resources. (Sometimes flailers actually get lucky and accidentally succeed. Unfortunately, such accidental successes only fuel their belief that superstition rules life rather than foresight and sweat.)
4. *Hole-Pluggers*, defensive fighters who solve problems as they arise. Whereas they may respond correctly and even effectively in the long run, they are always playing "catch up" because they respond only *after* a problem has fully manifested. (**Note**: This runs contrary to the advice of Sun Tzu, the *Tao Te Ching*, Machiavelli, and any other strategist worth their salt, all of whom know to deal with small problems—small enemies—*before* they become big problems—big enemies.)
5. *True Leaders*, on the other hand, deal with little problems before they become big problems—big enemies. Attacked, true leaders decisively

and effectively counterattack. They know that "the best defense is a good offense."

All of us fall into one of J. Paul Getty's five types. While it's theoretically possible for us to step outside the box and exhibit any of these responses, our core personality—our basic way of dealing with life—is built around one of these predictable reactions.

Our *enemy* too.

FLIGHT OR FIGHT?

When faced with a threat, physical or psychological, real or imagined, humans respond in one of four ways: Withdrawal, submission, seeking love, or seeking power.

Withdrawal

We run away. When we can't physically run away, we draw in our psyche and senses like a turtle withdrawing into its shell, or like an ostrich burying its head in the sand. (**Note**: The turtle draws himself into his shell as an effective defensive strategy, patiently waiting out his enemy.)

Hiding your head in the sand, on the other hand, whether figuratively or literally, can never qualify as good strategy. To quote Carolyn Shumway's favorite line from *Black Science*: "Even if you bury your head in the sand, you can still get your ass kicked!" (Lung and Prowant, 2001:171) Thus the difference between a "strategic withdrawal" . . . and running like Hell!

Submission

Unable to flee, we surrender. We submit to a "higher Authority" while trying to maintain a "low profile." We "go along to get along," hoping the bully won't pick on us. Sometimes we even help the bully pick on others so he won't pick on us. Pressed hard enough, we kiss ass.

Seeking Love

Ideally, we should each be able to "insulate" ourselves from the cruel world by surrounding ourselves with people who truly love and respect us.

When successful, we are blessed with family and friends and true love—

allies, which provide us with a sense of security that comes from having a strong, dependable support network.

When we fail to find genuine love and respect, we end up looking for love in all the wrong places—cults and gangs and toxic relationships.

Seeking Power

These first three—withdrawal, submission, and seeking love—are all simply ways of seeking the power to control our lives.

First of all, *power* isn't a dirty word. It is natural to seek to control a situation. From birth, we constantly struggle to gain power—power over ourselves (e.g., how to walk) and power over our environment (e.g., when and where to walk). Later, we seek power over our enemies. This is a natural drive, it's in our DNA. This *is* our DNA. The more power we exercise over ourselves and our environment, the better our chances of surviving long enough to pass our DNA on to another generation.

Ever heard of survival of the fittest? Adapt or die? Conversely, and as usual, "society" tries its best to beat this natural urge down with a monkey wrench.

Thus, we've all been taught to deny any thoughts of personal *power*. We're taught this by political and religious leaders because the power to think for ourselves—that first and foremost of powers!—means we will no longer need them to think for us.

When they warn us that "power corrupts and absolute power corrupts absolutely," they've only frightened themselves by looking too closely in the mirror (see *The Three Treasures*).

Besides, shouldn't "the power to choose" extend to the power to choose whether or not we want to be corrupted? Some people might choose to be a sonovabitch. And this would be a perfect way to discover who's sincerely a "saint" and who definitely ain't.

Look how many power hungry, but otherwise powerless piss-ants the world would never have heard of if Hitler hadn't come along and offered them a job. (See Bribery in chapter 3.)

But without power—if only the power to think for ourselves—our choices are more limited. And, all too often, those with the power make choices for us.

Oft times we shy away from the idea of *power* because we equate having power with being *responsible*. None of us wants to be the one left holding the bag, the person who's blamed when everything falls apart.

Suit yourself. No guts, no glory.

Life isn't about taking chances, it's about taking control. Of course, sometimes you have to be willing to take a chance in order to get control!

THE FIVE KINDS OF POWER

Power is properly defined as "The possibility that one actor within a social relationship will be in a position to carry out his own will despite resistance." (Ashley & Orenstein, 1990)

Black Science defines *power* as the ability to get your way, to exercise your *will*.

Freidrich Nietzsche (1844–1900) said all people have within them an innate *creative* urge he called the "will to power."

This will to power drives us to become more than what we are at the present moment, to test limits, to push against our walls—no matter how comforting those walls might at first glance appear, to seek power—first over ourselves, and then over the universe at large.

When we feel a vague (and sometimes not so vague) dissatisfaction with ourselves, it is because we are denying this instinctual drive within us. In other words, we're not living up to our potential.

We've already established that human beings only use their brains 10 percent efficiently. Another way of putting this is that far too many of us only use our lives 10 percent effectively. This is bad news for you if you're one of these people.

On the other hand, this is good news for you because the odds are your enemy is also one of these people.

Nietzsche goes on to say that power and pleasure are intricately linked. Power brings us pleasure. Pleasure, in turn, gives us a feeling of power. Look at your own life. When you are performing at your best, at your peak, you feel "powerful," like you can do no wrong.

Athletes call this feeling "being in the zone," where you perform flawlessly, where your years of study and sweat finally pay off. Remember: Chance favors the prepared mind.

Where does your enemy draw *his* power from? From an inner reserve of true self-esteem and self-confidence, or merely from the uniform he wears? (See False Position later in this chapter.)

What gives your enemy pleasure?

Can you "influence" him by offering him more of his preferred pleasure, or by threatening to cut off his source of pleasure?

How convenient for you when your enemy's favorite "pleasure" is considered "taboo" by current society standards. (See Blackmail in chapter 3.)

Where does your enemy run to when feeling "powerless"? To his Bible or to the bottle? To his priest or to his hooker? When his power base is threatened, will he run for his gun or run for the hills?

Remember that Sun Tzu teaches us to always leave the enemy a way out . . . if only so we can better ambush him farther down the road! What the inferior man seeks in others—including power!—the superior man seeks in himself.

The five basic sources for power are love and respect power, carrot power, stick power, expert power, and position power.

Love and Respect Power

This power depends on how much you are liked by others. It is genuine power, flowing from people who care, support, and follow you out of love and loyalty rather than those who kiss your ass for personal gain and/or from fear.

(**Note**: Ask whether it was better for a prince to be loved or feared, Machiavelli replied it was *safer* to be *feared* since, in the long run, it offers the prince more security. Machiavelli went on to remind us there's a big difference between being feared and being hated [Machiavelli, 1532:XVII].)

Carrot Power

Carrot power (aka "reward power") comes from your ability to manipulate others by dispensing rewards. Exercising this kind of power, you control "the carrot."

Example: Cult offers love and "family."

Stick Power

Stick power (aka "coercive power") comes from your willingness to wield "the stick," to threaten and to punish others, your ability to open up a can of whup-ass!

Example: Cult leader withholds his "love" until you start goose-stepping with the rest of the "chosen." (See The Cult Craft in *Black Science*.)

Sometimes the stick is simply a piece of information you hold over another person. (See Blackmail in chapter 3.) Other times you have to resort to a more *literal* "stick". (See *Bully* in chapter 3.)

Expert Power

Expert power comes from your special skills, unique abilities, or special intelligence you've collected, or can get your hands on. In a crisis—one naturally occurring or a crisis of *your* manufacture—your expertise (special skills and/or information) is suddenly in demand and you "humbly" accept your due.

A "leader" who steps forward in times of chaos, with just the right plan (expertise and/or equipment) to "stop the madness" fits this category.

A ninja spy and an insider trader on Wall Street can also fit this category when, by hook or crook, they come into possession of valuable pieces of information, information that can give them power over others, and/or influence over events (e.g., the outcome of a battle).

Often the person wielding this kind of specialized information becomes "the power behind the throne." Ever hear of Martin Bormann (1900–?)?

In medieval times, the court jester was often the most informed man in a kingdom because—thinking him the fool—everyone talked freely in front of him. Read *I, Claudius* by Robert Graves (1895–1985).

Position Power

Position power comes from a person's recognized and agreed upon right to issue commands and make demands of others.

For example, we all agree police have the power to arrest and that the president has the power to make war. The office and rank they hold—and our consent—give them their power.

Position power is thus dependent on and derived from others who "obey" you because they believe it is their duty and/or obligation to recognize your position within the social pecking order.

There are, however, two drastically different variations of position power:

Legitimate position power. This power comes from your having "won" a position, either through some sort of election process, or else by universal acclamation after you "seize" power, albeit with the blessing of the masses.

Julius Caesar fits this category, but so does Hitler—both "seizing" power in "troubled times" *with little resistance* because they were hearlded as "deliverers" (or at least the lesser of two evils) at the time.

(**Note**: "Legitimate" in this sense simply means the ability to get power and to hold on to it.)

False position power. On the other hand, false position power comes from simply wearing a uniform. This uniform can be anything from an actual military, police, or guard's uniform, to that silly hat your cult makes you wear; from your gang's tattoo, to that all-powerful bureaucrat's rubber stamp you swing around like it was the Grim Reaper's scythe!

Never mistake position for power. Mythology tells us Lucifer had power . . . but did he? He had a position in Heaven. But any "power" he exercised could be taken from him—and was!—at the whim of his schizophrenic, sexually repressed boss.

Sometimes it really is better to rule in Hell.

Any power that depends on the car you drive, the key you turn, the uniform you wear, or the desk *they* give you to sit behind, ain't worth squat since *they* can take it from you at any time.

3

The Killer "B's"

At first glance the task of studying, let alone mastering, all the ancient and modern methods of mind control appears impossibly daunting.

Indeed, there seems to be no end of approaches to mind-manipulation ancient and modern, East and West.

Nor will we any time soon find ourselves lacking for "masterminds", Black Science adepts, deserving of our study.

Don't be intimidated.

Truth be known, whether gleaned from a recently unearthed Tibetan scroll or downloaded just today off the Net, whether the "mystical" mutterings of some ancient Master Magi or the latest in highfalutin psychological jargon, all mind control schemings, skulduggery, and strategies boil down to the six killer "B's" (see Figure 11.):

BLIND

Sun Tzu taught that the ultimate accomplishment was to overcome your enemies without fighting, defeating your enemy before the actual battle is joined.

In other words, we need to *psych* him out. This psyching includes obscuring our objective, blinding him to our purpose.

Rather than having to resort to bludgeon and blade and bullet, Black Science adepts prefer to bamboozle and befuddle their enemies with bullshit, to frustrate and sow confusion in their enemy's mind, causing him to choke

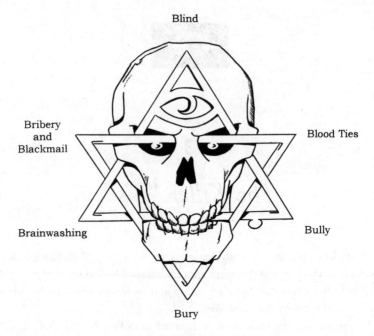

Figure 11. The Killer "B's"

at a vital juncture in a negotiation, to hesitate at mid-stroke during the heat of battle.

To accomplish this, we must "blind" him with emotion and make him doubt his own senses, his perceptions.

Ideally, we so blind our enemy as to leave him no option but turn to us for relief from his confusion, to turn to us for his salvation.

Whether a confidence scam designed to separate Aunt Matilda from her purse, or a murderous plot designed to separate a bloody tyrant's head from his body, the preparation and "execution" (heh-heh-heh) of such an operation is always the same and always begins with blinding your target to your true intention. This is classic Sun Tzu:

All warfare is based on deception. When strong, appear to be no threat. When on the march, make it appear you are still encamped. When drawing close, make him think you are still far away. And when still far distant, make him feel you are breathing down his neck.

The modern English word *glamour*, meaning beauty, charm, and romance comes to us from the Latin *grammar*, meaning "words," especially words used in casting magic spells:

> *"The Latin word in medieval times denoted not just literacy but learning in general, including knowledge of such occult sciences as astrology and magic."*
> —Webster's II New College Dictionary

By the time *glamour* made its way to ancient Scotland, it had come to mean the ability to control another's mind (hence their fate) through bedazzlement and confusion.

Still today, glamour retains much of its magical meaning. Don't *glamorous* movie stars and models have a seemingly *magical* charm to dazzle us?

To dazzle an enemy with glamour, to pull the wool over an enemy's eyes, thus to successfully hoodwink him, we call upon those twin-handmaidens of mind-manipulation: *Mis*lead and *Mis*direction.

Thus, no matter how seemingly complex a Black Science plan, from a skid-row confidence scheme, to a palace coup, all such operations use this most basic magicians' sleight of hand where we (figuratively and literally) make our enemy follow our finger pointing in one direction while the "magic ball" (i.e., his money, his life) heads in the opposite direction. (See Figure 12.)

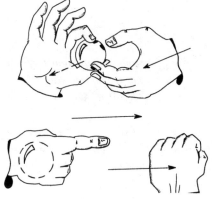

Figure 12. Sleight of Hand.

Once we understand this simple magician's principle, we can then use this unbeatable combination of *physical distraction paired with psychological doubt and distress* to mislead and misdirect any enemy down whatever blind alley we choose.

The simplicity of this principle has allowed it to be used in a thousand different ways down through the centuries—Black Science tactics and techniques ranging from the merely tricky, to the downright treacherous, by street hustlers panhandling their next meal, to bold freebooters plotting empire.

Again, it first appears that there's an endless number of ways to blind our enemies to our purpose and, indeed, it is a formidable list. But the more we study, the better we will become at spotting the similarities and discerning the patterns of successful tactics and techniques used by masterminds down through the ages; successful "blinding" tactics and techniques we will soon be calling our own!

BRIBERY AND BLACKMAIL

Use the words *incentive* and *inducement* if *bribery* and *blackmail* insult your sensibilities.

In simplest terms, bribery and blackmail are merely opposite sides of the same Janus-headed coin, that shining piece of literal or figurative silver coin we slip into another person's palm in exchange for his doing something for us (e.g., unlocking a door) or else for his not doing something he's supposed to do (e.g., locking a door).

Bribery

> *"If you give people exactly what they want,*
> *they'll kill themselves with it."*
> **—Marilyn Manson**

It only took thirty pieces of silver (roughly twenty dollars American) for Judas to betray the son of God Almighty, so what chance do the rest of us heathens have that someone close to us can't be bribed into selling us out for a handful of shekels?

You see there's no such thing as "altruism," no such thing as a truly selfless act. We always get paid, one way or another.

For example: We stop to help a stranded motorist. Why? Because it makes us feel good about ourselves, because we've been taught from childhood that helping people is what good people do.

I help, *ergo*, I am a good person. So we "get paid" with a good feeling.

Mother Teresa sacrificed her whole life caring for the sick and downtrodden in India. What was her pay-off? First, she got the same good feeling you get from helping that motorist. Second, "good people" go to Heaven—the *biggest* "pay-off" of all.

Here then is the key to getting people to do what you want: Always tell them what's in it for them, how they will gain by helping you and/or by following your plan.

Assume all people are "mercenary" and proceed from there.

Of course people are not always aware (i.e., thinking consciously about) how they are getting paid in every situation.

Still other people are always aware of how much *you* owe *them*. These people "credit bank," that is, they do something nice for you, "out of the kindness of their heart" . . . so they can *obligate* you later to do them a favor.

Psychologist Carl Rogers (1902–1987) said that we judge all actions and experience in terms of their value for facilitating or hampering or actualization growth, in other words we want to know "What's in it for me?"

Far from being a cynical view of mankind, this is a vital survival mechanism that evolution has programmed into us.

Ultimately, we all look out for number one—or should (remember, you're not much use to others unless you first get your own house in order).

And, yes, we never do anything unless there's ultimately "something in it for us." But, sometimes helping other people works to our advantage. The point to all this? *All of us have our "price."*

The good news is, chances are, you'll never be tempted by an enemy waving that one particular bribe you are especially susceptible to.

Hopefully your enemy isn't that observant, nor that adept at research.

Your particular bribe might not be something concrete, like money or sex. It might be something more abstract, like . . . ending world hunger. But rest assured, there's a bribe out there with your name on it!

Realizing—and *accepting*—this "night-side" flaw in yourself means you will now be armed against conmen, cult leaders, and would-be dictators blind-siding you with that one bribe you will be unable to resist.

Using bribery yourself is as simple as finding out what your enemy needs or wants and then offering it to him . . . with strings attached.

Buddha said: "A man's suffering begins with desire." Some people offer you *concrete* bribes: sex, drugs, money, revenge against *his* enemies. Others tempt you with *abstracts* like love, power, and "family."

When you can't directly bribe your enemy, you "Cut at the edges" by bribing someone close to him. (See Know Your Environment in chapter 1.)

> *"I can resist anything but temptation."*
> —Oscar Wilde (1854–1900)

Blackmail

> *"Some things are secret because they are hard to know, and some because they are not fit to utter."*
> —Francis Bacon (1561–1626)

In *Black Science*, in the chapter titled Digging Up Dark Secrets, we gave you a "dirty laundry" list of the seven kinds of "secrets" people keep.

Some of these are secrets because they are personally embarrassing (e.g., youthful indiscretions, body flaws, mental health concerns). Others are social and/or moral no-no's (e.g., sexual taboos and fetishes). Still other secrets are downright dangerous and illegal (e.g., crimes you or your outlaw in-laws have committed).

Blackmailing people is easy. You simply threaten to expose:

Something they did. Remember how your little sister threatened to tell Mom and Dad about your sneaking back into the house late unless you gave her a quarter and promised to do her chores . . . for the rest of your life?

Same principle when you offer to sell your enemy a full photo spread of him and his new girlfriend (or boyfriend!) . . . before you sell them to his *wife*.

Something you make them think they did. Using this approach, your enemy makes you feel responsible for an actual screw-up, or for a staged incident. This arranged accident could be anything from you crashing the boss's computer files, to making you think you inadvertently injured someone.

"Bump-n-hump" artists specialize in staging fake auto accidents. First they "bump" into you, then they "hump" (i.e., *screw!*) you by making you think you've given them whiplash or some other unseen injury.

Other hustlers stage stuntmen-like accidents (pratfalls, store displays collapsing onto them, etc.) making it look like you or your business are to blame.

All too often, in order to avoid trouble (or scandal) for ourselves (or for our business, etc.), we quickly settle out of court.

Something someone close to them did. We drop everything to come to the aid of loved ones. This action holds true when someone threatens to expose a friend or loved one's misdeeds (for example: that guy your alcoholic brother doesn't remember beating into a coma; that visit to the abortion clinic your little sister doesn't want your parents or priest to find out about).

Something you make them think someone close to them did. Same strategy as making your enemy think he did something.

The "hint" of scandal. For some people (e.g., politicians) the mere hint of scandal is enough to scuttle a promising career. Remember Chappaquiddick?

Remember Chandra Levy? No real blame ever attached itself to Congressman Gary Condit. But the scandal itself was enough to effectively ruin Condit's chances for reelection.

Likewise, Michael Jackson was never caught with any actual impropriety against children. Yet once the allegation was lodged against him . . . years later, he is still the butt of jokes.

Thus, merely the *threat* of having his name (or the name of a loved one) associated with such scandal is sometimes enough to bring an enemy around to your way of thinking.

For example, in June 2002, the FBI charged three men from Ohio and Kentucky with conspiracy to extort money via e-mail from people across the country. The men specifically targeted visitors to a child-pornography website.

The extortionists, calling themselves "Hacker Group 109," made contact with their targets in Internet chat rooms by expressing an interest in discussing child pornography. The men then "followed their targets home" via e-mail, sending them a blackmail letter threatening to expose their dirty little secret to the police unless they paid through the nose.

Twenty-one people, from as far away as California, reported the attempted extortion (AP 6/14/02).

(**Note:** If twenty-one people reported the attempted blackmail, you can bet twice that many were actually targeted. The best ally blackmailers have is the silence—fear or shame—of their targets.)

BLOODTIES

As the name implies, bloodties "tie" you to another person or to a group because they know some deep, dark secret about you.

Simply put, bloodties are just another—albeit specific—type of blackmail.

Cults, savage street gangs, and other killer cadre require prospective members to "make their bones," that is, do crimes or commit heinous and taboo acts, up to and including murder, to prove their dedication and loyalty.

The real purpose of demanding such acts from recruits is to give the person running the show a sword of Damocles they can hold over the new member's head.

Ironically this kind of "test" in itself indicates an inherent weakness in the group and in their leader, that their "teaching" and/or claim of "brotherhood" in and of itself isn't enough to insure the loyalty of their members.

Depending on the particular group, these bloodtie tests range from the bizarre to the brutal and bloody.

For example, two killers committing a murder often make sure both of them pump bullets into the victim, so both have as much to lose—and to *tell!*—when caught.

Likewise, cults often have members perform acts considered shameful by society's standards. This further helps the cult alienate the new recruit from "civilized" folk who would understandably look upon such taboo behavior with scorn and horror.

Documented cult tests of this sort include taboo sexual practices up to and including incest and pedophilia, obsessive ritual cleansing (e.g., shaving of genitals and anus, wiping with stones rather than toilet paper), and even self-mutilation (up to and including castration).

Most times a cult's bizarre initiation rituals and inner teachings are kept secret, supposedly because they are too sacred for the prying eyes of nonbelievers, but mainly because the cult's methods and mythologies are unable to stand up to the light of logic and are unacceptable, if not outright illegal, by society's standards.

Recall that the Heaven's Gate UFO cult demanded first castration, and ultimately suicide from its members.

Likewise, another UFO cult, Louis Farrakhan's so-called Nation of Islam, teaches its "inner circle" that a gigantic, invisible spacecraft called the "Mother Wheel," built by advanced Afrocentric technology, orbits the Earth.

While Farrakhaners never tire of bragging among themselves how this stealth UFO will one day (soon!) rain death and destruction down upon the Earth, cleansing it of all the Nation of Islam's enemies, NOI members never discuss the Mother Wheel with outsiders and are (understandably) embarrassed when asked about this ridiculous belief.

Louis Farrakhan himself claims to have been taken aboard this UFO in 1985. (See NOI's official newspaper *Final Call*, November 1989.)

Belief in the Mother Wheel (sometimes called the "Mother Plane" and the "Mothership") is bolstered by NOI's founder Elijah Poole's claim that the black race originated on *the moon* 66 trillion years ago.

As with most cults, showing one face to the public while showing another—presumably your *true* face and intention—to your fanatical followers is a time-honored tradition with NOI leaders. Its founder, Elijah Poole, alias Elijah Muhammed (1897–1975), was himself a follower of a *true* Black Science mastermind named Noble Drew Ali, founder of the Moorish Science Temple. But when the time came for Poole to concoct a "mystical lineage" for *his* newly found Nation of Islam in 1931, instead of crediting Ali with his instruction and inspiration, Poole manufactured a fictional mentor named W. D. Fard (nowadays written "Farad").

Today, while Nation of Islam revisionists go to great lengths to find candidates for a historical W. D. Fard, the true English—not Arabic—origin of the name "Fard" tells the real tale: "Fard" means "to paint the face," "to gloss over," especially to gloss over the truth. In other words, to wear one face for your followers while wearing another (false) face for the world at large.

That being said, the history and mythology of the Nation of Islam is a required course of study for any serious student of the Black Science. With the possible exceptions of the Mormons and the Jehovah's Witnesses, you'll not find a better—more bizarre!—example of a successful home-grown American religious cult. (See part III.)

Sharing in such a charade (let alone actually *believing* such fantasy!) further ties members to a cult, just as certainly as do more brutal "bloodties."

BRAINWASHING

The goal of brainwashing is twofold but simple: I strip your identity from you, and then I give you a new identity, one more suited to my purposes.

My strategy to accomplish this has two steps:

> Step One: I break you down.
> Step Two: I build you back up.

Following are numerous tactics and an endless variety of techniques I can incorporate into these two steps.

Love and Brainwashing

Being brainwashed is a lot like falling in love . . . with an emphasis on *falling!*

When we first fall in love, we tend to *overlook obvious flaws* in our significant other, those "little things" that, later on in the relationship, will drive us nuts!

Head over heels in love, we sacrifice our own wants and needs to make the other person happy. Only later will we come to lament all the lost opportunities, that promising career we passed up.

Soon the other person begins to change who we are; "just a little" at first. But before we realize it, we're dressing differently, talking differently—thinking differently. We shave our beard, or grow one, just to please the other person. Ultimately, in a "toxic" love affair, we alter our identity to please the other person.

These "symptoms" of love mirror the steps of brainwashing:

* *We overlook obvious flaws*, both in the "message" and in the "messenger."
* *We sacrifice our own wants and needs* to make our brainwasher happy.
* *We change who we are, altering our identity* to fit the reality crafted by our brainwasher.

The Identity "Stick"

There's a lot of worry today about identity theft, someone stealing your credit card or your Social Security number. But brainwashing is the *real* identity theft.

Where does your enemy get his identity? There is an intricate connection between identity and power. (See The Five Kinds of Power in chapter 2.)

Once you figure out what your enemy "identifies" with—because what we identify with *is* our identity—you can then use one or more killer "B's" strategies to first steal that identity from him, and then offer him a new identity more suited to the new reality you have created for him.

Ultimately, brainwashing gets its power from "the stick," the power to punish the victim. Initially this brainwashing stick may be actual *physical* punishment, but as the brain washing process progresses, physical punishment ("incentive") gives way to *mental* punishment, a more subtle, and much more insidious stick than that used when we simply bully someone.

When I "bully" (our next killer "B"), I punish you with the stick for not doing what I demand.

After I successfully brainwash you, I confidently hand you the stick, and you punish yourself for not living up to *my* expectations!

Making another person doubt themselves, change themselves, and even punish themselves is ultimate proof you've successfully brainwashed them.

How to Tell If You've Been Brainwashed

Number one clue: You're afraid to ask questions. Sometimes it's not what you do that proves you've been brainwashed, it's what you don't do.

If you ever hold your tongue when you know someone (your boss, political leader, preacher, or teacher) is dead wrong, or if you catch yourself making excuses for them, trying to help hide or rationalize away contradictions in their behavior, then you've already experienced some degree of brainwashing.

While researching for *Mind Control*, I had cause to investigate members of a Muslim cult in northern Ohio whose *Imam* (leader) teaches them to pray towards Mecca by facing northeast.

Yet no amount of evidence (gloves, maps showing latitude and longitude) is sufficient to convince the followers of this Imam otherwise.

More ominous still, his followers—even those in the inner circle who know better—are afraid to question their leader. These followers fear that if they prove their leader wrong on something so obvious as being able to correctly read a simple map, odds are he's also wrong about being able to interpret the slightly more arcane "Will of Allah."

(Hopefully none of this Imam's unquestioning followers know how to pilot a jet airliner!)

Clue two that you've been brainwashed is when you catch yourself doing things you'd never have been caught dead doing a year ago—not good things, bad and bizarre things.

For example, if someone's convinced you "salvation" requires you to perform strange rituals like wiping your ass with seven stones, or doing an impromptu circumcision on yourself with rusty garden shears . . . you *might* be just a little brainwashed!

Yet, even when a brainwashed cult member suspects he's been duped, rather than fleeing the cult, he all too often redoubles his efforts to recruit others into the cult's fantasy world. This is his way of proving everybody is as gullible as he was and still is.

Misery loves company . . . and so does stupidity.

Cults know the more sheep in their flocks the more "legitimacy" they'll have as a "recognized religion."

And the more members my cult has, the more I can claim a monopoly on "the Truth."

Majority makes reality. But always remember: Just because a billion people belong to a cult, that doesn't make it any less of a cult.

Sometimes even the greatest of Galileos, the most lucid of Leonardos, must bite their tongue in order to avoid becoming the next faggot to feed the bonfires of the ignorant.

How to Prevent Yourself from Being Brainwashed

First, never stop asking questions. Never bite your tongue. Second, never just "go along to get along." Never let them talk you into "just pretending." Never convince yourself "It can't hurt to just go to one meeting, to just listen to what they have to say, to just play along for a while."

Chapter 1, verse 1 of the *Brainwasher's Bible*: "Saying is believing. Believing leads to behaving. What we do, we become."

Third, get a real identity, not a half-assed identity that depends on externals (e.g., on how many body piercings you have, the size of the Bible tucked under your arm, that funny robe or hat you're required to wear, how long your beard is, that foreign language you speak more fluently than your native tongue). (See Position Power in chapter 2.)

Remember: All true power comes from within.

Modern interest in "brainwashing" began in earnest after it was revealed that North Koreans were using Chinese *Hsi hao* indoctrination techniques on NATO POWs. Worried that Communist countries might get the upper hand when it came to mind manipulation, Western intelligence agencies began pouring billions into the study of the Black Science, researching everything from psychological warfare to psychotropic truth serums, from ESP assassins to *psychotronic* devices designed to overshadow the mind. This research has continued—unabated—down to the present day. Only the names—not the *aims!*—have changed.

But while the term "brainwashing" itself is barely fifty years old, techniques of brainwashing have existed for ages. (More of this in part III, Masterminds and Madmen.)

Reread *Coming Clean about Brainwashing* in *Black Science* (Lung and Prowant, 2001).

BULLIES

*"Often the mind-slayer's craft comes down
to simply making threat."*
—Lung and Prowant, *Black Science*

Whether it's a grade school threat of "Give me your lunch money or I'll give you a wedgie!" or "Mess with me and mine and we'll nuke your whole friggin' country!", from the playground to the battleground, the "Bully Game" is alive and well.

The bully's power is the "stick." (Nukes are just a bigger more radioactive stick!) Deciding to bully your enemy, you have the choice of using a *psyche* ploy or a *Nike* ploy? In other words, you can head him off at the pass with a psychological ploy—attacking his *psyche*. Or else, you can get *physical* and kick off in his ass with a size-13 *Nike*!

Mental Bullies

*"By directing the first prong of attack into our foes' mind, we
might eliminate the need to 'follow through' with an actual
physical attack."*
—Lung, *Cao Dai Kung-fu*

In medieval European churches, religious paintings and icons were crafted using a technique called *trompe l'oeil* (French for "deceive the eye") to make it seem the eyes of Jesus, the Virgin Mary, and all the saints were "following" parishioners around the room.

This subtle form of bullying was (and still is!) enough to guilt most parishioners into digging a little deeper into pocket and purse when the collection plate was passed.

That famous World War I (the one fought in 1914) poster with our stern Uncle Sam pointing his promising (or warning?) "I want you!" used this same eyes-locked-on technique. Modern billboards, where that scantily clad babe just can't seem to take her eyes off you . . . until you buy whatever it is she's hawking, also use this approach.

Of course *you* would never be susceptible to such "obvious" Madison Avenue manipulation. (Heh-heh-heh.)

You'd be surprised to learn just how many psychological "bully ploys," some subtle, some more overt, are aimed at you every day. More still, how many of those ads hit the mark:

Novelty. If it's "new" and "improved" we gotta have it.

Scarcity. Diamonds are rarer than rocks, so diamonds are more expensive, so we want diamonds. If it's "one of a kind," "a collector's item," we gotta have it.

The less there is of something, the greater the chance "They'll run out of it!" and the quicker we gotta have it.

Advertisers—and conmen—know this, that's why they're always warning us that whatever they're trying to sell is rare, or running out fast.

Time. Every day we get bullied by limited time offers, or we have to scramble before we miss out on the "sale of the century." This rush game is one of advertisers' favorite approaches.

Criminal masters of the short con also force their "marks" into making snap decisions, denying their victims time to realize they've been targeted for a scam.

Likewise, religious cults never tire of reminding us that salvation is a "limited time offer," that "the end is nigh!"

Most people don't work well under pressure. Grace under fire is an acquired skill. Calculations against our enemy must be painfully slow. Operations against our enemy, blindingly swift!

Age. Age is the way time bullies us personally. Advertisers know this and make billions by promising to show us how we can avoid aging, slow aging, and even reverse the effects of aging.

And even if we succeed in convincing ourselves that growing old doesn't bother us, that "age doesn't matter," the truth is *age does matter*, if only to the people we deal with on a daily basis who are all too quick to make assumptions based on our apparent age.

We stereotype people according to age; teenagers are anxiety ridden and rebellious, middle-aged men go through a midlife crisis. Women pushing thirty hear their biological clock ticking. Later, after their grown children leave home, these same women experience empty-nest syndrome. And senior citizens—they're all old fashioned, set in their ways, stubborn, and senile.

Stereotypes, sure. But like many stereotypes, these have some basis in fact.

According to psychologist Erik Erikson (1902–1994) human beings go through eight "psychosocial stages" during the course of their lives. At each stage there is a task or goal to be accomplished. Accomplishing each "task" (at its proper stage) better prepares us to move on into the next stage of life. Failure to accomplish the task assigned at each stage stifles our overall development, produces neurosis, and interferes with our ability to cope with life in general.

Nietzsche would say that our *need* to accomplish these "tasks" is just further proof of our "Will to Power," that innate drive that compels us to acquire new skills and more power, both of which, in turn, better prepare us for survival and further conquest. (See The Five Kinds of Power in chapter 2.)

From a Black Science perspective, knowing the age/stage of the person we have in our sights helps us craft a strategy specifically designed to exploit his *need* to fulfill the Erikson task immediately obsessing him.

We thus shape our language and demeanor to suit the person's age and stage: We talk differently to a teenager (struggling to establish his identity) than we do a man in his fifties who needs to feel he can still contribute something to life.

Conformity. "Public opinion" is just the adult name for "peer pressure."

Experiments done by psychologists have shown repeatedly that an individual human being will all too easily yield to the will of the majority at least one-third of the time. (Blass, 2002:71)

We all like to think we're rebel souls, loners who don't care what other people think. But the truth of the matter is other people—and what they think of us—have a lot to do with defining our identity, hence our reality.

When everybody's doing it, it's hard for us to stand alone and resist the temptation. When the bandwagon's parading out the gate, it's hard to resist jumping on board.

The psychologist Erich Fromm's (1900–1980) research led him to conclude that most of us take our identity from our association with others. So we *do* care what others think.

Our church, job, school, social clubs—all influence us, subtly and sometimes not so subtly bullying us to conform to the will of the majority. (See Know Your Environment in chapter 1.)

Nineteenth-century anarchist Max Stirner railed against "the tyranny of the masses," against the way the voice of individuality is all too often drowned out by the incessant mutterings and mental meandering of the ignorant masses.

This would be the same spirit-stealing majority Nietzsche dubbed the "herd."

Remember: Majority makes reality. And it is the rare individual indeed who can stand against the obese obnoxiousness of the mindless majority.

Status. A recent San Francisco study found that frustrated motorists honked less or waited significantly longer before honking at *luxury cars* lingering at green lights.

Admit it or not, we kowtow to those of real or imagined higher status. Sometimes we do this consciously, all too often we do this unconsciously. (**Note**: It's only "ass-kiss'n" when you're unaware you're ass-kiss'n. Otherwise, it's *strategy!*)

Rather than being rooted in some modern vanity, our obsession with our place in the "pecking order" is a natural holdover from less-evolved times when the top dog always ate first, and the slowest and lowest in pack and pride went hungry.

Authority. Blass (2002) stated: "We didn't need Milgram to tell us we have a tendency to obey orders" (page 73). In June 2002, the short-lived television program *SPY-TV* (think *Candid Camera* . . . on crack!) aired an episode where three unsuspecting men (curiously enough a black, a white, and a Hispanic) were hired as night watchmen to guard a seemingly innocent warehouse.

One by one the men were set up in a security booth outside the warehouse and instructed by their new boss to call him on the walkie-talkie should anything "out of the ordinary" occur. None of the men bothered to ask *what* they might be guarding in the warehouse.

No sooner did the boss exit than a man *apparently being held prisoner* (!) began begging through a broken window for the respective guard to release him.

Though obviously confused, rather than rush to free the pleading men, all three guards instead radioed the boss.

While the guard(s) waited outside, the boss stormed into the warehouse. And even though the guard(s) could clearly hear the prisoner screaming as the boss apparently tortured him, still the guard(s) made no protest. Later, the guard(s) each spot another prisoner escaping down a ladder on the side of the building. Again, all three guards call the boss who runs out and begins torturing the escaping man with what appears to be a powerful stun gun, before boldly dragging the battered prisoner back into the building.

Even after such a horrific display, only the Hispanic guard mutters a weak protest. Despite this, all three go back to work guarding the building, but not before the boss shows them a switch he says will trigger a 50,000-volt electrical barbed-wire-topped fence surrounding the warehouse.

No sooner does the boss disappear around the corner than a pack of "prisoners" suddenly burst from the building and start climbing the fence, obviously desperate to escape.

Without hesitation, two of the security guards throw the switch triggering the "electrified" fence. The two, the white and the black, then stand by and watch as sparks literally fly and the prisoners writhe in the fence, "sizzling" in obvious agony.

Only the Hispanic guard rebels against authority, not only refusing to throw the switch, but physically preventing his returning boss from throwing the switch himself, while verbally encouraging the prisoners to flee.

However humorous this *Spy-TV* episode, it only reaffirms what psychologist-slash-showman Stanley Milgram (1933–1984) proved back in the '60s with his experiments in obedience.

Milgram successfully compelled students to willingly inflict what they believed were painful shocks to fellow students. Milgram accomplished this using "no coercive powers beyond a stern aura of mechanical and vacant-eyed efficiency" (Blass, 2002:70).

We're trained from birth to obey authority: our parents, teachers and preachers, football coach, drill sergeant, bosses, police and politicians.

Great societies are envisioned by a handful of enlightened minds; they are won by the sweat, blood, and tears of a brave few; but inevitably societies are maintained by the day-to-day drudgery and unquestioning obedience to authority given by the mundane and mindless millions.

Again, evolution is to blame: In the wild, you only get one chance to challenge the top dog. Fail, and you don't have to worry about where the pack's next meal is coming from . . . because *you* are their next meal!

Perhaps you need reminding again of the old Chinese adage: Never strike a king unless you're sure you can kill him. (Rebels tend to live very exciting, *very short* lives.)

Physical Bullies

> *"When you've got them by the balls, their hearts*
> *and minds will follow."*
> —G. Gordon Liddy

When the *threat* of force fails, there's always the *force* of force!

The other Killer "B's"—Blind, Bribe, Blackmail, Bloodties, Brainwashing, and even *mental* Bullying—all rely on "messing" with your enemy's head.

Physical Bullying, on the other hand—actually, on the other *fist*—doesn't "mess" with your enemy's head . . . it *crushes* it!

Let's not waste time repeating cliches like "Violence is the last refuge of the ignorant" and "Violence never settles anything." Sure it does.

History is full of examples where well-placed violence has stopped wars, ended the tyranny of mad dictators, and prevented the rise of their would-be replacements.

Mao Tse-Tung (1893–1976) knew the magic formula: "All political power comes out the barrel of a gun." In other words, political power comes from the threat of violence, or else from the actual use of violence.

If this comes as a major shock or affront to your sensibilities, maybe you should be reading *Harry Potter*, not *Mind Control*.

Grow up. Violence is all too often how business is done in the real world. From womb to tomb, we live under the threat of violence.

All the progressive parenting classes in the world won't change the fact that, when all else fails, Mommy and Daddy have the power to administer some "violence" to your backside.

In some places teachers can still paddle students. Do you think that cop is kidding when he screams, "Halt, or I'll shoot!"? And what "business" do you think the Armed Forces are in?

Religious cults talk a lot about love, but behind it all is the violent threat of the ass-whipping their blood-crazed deity is gonna slap on we nonbelievers at the Judgment.

Terrorists are bullies too. Look at what a few such bullies—not afraid to use violence—accomplished on 9/11.

Sadly, the fact remains that violence—physical bullying—is a great motivator once "civilize" negotiations break down . . . or when the previous Killer "B's" fall on deaf ears. Machiavelli stated in the *Discourses* in 1531:

> Men are mainly moved by one of two emotions: love or fear. A prince has a choice to make himself loved or to make himself feared. In the end a prince who makes himself feared is usually better obeyed, his orders more quickly and closely followed, than a prince who depends on being loved. (III:2)

BURY

"When society was in its infancy, men distinguished themselves by the amount of brute strength they could muster. Today, at what we fondly refer to as 'the height of civilization,' we do the same— only less directly."
—**Marquis Donatien Francois Alphonse De Sade, 1797**

Observation and prediction: Gunpowder changed warfare forever by substituting chemical energy for physical strength. So, too, today we find ourselves in a rapidly changing world where information is slowly replacing all other forms of "persuasion."

Yet it is doubtful there will ever come a time in the affairs of man when reasoning alone will settle all our problems and assuage all our differences.

No matter how obvious a solution, no matter how untenable their position, there always seems to be that one knucklehead standing in the way of progress, one asshole who won't listen to logic and who refuses to realize the bell is tolling for *him*. No amount of persuasion is enough for this guy. . . .

And that's where *Hasan's Rules* come into play. Hasan ibn Sabbah, founder of the dreaded eleventh-century Middle Eastern cult of the *Assassins* (Hashishin) taught his followers that all problems could be solved either through (1) *education* or through (2) *assassination* (Lung, 1997b).

Simply put, you should first try to "educate" anyone who gets in your way.

Any official getting in Hasan's way would wake up one morning to find a dagger sticking in the pillow next to his head. Anyone (and there weren't too many!) failing to be educated by Hasan's timely lesson were then simply killed.

A similar attempt would be made to educate whoever the lucky stiff (. . . ahem) was who replaced the dead man . . . *ad infinitum*, until someone took the official's position who was willing to be "educated." Machiavelli (1531) said, "No prince should be quick to shed blood, unless no other course presents itself, and this is seldom the case" (Discourses, III:19).

Last but not least, there's one final Killer "B" to take notice of, the *most important* Killer "B."

This "B" stands for "better" . . . as in "You *better* watch your ass!" And, you *better* study your enemy *before* your enemy succeeds in mastering these Killer "B's" before—and better—than you do!

> *"In warfare, the more you can disguise your intent and angle of attack, the better your chances of first befuddling, battering down, and then burying your enemy."*
> —Lung, *Cao Dai Kung-fu*

Part II

MASTERING
THE GAME

*"We became flexible, adaptive and versatile—adept at
improvisation and innovation—if for no other reason than
because we had to in order to survive."*

—J. Paul Getty

 ## Introduction

In part I, *Perception and Power*, we learned some of the overall approaches and
strategies employed in mind control.

Now in part II, *Mastering the Game*, we'll hone our acuity by concentrating on more specific insights and *tactics* designed to help us more easily steal
away the methods of mind control and manipulation used by the *Masterminds
and Madmen* we'll meet in part III.

Yes, I did say "steal" their methods.

Given half a chance, it's the least such merciless masters of mental
mayhem would do to us!

4

Mind Control by the Numbers (Redux)

Down through the ages any number of Black Science schools have established curriculum—schema and schemes—some far-reaching, others merely far-fetched, but all designed to help pry open the stubborn oyster of the mind. Some of these methods were shaped by, and perhaps better suited to, dealing with the realities of their particular time and clime.

Other methods have more universal application and are just as viable—if not villainous!—today as they were when conceived of centuries ago.

Either way, for Black Science scholars, all are deserving of our study.

SHUHARI: THE ONE CIRCLE

"When you find you're ass-deep in alligators, just remember you came to drain the swamp."
—Lyndon Baines Johnson

In medieval Europe, whenever a dispute between villagers threatened to disrupt a community, those bickering were admonished to "Keep the church in the middle of the village"; in other words, *focus* on the big picture, in this instance, to think about how their petty dispute was affecting their community and neighbors.

Focus is always job one. The minute we lose our focus, no matter what our goal, all is lost.

If our enemy can distract us—even for an instant—that is all the time he needs to slither his dirk between our ribs—be he armed with a physical blade, or a dagger of the mind. Distraction is the doorway to death.

Thus the "art of distraction" is a required course of study at the "Black Science Institute."

From psychological warfare experts to petty conmen, from a magician making a dove disappear to a conspirator making you disappear, so much of the Black Science (mind control) comes down to simple *distraction*.

Tao You See It, Tao You Don't

Modern physics keeps looking for what it calls the "Unified Field Theory," a single equation that will tie together and pretty much explain everything in the universe.

Chinese Taoists have had their own Unified Field Theory for centuries. They call it *Tao*.

Tao is the one singular force in the universe. In fact, Tao is the universe. Like a balloon both filled with air and surrounded by air, so, too, Tao envelops us, fills us, and animates us. Tao *is* us. Tao is symbolized by what Westerners call the "yin and yang":

Figure 13. Yin and Yang/Tai Ch'i

Most non-initiates, when looking at the yin and yang symbol, see the obvious: *opposite sides*, each containing the seed of the other.

Yin and yang are hot-cold, light-dark, masculine-feminine, an endless list of opposites. Everything in the universe is assigned a place on one side or the other of this equation. Depending on time and circumstance, event and effect, either yin or yang dominate. Or at least that's how it appears to most people.

But according to Taoist masters, such *dualistic thinking* is flawed. Any time we embrace one side or the other of this yin-yang, good-bad equation, we set ourselves up as the enemy—and victim—for its opposite.

For example, when I'm content, my enemy can make me discontent. If I'm depressed, I am more vulnerable to anyone promising me eternal bliss.

The key, say the Taoist masters, is to realize that while yin and yang are constantly jockeying for position, symbolizing the ever-changing nature of life, *the circle remains constant*—symbolizing the true nature of a universe that never changes. To Japanese *sennin* (mind-masters) the tao is *shuhari*, meaning "circle." Shuhari includes both literal circles and philosophical ones.

For example, there is the physical shuhari martial arts students "draw" around themselves, the protective parameter that surrounds them. In combat, an enemy is never allowed to trespass into your personal shuhari unchallenged.

There is also a physical circle around you composed of your family and friends. An enemy can attack you by infiltrating this circle, either by pretending to be your friend, or else by befriending (i.e., targeting) your intimate circle.

This intimate shuhari exists inside an even larger circle that encompasses everyone—no matter how seemingly unimportant—you come into contact with on a daily basis. As already mentioned, an enemy can also get at you through these "little people."

We have still another more abstract—but no less real!—circle composed of the totality of our life, including our intimate and extended circle of associates as well as our attitude and outlook. Big surprise: A shitty attitude attracts more negative "flies" into your life circle.

Thus, in the same way we need to focus on the circle of the yin and yang and not be distracted by its opposites, so too we need to tighten our circle, examining our close associations and attitudes to discover our innate strengths and most important, any potential chinks in our mental armor. Such realistic self-assessment is rare because it demands focus.

Three Monkeys Practice

Before trying to influence the mind of others, we first must rein in our own restless and undisciplined mind. In the East, the uncontrolled mind of man is symbolized by the scampering, easily distracted monkey. Rather than being "deaf, dumb, and blind," the three "hear no evil, see no evil, speak no evil" monkeys of the Far East are actually a Buddhist depiction of the proper way to meditate by closing off the senses and eliminating distractions, thus calming and focusing the mind.

To increase your own powers of focus, sit in a comfortable position and breathe in slow, deep, and deliberately several times while concentrating on the mandala in Figure 3, page 3.

After concentrating on this mandala for thirty seconds, close your eyes and try to hold the *after* image of the mandala in your mind's eye as long as possible.

Once the after image fades, open your eyes and repeat the process. Soon you will be able to retain the after image for longer and longer periods of time. Don't forget your slow, deep, and deliberate breathing while "visualizing" the mandala.

The calming effect of this concentration/meditation exercise alone makes it worthwhile, but the ultimate goal and benefit will be your reaching the point where, without having to look at the mandala, you can visualize this calming image—or anything else you choose to visualize—simply by closing your eyes and concentrating.

The lesson of the Tao yin yang (also called the *T'ai Chi*—"Supreme Ultimate") and the shuhari is to never take your eyes off the prize, never allow yourself to be distracted from the goal.

And the goal in mind control is to be the "distract*or*" and not the "distract*ed*."

As with the physical battlefield, so too the hazards of mental minefields; a single misstep is all it takes, a casual lapse in concentration can make you a casualty.

According to Norris (1998):

No one, not even a lover, looks at you as intensely and closely as someone who intends to knock you out in the ring. I could actually feel my opponent's eyes drilling into me, examining my slightest movement, measuring my breathing, calculating my physical condition. And I did the same to him. It's no exaggeration to say winning and losing a bout is directly related to concentration. A gap in your concentration is a hole in your defense—and your competitor will spot it immediately and make his move. (page 41)

TWO HEADS ARE BETTER THAN ONE

We've been taught "There's two sides to every coin." What we're not taught is that, in the hands of a Black Science adept, both sides are sure to be *head*s . . . or both sides *tails*, thus both definite winners—or losers— dependent upon our knowing what to call *beforehand*.

In plain English this translates to our needing to see both sides of an issue while not allowing ourselves to get caught up in (or *manipulated* into) the "illusion of opposites," into seeing life as either/or.

We're constantly told "You can't have it both ways," "you can't have your cake and eat it too," and "You have to choose one side or the other." But is this *always* true?

Has there ever been a war where both sides were wrong, conflicts where there were no clear-cut good guys or bad guys? All too often our enemies succeed in making us think we must reflexively embrace who they assure us is the "good guy" in a conflict, while summarily dismissing the other side— despite what we might be able to gain in the long run by allying ourselves with the "bad guy."

- Never let someone else pick friends—or enemies—for you.
- Some people are never satisfied . . . be one of those people!

Two heads really are better than one. To know the thoughts of your enemy as well as your own doubles your chances of victory.

The ability to see both sides of an argument allows you to manipulate factors on both sides, adjusting your own thinking to compensate for rapidly changing conditions and allowing you to "adjust" your enemy's thinking to better suit your purpose.

This is where "know your enemy"—being able to think like he thinks— spells the difference between your carrying the day . . . or your being carried out today!

Whether we choose to exercise it or not, we all possess the ability to see our mistakes after they happen. But even animals have this hindsight and learn from their mishaps and mistakes. What we need to acquire is *foresight*.

The Roman god Janus was two-faced—literally—symbolizing his ability to see both past and future. Janus was the god of Doorways hence the god of Opportunity.

No clichés can actually "turn stumbling blocks into stepping-stones," wrest advantage from disadvantage, or squeeze asset from deficit. Only the singular keen and concentrated eye of determination can accomplish that.

Consider the waste of war. Look at wars we've fought, just in the twentieth century alone.

Those once our blood enemies, those we once villainized and dehumanized with scathing propaganda as subhuman savages and brutal killers just scant years ago, are now our closest allies.

Likewise, today we make ill-advised alliances with petty dictators, arming them with the same knife that tomorrow they'll use to stab us in the back.

So much international turmoil comes from shortsightedness, self-promoting politicians incapable of looking ten or twenty years ahead toward crafting a more lasting peace and prosperity.

Although individually we may not be able to impact much on world politics, we can control our own little corner of the world by preventing this same pitiful and myopic scenario from playing out in our personal lives.

Too many of us consistently waste our *bio-resource*s (i.e., people) by allowing jealousies, lingering resentments, and petty prides and prejudices to prevent us from recognizing and exploiting (Oops! I mean "utilizing") the unique skills of those around us.

Everyone of us has grievances stemming from the way we've been treated by others, the boss, the government, and life in general; complaints that a perceptive and oh-so-sympathetic enemy mind-slayer can use to get close to us.

Flipping this coin over, we realize we can also use the resentments people secretly (and sometimes not so secretly) harbor to our advantage in recruiting "agents" to our cause. Thus:

- The underappreciated can be turned into our willing agents when we show them how much more appreciated they will be in *our camp*.
- The abused can be comforted by our "sympathetic ear" and waterproof shoulder.
- The bitter, battered, and falsely convicted can be given a blueprint for

revenge against all those who crossed him, stood in his way, or were just too slow to recognize his "obvious genius." (Once again: The enemy of my enemy is my friend.)

Sun Tzu devotes an entire chapter to the recruitment of such disaffected and estranged personalities. Appropriately enough, chapter XIII.

The Two Schools

For Black Science and mind-control study, modern psychology can be broadly divided into two schools of thought which we shall call the "Inner School" and the "Skinner School," corresponding to two very different ways of dealing with psychological healing.

The Inner School. This school is represented by *Psychoanalysis*, founded by Sigmund Freud (1856–1939).

Freud theorized that disturbed and deviant behavior could be explained by internal events: feelings and phobias, desires and dreads, the traumas and drama stumbling around on the subconscious stage inside our skull. (See Getting to Know his "Night-Side" in chapter 1.)

Freud was convinced a person would stop acting screwed-up (effect) as soon as he exposed the underlying (i.e., subconscious) cause.

Most times, according to Freud, why we do half the stuff we do is a mystery, even to ourselves. That's where spilling your guts on the shrink's couch comes in. Talk long enough and you eventually give yourself away to the shrink and he figures out you became a serial killer because you were improperly pottie trained.

(The good news is, the Inner School says you can blame all your adult problems on your equally screwed-up parents . . . and that's kind of therapy in and of itself!)

The Inner School follows Freud's theory that we have in our heads an "id" (our subconscious "inner brat" that wants everything it sees and won't take "No!" for an answer), the "ego" (our conscious mind, responsible for telling the id "No!" because ego doesn't want to go to jail for something id did) and the "super-ego" (our "conscience" who sets impossibly high standards that ego can't possibly reach, causing ego nearly as much *anxiety* as does id).

This "unresolved" anxiety pops up in all kinds of ways, not the least of which are phobias, neurosis (nervous disorders), and psychosis—think "Hannibal the Cannibal."

The id, ego, and super-ego seldom agree and often subconsciously sabotage one another. Thus embarrassing trip-ups of the tongue occur when ego is saying one thing but id is "thinking" something else.

Inner School shrinks delight in hearing such "Freudian slips" since these, and other subconscious verbal and physical tells (our body language, etc.), give them insight into what you are really thinking. (See Shadow-Talkers in chapter 5.)

Needless to say, correctly discovering and deciphering your enemy's subconscious drives and desires before he's aware of them himself puts him pretty much at your mercy.

Conversely, we must take pains to clean out any subconscious skeletons still skulking in our own closet . . . *before* you-know-who does.

The Skinner School. Named for B. F. Skinner (1904–1990), the most outspoken and controversial follower of Behaviorism, the Skinner School considers deviant and disturbed behavior (effect) to be caused by external events ("stimulus" from the environment) and to be maintained (positively reinforced) by its consequences. In other words: "It felt good the first time I did it, so I want to do it again."

Change the stimulus (i.e., cause) and you change the response (i.e., effect): "It used to feel good to do it, now it hurts to do it, so now I'm not going to do it again!"

Thus neurotic and even psychotic behavior can be explained as inappropriate or insufficient learning. In other words: too much stick, not enough carrot. Or too much carrot, not enough stick.

J. B. Watson (1878–1958), founder of Behaviorism, urged students to stop looking for a patient's inner feelings, subconscious thoughts and motivations, and Freudian hobgoblins like the id, ego, and super-ego. Instead Watson taught his students to concentrate on how organisms (including human beings) respond to stimuli in their environment.

Nobel Prize winner I. P. Pavlov did just that. Yeah, *that* Pavlov: Ring the bell, feed the dog. Ring the bell, feed the dog again. Ring the bell a third time, don't feed the dog, Rover *still* slobbers all over the place. Classic conditioning. Works with people too. (And, of course, *you* are 100 percent sure it *won't* work on you. Heh-heh-heh.)

In the 1920s Watson successfully produced a phobia in an eleven-month-old infant named Albert by making a loud noise every time he showed the boy a white rat.

Big surprise, the poor kid was soon cringing in terror, not only every time he saw a real rat but any time he saw anything even remotely resembling a real rat: other furry animals, a bushy coat, even rough cotton and wool fabrics (Journal of Experimental Psychology, 1920).*

On at least one occasion (the one occasion we *know* about) Skinner himself used his discoveries on just how easy it was to shape desired behavior in humans, to subliminally manipulate others (Lung and Prowant, 2001:101).

The Inner School believes you must first find the source of your negative feelings and phobias, the neurosis or psychosis beleaguering you. By unearthing the roots of the problem (usually either trauma or your mamma!), you'll then change your feelings and attitudes, which in turn, will make you stop acting so damned crazy. In other words, *revelation* leads to *rehabilitation*.

The Skinner School, on the other hand, doesn't concentrate on what or who screwed you up in the first place. They maintain that if you disrupt (i.e., change, stop positively reinforcing) the undesired behavior, feelings will follow. *Ergo,* change the person's behavior (their actions) and you also effect (change) their attitude as well.

Thus where a therapist from the Inner School might delve into a patient's early life to find the source of that patient's phobia of elevators, a therapist from the Skinner School would concentrate on getting that patient to actually ride the elevator, desensitizing the patient, knowing that changing the patient's behavior would change his feelings, thus eliminating his phobia.**

Recall that this is a basic principle behind brainwashing, that is, changing a person's behavior (e.g., making a person perform an act, no matter how superficial) is the first step to changing that person's beliefs.

Simply put, according to the Skinner School, you can change anyone's

---

*No, Watson didn't get arrested for child abuse. And no, we don't know if poor little Albert grew up to be a cross-dressing serial killer!

**Albert Ellis, founder of Rational-Emotive Therapy, once made a patient who was terrified of being humiliated walk around in New York City while dragging a banana behind him on a leash like a dog. Predictably, people did laugh at the man, but when the man realized that people laughing at him wasn't the end of the world, he started laughing too. Patient cured.

mind, and pretty much make anyone do anything, as long as you have a sweet enough carrot or a big enough stick.

Said J. B. Watson (1924):

> Give me a dozen healthy infants, well-formed, and my own speci-fied world to bring them up in and I'll guarantee to take any one at random and train him to become any type of specialist I might select—doctor, lawyer, artist, merchant-chief and, yes, even beggar-man and thief, regardless of his talents, penchants, tendencies, abil-ities, vocations, and race of his ancestors.

The Thinner School. Here at the "Black Science Institute" cafeteria, we like to have our cake and eat it too. So instead of choosing one school of mental mastery over the other, Inner School versus Skinner School, we take the best of both in order to create what we like to think of as the *"Thinner School,"* so-called because its methods and motivation are directed towards a singular goal: making us the winner while making our enemy's wallet, waistline, and ultimately his lifeline, "thinner"!

Thus, we freely mix and match tactics and techniques from opposing schools of thought until arriving at just the right tonic (or toxin!) guaranteed to cure whatever "ails" our enemy. (And when this prescription is properly administered, our enemy will no longer ail us!)

We can thus use the Inner School carrot of feigned friendship and pre-tended concern to get him to open up, to lay bare his psyche, allowing us to uncover the subconscious desires, dreads, and dirty little secrets he hides even from himself.

Like a wily poker player reading the tells his opponents unwittingly bring with them to the table, so, too, we can learn to read our enemy's subcon-scious, allowing us to confidently double our bet (investment) . . . or fold and flee to fight another day.

We can then borrow the "stick" from the Skinner School and use it to gently prod our subject into scurrying like a blind rat through physical and mental mazes of our crafting.

The means to accomplish this is surprisingly simple math: We either add stress to our enemy's life (the stick), or we offer to take away his already existing stress (the carrot).

Different events effect each of us differently. Some types of stress (e.g., horror movies, bungee jumping) we volunteer for. This is the acute adrenaline rush type of stress.

Chronic stress on the other hand is more insidious, lasting, and seldom invited. Anything from divorce to the collapse of the World Trade Center fits in this category, as does posttraumatic stress disorder (PTSD).

While new scales continue to be developed to more accurately measure stress, most are merely variations of the famous Holmes and Rahe Stress Test. (See Figure 14.)

Figure 14: LIFE STRESS EVENTS

Life Event	Pressure Points
Death of a spouse	100
Divorce	73
Marital separation	65
Jail term	63
Death of a close family member	63
Personal injury or illness	53
Marriage	50
Fired from work	47
Marital Reconciliation	45
Retirement	45
Change in a family member's health	44
Pregnancy	40
Sexual difficulties	39
An addition to the family	39
Business readjustment	38
Change in financial status	38
Death of a close friend	37
Change to a different line of work	36
Change in the number of marital arguments	35
Mortgage or loan over $10,000	31

Foreclosure of mortgage or loan	30
Change in work responsibilities	29
Son or daughter leaving home	29
Trouble with in-laws	29
Outstanding personal achievement	28
Spouse begins or stops work	26
Starting or finishing school	26
Change in living conditions	25
Revision of personal habits	24
Trouble with the boss	23
Change in work hours, conditions at work	20
Change in residence	20
Change in schools	20
Change in recreational habits	19
Change in church activities	19
Change in social activities	18
Mortgage or loan under $10,000	17
Change in sleeping habits	16
Change in the number of family gatherings	15
Change in eating habits	15
Vacation	13
Christmas season	12
Minor violations of the law	11

Total Pressure Score: ——

Scores 0 to 149 are reasonable, and indicate a relatively healthy state of normal stress.

Scores of 150 to 300 indicate that you are 50 percent more likely to experience illness within the next six months since stress reduces the body's ability to fight off illness.

Already besieged by one or more of these stressors, your enemy will be all too willing (gullible) to listening to anyone promising anything and everything designed to relieve his stress, from popping a pill to joining a cult. Conversely, should our enemy seem to possess little or no stress (highly unlikely!), it is a simple matter for us to use our mind control to give him some!

The Two Types of Intelligence

"Precision personal intelligence can be more critical than precision-guided munitions."
—**Count de Marencnes, former chief of French Intelligence**

Black Science (mind control) is first and foremost "the science of intelligence." And when speaking of intelligence, we distinguish between two types: *Innate* intelligence and *gathered* intelligence.

Innate Intelligence. The intelligence potential you are born with, as well as the intelligence (experience, education, and skills) you acquire over the course of your lifetime, is known as innate intelligence

Big surprise, most people never come close to actually reaching their intelligence potential.

The biggest single determinant of how close we come to operating at our peak intelligence potential is how diligently we teach ourselves to accurately perceive and process information about the world.

Remember that we human beings have two "sides" to our brain: a left half that does our linear and logical thinking, and a more abstract, artistic right half.

While we all use both halves of our brain, we're either right- or left-brain dominant.

Left-brain dominant people are more methodical in their thinking, they like to organize and accomplish things in their life step by step. These kinds of people make good, no-nonsense managers, but seldom receive awards for being creative or innovative.

It's easy to spot whether someone is right- or left-brain dominant by the verbal and nonverbal clues they exhibit. (See Figure 15.)

LEFT-BRAIN / RIGHT-BRAIN TRAITS

Left Brain	Right Brain
Verbal, uses words to describe things. **Temporal,** keeps good track of time. **Analytic,** figures problems out step by step and part by part. **Abstract & symbolic,** uses symbols and word representations easily.	**Nonverbal,** uses hands, draws pictures and designs in the air when talking. **Non-temporal.** Has no sense of time. Not good with schedules. **Synthetic,** sees the "whole", the big picture just by looking at the parts. **Concrete thinking,** relates to things as they are at the present time. **Intuitive, a good guesser! Makes cognitive leaps.**
Logical & linear. **Sequential** (A-B-C . . . .)	
Objective	**Subjective**
Catchphrase: HMMM . . .	**Catchphrase: AHA!**
Mathematical (uses numbers to measure and count his world)	**Metaphorical** (uses images and metaphor and simile to describe his world)
Most left-brain dominant people are **Listeners**	Right-brain dominant people tend towards being **Watchers and Touchers.** Listen for his use of words and phrases indicating his **W-L-T** orientation.

Figure 15.

Determining whether our enemy is right- or left-brain dominant tells us how our enemy perceives, procures, and processes intelligence about his world:

- Is he an abstract thinker or a more concrete (literal) thinker?
- Does he employ scientific reasoning before coming to a decision, or does magical thinking (e.g., Lady Luck and the Lottery) rule his world?

- Is he capable of being objective or is he always subjective in his dealing with others?
- Is he inner-directed (Jp. *Jodomon*) or outer-directed (Jp. *Shodomon*)?
- Is he a loner who prefers operating on his own, or does he need the safety of the crowd, making him curry the favor and validation of others?
- Is he spurred by conscious ambitions, or is he driven on by subconscious Night-side motivations he's unaware of?

The more of these inclinations and motivations you can discern the easier it will be to slip a ring through your enemy's nose.

Gathered intelligence. On the other hand, gathered intelligence is bits and bites of information you glean in order to accomplish a specific objective.

The best example of this is, obviously, deliberate intelligence we set out to gather about our enemies, his "camp," and his intentions.

We gather this kind of intelligence about our enemies using two methods:

- *Observation* (including in-depth research)
- *Insight* into our enemy's thinking that he gives us himself—freely, inadvertently, or after we apply sufficient . . . incentive

Having gained intelligence via observation and insight, we are then free to apply that intelligence using two types of techniques.

Error or Terror?

Basically, mind-control techniques rely on elements of either error, terror, or a combination of both.

Error. Using an *error* attack plan, we first uncover and quickly take advantage of any and all error we find in our foe—faults in his perception, flaws in his personality, fatal oversights in any plans he has for the future.

Bluntly, this means ruthlessly exploiting any weakness we discover in him or in his world, using deceit to play on his conceit, and filling his already swooning head to overflowing with doubt. According to Lung (2002):

> Doubt is the doorway to death. Make a man doubt his abilities and
> the validity of his battle plans, make him doubt his best friend, and
> you have already defeated him. Read *Othello*.

The first four Killer "B's"—Blinding, Bribes and Blackmail, Brainwashing, and binding him to you with Bloodties—all hinge on this element of error.

Terror. The two remaining Killer "B's"—Bully and Bury—rely on an element of *terror* to accomplish their ends. Lung said: "A dagger of fear can kill quicker than a dagger of steel. The right word in the right ear accomplishes much, and often wins a battle before that battle begins."

Crude as it may sound, you'd be amazed what just the right bludgeon—strategically poised over just the right head at just the right time—can accomplish.

Likewise, you'd be shocked how quickly just a few amps of electricity—correctly applied—can jump-start stalled negotiations!

So much confusion, waste, and wantonness exist in the world today simply because too much time is allowed to elapse between a clear-cut crime and an even clearer-cutting punishment (Lung and Prowant, 2003).

The carrot or the stick, sooner or later we all succumb to one or the other . . . or both. Try as we might to break the leash, we're still Pavlov's pups.

THE THIRD EAR

Depending on circumstance and flux, human beings process the information they get from the world analytically, emotionally, or instinctually, represented respectively by head, heart, and hearth.

Head

Our ability to reason and analyze is what puts us at the top of the food chain. Sadly, so many human beings make little or no effort to actively lay claim to this "birthright." While this is a sorry comment on the human race in general, the fact that 95 percent of human beings make little or no effort to improve their intellectual capacity or their reasoning ability is actually good for us individually so far as our Black Science craft is concerned.

Heart

The heart was long thought to be the seat of emotions. Today, we know its chemicals in the brain that actually cause our mood swings.

For example, when a person falls in love they experience passion and a sensation of euphoria because of an increase of brain neurotransmitter called *dopamine*. This euphoria can last for months, up to two years, and gradually settles down to a feeling of warmth and attachment as a hormone called *oxytocin* increases in the body.

During this initial euphoric stage of romantic love, our judgment is often clouded, preventing us from seeing flaws in our lover (reported in *Awake!*, August 8, 2002).

However, don't count a "feeling" heart out just yet. Interestingly, there may actually be some credence to the belief that the heart influences emotion since the thymus gland (situated close to the heart) is associated with love and compassion. (See The Seven Wheels of Power, later in this chapter.)

Recall from our initial discussion on "perception" that having access to all the cold, hard facts in the world doesn't mean squat so long as we filter those facts through our all too fallible emotions.

Allowing undisciplined emotion to rule us is the same as putting a gun to our head and insures we've lost the battle before it begins. On the other hand, encouraging (i.e., forcing) our foe to filter all his incoming intelligence through his faulty emotional filters insures your victory.

Tempting an enemy's lust and greed, fanning his fears, pissing on his pride, or playing on his sympathies can all cause him to react subjectively and emotionally, from the heart, rather than objectively, examining facts and acting from the head. (See *Five Flags, Five Fears*, later in this chapter.)

In the final analysis, the heart is no substitute for the head. Facts should never take a backseat to fantasy.

This doesn't mean that we should be an unfeeling bastard, lacking compassion for infants and old folk, quite the opposite. Whether as a motivating factor for ourselves and our troops, or as a milestone marking the road to our foe's downfall, the play of emotion must be factored into any mind-control battle plan.

Hearth

According to Norris (1996): "There will be times when you don't know what to do, when your head dictates one course of action, your gut another. Which to follow? Always go with your gut" (page 166).

The English word "hearth" comes from the Sanskrit *kundayati*, meaning "he singes" and may be related to another East Indian word, *kundalini*.

Today we use hearth specifically to mean a fireplace, and more generally as a synonym for home.

Metaphorically speaking, our hearth is our gut, our instinct, untainted, untamed, un-trampled by society.

When something touches our feelings deep down, we say it hits us where we live, at gut level.

Some cultures in the East maintain that the seat of the soul is physically located three fingers' width below the navel, what the Chinese call *tan tien* and the Japanese call *hara*, as in *hara-kiri* (belly cut).

In fact, when a Samurai committed hara-kiri (more properly called *seppuku*) they were symbolically exposing their soul (literally their guts!) to public scrutiny. Therefore, to "go with your gut" means to trust your instincts.

In this tepid age of political correctness, where every innovative idea must first be double-checked by an equally tepid censor whose own taste buds were neutered long ago, where every joke is now a potential indictment, we've become so terrified to question another's motive and dare not openly show suspicion for fear of being branded a chauvinist, racist, reactionary, or worse.

This fear of what might happen all too often blinds us to the immediate danger of what is happening. Skinner (1995):

> Don't let *courtesy* get you killed. Rules of social etiquette were established a long time ago. Unfortunately, we live in *today*. . . . We should examine *our father's* rules of etiquette—drawn up in more civilized times—to make sure they still apply to today's savage streets. When forced to choose between courtesy, or street smart survival, the bottom line remains: Better to *offend* than have to *defend*. (page 61)

Better *red* than *dead*. Trust your instincts.

If it makes you feel better, think of your gut as halfway between your head (reasoning power, yang) and your heart (emotions, yin)—a balance of the two.

Just as our subconscious mind picks up on subtlety and nuance (i.e., "shadow-talk"), which then in turn influences our conscious reasoning, so, too, our physical body awareness often picks up on barely perceptible shifts in another person's attitude, their balance, or their release of pheromones (e.g., we smell their fear).

Some people believe in ESP. Whether or not such a "sixth sense" truly exists is moot, since the full use of our five existing senses can intimidate our enemy into thinking we indeed have extrasensory "powers."

Often we subconsciously pick up on verbal and nonverbal signals others give off subconsciously. (See Shadow-Talkers, in chapter 5.)

We get spooked or feel bad vibes. And we notice the hairs at the nape of our neck standing up (a carryover from less-evolved times when the thick fur on our bestial backs bristled up to make us look bigger and more fearsome than we actually were).

Hearth is therefore our "third ear." And we should listen. If you ever get a feeling something isn't right, that you're being watched . . . *go with your gut.*

Your gut, your animal instincts, evolved millions of years before your higher (all too often over-analyzing) human brain. If nothing else, your "gut" has seniority. Norris (1998) said:

> As a husband and father, friend, brother, and son—as a human being living among others—I know that many of my most important moments in my personal life were when I responded not in accordance with what I had reasoned to be the best course of action but when I acted in accordance with the urging of my gut or heart. (page 166)

THE FOUR HUMORS

No, the "Four Humors" are not the Marx brothers.

The concept of the Four Humors originated with Sicilian philosopher Empedocles (490–430 BCE) who theorized that everything in the universe is composed of four elements: Earth, Air, Fire, and Water.

Empedocles maintained these four elemental energies appear in the human body as four bodily fluids: phlegm, blood, choler (aka yellow bile), and black bile.

In order to maintain continued good health and proper disposition (literally good humor), a just balance of these four humors is required.

Conversely, a preponderance of any one of these four creates ill humor, physical sickness and/or maladjusted attitude.

For example Blood Humor (characterized by things hot and dry) makes us sanguine, thus confident, active and enthusiastic. However, when Blood Humor predominates we become overbearing and domineering, even dangerous and bloodthirsty *in extremis*.

Phlegm Humor (associated with things cool and moist) makes us phlegmatic (i.e., calm and stolid, objective and unemotional). Too much Phlegm Humor however makes us mentally lethargic and physically lazy. Taken to extremes, too much Phlegm Humor turns our useful objectivity to ruthlessness.

Black Bile Humor normally creates a pensive introspective mood, often resulting in feelings of nostalgia. An excess of black bile results in debilitating guilt and depression.

Yellow Bile Humor makes us excitable and filled with choleric energy. Taken to extremes, we become irritable and hot-tempered.

Ancient healers who subscribed to this Four Humors theory to explain illness cured patients via enantiopathy (i.e., applying the opposite element, for example treating fever with cold. (Hmm . . . this smacks of yin and yang!)

Since one of these four humors dominates in each of us, determining our overall temperament of mind and body, discovering which particular humor dominates our enemy allows us to more easily manipulate him.

Thus an enemy with balanced humors (i.e., in good health and spirit) must be pushed "off balance" and into an ill humor by applying a physical poultice or a mental ploy, designed to give him an excess of one of the four elements specially chosen to lead him in the direction you choose (e.g., giving him too much phlegm to make him lose his objectivity, or too much yellow bile to make him go postal).

This is accomplished by introducing various chemical potions, charms, and even specially crafted words and phrases (i.e., spells)—each corresponding to a specific Element/Humor—into his world.

(**FYI:** Basically, this is what most "*witches*" burned at the stake during the Middle Ages were accused of doing.)

Empedocles' Four-Element Theory, including its application in the human body as the Four Humors, continued to be used up through medieval times to the Renaissance, until finally displaced by more detailed discoveries in biology and medicine, and the development of true scientific disciplines like chemistry.

FIVE FLAGS, FIVE FEARS

"The five colors blind the eye. The five tones deafen the ear.
The five tastes seduce the tongue."
—Tao Te Ching

Empedocles' western Four Elements bares a striking resemblance to the Japanese *Gojo-goyoku* Five Weaknesses strategy discussed in detail in *Black Science* (Lung and Prowant, 2001).

In addition to Gojo-joyoku used by Ninja, down through the ages masterminds both East and West have made a multitude of calculations and compilations of human faux pas, faults, and fallacies, any and all of which can be useful to us today.

For example, many argue that Siddhatha Guatama the "Buddha" should be given the additional title of "Father of Psychology" since his insights into human nature were made 2,400 years before Freud lit up his first cigar.

Indeed, the *Dhammapada* ("Collected Sayings of Buddha") lists five weaknesses to be avoided if Nirvana (enlightenment) is to be achieved: "Ignorance is the greatest of taints . . . There is no fire like lust, no spark like hatred, no snare like folly, and no torture like greed."

(**FYI:** The next verse in this Buddhist "Bible" cautions: "The faults of others are easy for us to see, but our own faults are hard to see.")

Later Buddhist masters would identify the "Five Poisons" that plague man: Delusion, Wrath, Passion, Envy/ Greed, and Malignity (i.e., ignorant and injurious actions).

Again we note similarities between these observations and conclusions drawn by other schools of Black Science, East and West.

FLAGS

There's a Zen *koan* that goes:

> First monk: "Look, that *flag* is moving."
> Second monk: "No, the *wind* is moving."
> Third monk: "It is your *minds* that are moving."

In other words, our minds are constantly moving, an undisciplined monkey leaping from place to place, constantly chattering. When this monkey is our own mind, we are in constant peril, easily distracted and led astray. When this monkey-mind belongs to our enemy, half our objective has already been accomplished!

Like a flag incessantly flapping in the wind, turning first one way then the other, straining after every distracting breeze, so too the undisciplined mind dances around, captive to the arbitrary wind of the moment.

Recall from the book *Black Science* that FLAGS (as in warning flags) is a mnemonic device for remembering the "Five Weaknesses" we look for in our enemies: Fear, Lust, Anger, Greed, and Sympathy.

Fear

Fear is the first of the "Five Weaknesses."

According to the Buddhist *Avatamsaka Sutra* (sixth century BCE) human beings have five primary fears:

Fear for not having enough. This fear includes physical fears of poverty and hunger, as well as more psychological fears of inadequacy.

Fear of getting a bad reputation. On the positive side this fear makes us closely guard our personal honor. On the negative side, this kind of fear can drive us crazy worrying about what others think. (See Shadow-Talkers in chapter 5.)

Fear of death. This fear is not just the fear of physical death that all sensible people have, but also specific individual fears people have of dying a "useless death" after a wasted life.

This fear can also be the warrior afraid of dying with a black stain on his honor (e.g., before exacting revenge against his enemies, or concluding a promise).

Fear of falling into evil realms. Many Easterners belive in reincarnation, and for them this is a real afterlife fear (e.g., coming back as an animal, or as a *preta* (hungry ghost).

This kind of fear is also found among religious-minded Westerners fearful of going to Hell because they've sinned.

More mundanely, falling into evil realms can refer to descending into disgrace and/or losing a coveted position.

Fear of the authority of the crowd. On the one hand this fear manifests in a need to be recognized (i.e., loved and respected) by others, a need for social acceptance, to feel we fit in, to be part of the in-crowd.

On the other, we can actually fear our individuality being stampeded underfoot by the same maddening, mindless "herd" that so oppressed Max Stirner and Nietzsche.

Collectively, these five fears stack up well against Abraham Maslow's (1908–1970) Psychological Needs Pyramid, whose levels lead from *physiological* and *safety needs* (fear of not having enough), to *love and belongingness* (fear of the authority of the crowd), to *self-esteem needs* and *self-actualization* (fear of getting a bad reputation). (See Lung and Prowant, 2001:166.)

THE SIX DUSTS

A mirror is used in both Buddhism and Japanese *Shinto* to represent our pure "original mind," a mind unstained by worldly desires.

Unlike Western religions which teach that man is "born into sin" with two strikes already against him, Buddhism maintains that the original nature of man is perfect, that our mind is like a beautiful mirror crafted to perfectly reflect the will of The Universe.

Unfortunately, "dusts" obscure our otherwise perfect mind-mirror, preventing us from seeing our *true* self reflected.

The goal then is, via meditation and other Buddhist practices, to gradually wipe away these worldly dusts in order to accurately reflect reality as it is, rather than as we'd like it to be.

With all due respect to the Buddha, first comes survival, then comes enlightenment.

While the Buddha would undoubtedly frown at our "misusing" his insights and observations for personal gain, from a Black Science perspective, the more dust we can blow into our enemy's eyes, the better for us.

Six kinds of worldly dust prevent us from seeing correctly: Form, Sound, Scent, Taste, Touch, and *Dharmas* (i.e., external opinions and views). These dusts are similar to the mind "filters" we talked about in part I, Perception and Power.

Esoteric Tibetan *tantricism* (often accused of being a somewhat "twisted" branch of the great Buddha tree) lists six such dusts, what they call *Sem yung,* "mental factors."

These Sem yung are the *Rtsa nyon,* six "root afflictions" that stand in the way of enlightenment: Desire, Anger, Pride, Ignorance, Doubt, and Afflicted views (i.e., egotism and attachment).

Again, we easily spot similarities between these two compilations—Buddhist dusts and Tantric root afflictions—and the Japanese Gojo-goyoku.

(While we're stuck on "sixes", don't forget Cicero's Six from part I.)

THE SECRET OF SEVEN

The West has the classical Seven Deadly Sins, the seeds of weaknesses in man that are the bread and butter of the Black Science feast.

But just so we don't think the worst of ourselves and our fellow man, someone decided to try balancing these seven sins with seven virtues (See Figure 16).

In both East and West, the number seven holds an honored (i.e., superstitious) place.

It is in India that we find the secret of the seven power centers known as the *chakras*.

The Seven Wheels of Power

According to Indian Yoga masters, we have a mysterious, largely untapped energy in our body known as *kundalini*, symbolized as a serpent asleep at the base of our spine.

VIRTUE AND VICE

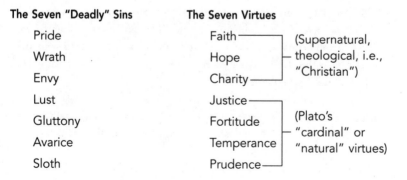

The Seven "Deadly" Sins	The Seven Virtues	
Pride	Faith	(Supernatural, theological, i.e., "Christian")
Wrath	Hope	
Envy	Charity	
Lust	Justice	(Plato's "cardinal" or "natural" virtues)
Gluttony	Fortitude	
Avarice	Temperance	
Sloth	Prudence	

Figure 16.

Once awakened—through yoga, meditation, and other disciplines—kundalini begins spiraling its way up our spine towards the crown of our head. Along this path, Kundalini's passing activates seven "power centers" called *chakra*s (wheels).

Each of these chakras controls various aspects of our physical and mental life—from basic survival needs to our desire for power, to our achieving ultimate enlightenment.

Kundalini energy, similar to the Taoist concept of chi, follows a natural, smooth-flowing course through the body unless interfered with by our personal hang-ups. According to Lozoff (1985):

> It's completely natural for power to flow into one chakra or another. The problem is, our fear and desires push us to unnaturally manipulate the power-flow, so that we don't allow the whole system to work as it should. (page 78)

Often compared to a flower opening and releasing its unique fragrance, as the ascending kundalini opens the petals of each chakra, unique energies are released, granting us enhanced physical and mental "powers" (*siddha*s).

In an effort to jump-start these chakra powers, over the centuries, yogin practitioners of both Kundalini Yoga and Tantra have experimented with countless ways to stimulate these power centers. These include physical disciplines:

- Contortionists' yoga postures
- Laying on specially designed beds of nails
- Burying themselves in earth up to the level of a specific chakra

Mental manipulations have included drugs, meditation, and hypnosis.

Extensive lists have also been complied of chakra correspondence, factors and formulas that can be introduced into a situation—into your own mind as well as the mind of your enemy—to help stimulate particular chakra and thus induce particular moods:

It's a two-way street: Our attitudes and actions help stimulate specific chakras. In turn, how we see the world depends on which chakra we're "looking through" (i.e., which chakra we are focused on), thus, which chakra is most active in us at any given time.

During the course of any day, even from minute to minute, our mood can change as energy vacillates from one chakra to the other.

In general, upper chakra are associated with higher levels of thought and action, while lower level chakra—though necessary for the survival of self and species—are associated with baser thought and action.

Much of our language reflects this natural aversion away from the lower end of this temperament totem pole: "Don't *go* there!" "Feeling *down* in the dumps," "Getting *down* and dirty," "lower expectations."

Conversely when things are going our way we feel "*up*beat," and "on top" because "things are looking *up*," which they actually are because we are focusing on the world through one of our upper chakra "filters."

Thus, when we feel good and compassionate about the world, we are dealing from our fourth heart/compassion chakra.

Conversely, when we worry over where our next meal is coming from, or fret about personal safety, we're stuck at our lowest root chakra.

You're engaged in a spirited conversation about philosophy and/or self-realization—your energy focusing through your sixth chakra. Suddenly a devastatingly beautiful blonde struts by in painted-on jeans and just as suddenly all your thoughts go south—literally south!—as your focus drops from your higher sixth chakra to your lower second chakra—the chakra controlling your uncontrollable libido.

But don't let this information *depress* you. (Heh-heh-heh.) We can easily use our knowledge of chakra to manipulate our enemy's mind-set and moods. For example, when we catch our enemy thinking higher thoughts, we simply bombard him with unexpected lower chakra images, instantly bringing him back *down* to thoughts of tribe, survival, and sex.

Determining the chakra level our foe is operating at—or aspires to operate at—gives us invaluable insight and takes us one step closer to our Black Science Ph.D. (In this case, Ph.D. = "plotting his downfall!")

For example, a common cult strategy when dealing with a religious-minded seeker who is trying to channel their energy through their sixth or seventh wisdom and enlightenment chakras is to tempt that seeker with third chakra images of power (e.g., forbidden secrets, the golden throne that awaits them).

Shakespeare's *Othello* provides us a perfect example of chakra manipulation. Othello truly loves Desdemona (fourth love and compassion chakra) but the scheming Iago craftily takes Othello down a notch, down to the next lower (third ego power and emotions) chakra where Othello's love is refocused into jealousy.

The energy Othello puts out is the same, only the chakra it is being *filtered* through has changed—with disastrous results.

The Seven Glands

While this chakra power centers concept might at first sound far-fetched to Westerners, modern scientific studies have found intriguing correspondence between ancient Sanskrit descriptions of chakras and the discovery of the human endocrine system, seven glands which pump their mood-altering chemicals directly into the bloodstream.

The part of the endocrine system most people are familiar with is the *adrenal*s, our "flight or fight" gland. (Remember? Mother lifts automobile off of her trapped child?)

(**FYI:** If you're a smoker, what you're really addicted to is an adrenal-based hormone called epinephrine triggered by the intake of nicotine. That's why just a few drags off a cigarette affects you so quickly, because the hormone is being pumped directly into your bloodstream. That's also why it's so hard to quit smoking, because what you're actually addicted to is a natural chemical in your body.)

Seven Squared

The seven chakras and the seven endocrine glands can also be compared to other "sevens," any and/or all of which can prove useful to Black Science (mind control) (see Figure 17).

THE EIGHT MINDS

Tibetan Lamaism teaches that six *Rtsa Nyon* (root afflictions) manifest through a collection of "minds" that we mistakenly think of as our one, single mind.

These eight minds, called *Nam She Tsoq Gye* in Tibetan, are: eye consciousness, ear consciousness, nose consciousness, tongue consciousness, overall body consciousness, mental consciousness, afflicted consciousness, and ground consciousness.

Eye Consciousness

We think "we" see things and we identify with the things we think we see.

SEVEN SQUARED

The Seven Passions (Vietnamese, That Tinh)	joy	sorrow	love	hate	lust	fear	anger
The Seven Deadly Sins (Western/Christian)	pride	wrath	envy	lust	gluttony	avarice	sloth
The Seven Virtues (Western/Christian)	faith	hope	charity	justice	fortitude	temperance	prudence
The Seven Emotions	stillness	desire	joy & anger	compassion	enthusiasm	emotions in dreams	understanding
The Seven Active Elements	earth	water	fire	air	ether	light	thought
The Seven Fears (Tibetan)	afraid of being afraid	cold	poverty	hunger	thirst	melancholy	fear of straying
The Seven Solutions to the Seven Fears	castle (Shelter)	garment	wealth	food	drink	a friend	focus
The Seven Precious Things (i.e., wealth*)	gold	silver	beryl	crystal	coral	red pearls	emerald

Figure 17.

Recall from part I, Perception and Power, that light impacts on the eye, sending signals to the brain/mind, which then deciphers said signals through our distorted mind filters.

Therefore "we" don't really see with the unfailing organ of the eye but with our all-too-fallible mind.

Ear Consciousness

Same as with the eye: "We" only think we hear because we identify with the organ of sound.

Nose Consciousness

Same as with the eye and the ear. Reacting to sex pheromones and the like, our sense of smell can instantly affect our mood and—literally—lead us around by the nose.

Tongue Consciousness

Same as the eye and ear and nose.

Overall Body Consciousness

Neither our sense of touch, taste, nor "our" other senses combined are really "us." They are simply impulses of sensation information sent to the brain for storage.

(**FYI:** These first five "minds" are called *Bang She* [No, they weren't named for your ex-girlfriend!].)

We receive sensations ("impressions") in through these five sense "minds" and falsely believe "*I* am seeing", "*I* am hearing," when it is merely the sense organ "mind" experiencing the sensation event.

The remaining four "minds" are mental processes (like a library) where we record and recall the sensations we experience through "our" senses.

Mental Consciousness

Tibetan masters disagree with Descartes (1596–1650) "*Cogito, ergo sum*" ("I think, therefore I am"), countering "You only *think* you are *thinking* because you *think* you actually have a "you" to do the *thinking* with!"

In actuality, say these masters, what we think of as "I" and "me" is only the restless monkey of the mind(s) playing with itself.

Afflicted Consciousness

Afflicted consciousness (i.e., attachment to self) means thinking there is a real I apart from the sensations we experience and identify with, a real I that lives, dies, and "feels" a whole lot of pain in between because of our attachment and desire.

Ground Consciousness

Ground consciousness binds these previous seven consciousnesses together to give us the illusion there really is an "us" apart from the sensations we feel.

This is where "the whole becomes greater than the sum of its parts." In effect, these seven separate minds, having come together, now falsely believe they are a single mind, a single being—an "I", a "me"—rather than simply a collection of parts.

In other words, our mind is an ever-changing stream of thoughts and feelings and *not* a solid, separate "self."

Or so the Tibetan masters tell us.

The bad news is, even if we accept this metaphysical idea that "*we*" *don't really exist* . . . we still have to pay taxes!

The good news is, our enemy also identifies with *his* "eight minds" sensations, meaning we can easily distract him by dazzling his five physical senses while masterfully manipulating his three mental consciousnesses.

5

Methods of Mayhem

*"Lacking the wherewithal to defeat a foe with bludgeon or blade,
you can always bury him beneath a steaming pile of bullshit!"*
—Lung, *Cao Dai Kung-Fu*

INTRODUCTION: "THE ART OF LISTENING"

Whether it's a fast-talking used-car huckster or that Middle Eastern gentleman in the airplane seat next to you who seems to be trying to light his shoe on fire, both for the sake of your wallet and your well-being, you must learn to read your enemy like a book, chapter and verse, before assigning him his Dewey decimal due on some back shelf or, better yet, relegating him— kith and kin, his kickback constituents, cohorts, and co-conspirators—to the recycling bin of history.

To accomplish this we must learn to hear—*really hear*—what our enemy is saying. This means learning to hear with all our resources—innate and gathered.

All the many skills employed in the Black Science (mind control) hinge on the singular *art of listening* to what our enemy is saying—or not saying. In other words, what he says is often not as important as the words that catch in his craw.

Thus, by listening—*really listening*—we see through his pretend pleasantries, practiced graces, and feigned friendship.

We study how he walks—and "shadow-walks."

We study how he talks—and "shadow-talks."

We listen—really listen—and we learn to recognize his attempts at word wizardry; all the while stockpiling our own arsenal of "word weapons" and assiduously mastering those other "black arts" necessary to assure us the firm upper hand with which to slap down our foe. . . .

And make him hear what *we* are saying loud and clear!

SHADOW-WALKERS

"What you are thunders so loudly that I cannot hear what you say to the contrary."
—Ralph Waldo Emerson

Mark Twain once said, "One learns people through the heart, not eyes or the intellect."

Ol' Sam was wrong. As a philosopher, perhaps he had the time and luxury to "peer into a stranger's heart," to decipher their true intent and motivation. The rest of us can hardly afford the luxury to take time to "get to know someone." Nature seldom rewards the indolent.

I know what you're thinking. On reflex, you're already regurgitating the warning: "Judge not that ye be not judged!"

What planet are you from? We judge and are judged in return. To wish it otherwise is perhaps forgivable. To imagine it is otherwise is at the very least foolish and, *in extremis*, fatal.

People see us as we approach from across the room or from across the street and, like it or not, we are first judged by our physical appearance.

I know what you're thinking. "Oh, *I* would never be that shallow." (Heh-heh-heh.)

Do you really feel the same when you are approached by a scruffy, perhaps smelly homeless person as when a sharp-dressed man in a three-piece suit hails you?

Can you really say with a straight face that you experience the same emotional reaction when a white teenager wearing a Boy Scout uniform walks up to you, as opposed to a black teenager wearing a gang bandanna and sporting a "gansta rap" T-shirt?

Relax. Nobody's implying you're a racist just because your eyes narrow, your mouth gets a little dry, and a lump the size of Rodney King suddenly materializes in your throat.

What these *natural reactions* mean is that you're cautious, and understandably so. The media . . . society . . . *"they"* bombard us with stereotypical images of adolescent "gang-bangers," most of who just happen to be *young* and *black* . . . huh, the gang-bangers that is, not the media.

Once these media stereotypes are firmly imbedded in our brain, it's natural for our body to react with flight or fight—easily overriding our "higher" reasoning—before we can rein in our irrational fears.

(**P.S.** Take it easy on yourself. Just because something's a "stereotype" doesn't mean it isn't true.)

Manipulators, from confidence men to cultists, *dress for effect*. So do street punks who like seeing the rest of us shit ourselves every time they cross to our side of the street.

Like the expert actors they are, adroit mind-slayers pick every stitch of clothing with care, every nuance of stance and gesture, all designed to "make a good first impression," to "get a foot in your door," and a finger in your wallet.

Posture

Miyamoto Musashi taught we should make our combat attitude the same as our everyday attitude. Like Samurai on the battlefield, we must always be alert and prepared to deal with danger—whether an actual physical attack or a psychological incursion into our mental space.

Likewise, we should carry our calm and collective attitude from home, our everyday life, out into the stressful world at large.

In seeking to balance these two "worlds," Musashi was as astute as he was honest enough to acknowledge the fact we "carry ourselves" differently at work than at home than at church.

We all wear different "faces"—*masks*, if you will—we hope will better fit specific situations.

Musashi used the word *attitude* to refer specifically to the way a Samurai held his sword and to the overall stance one took when facing a foe.

Of course while Musashi was perfecting his own combat attitude, you can bet he was studying the least little subconscious twitch of his opponents—seeking that one telltale narrowing of the eye, that subtle shifting of weight, signalling that his foe was about to strike.

What Musashi called *attitude*, Black Science calls posture. And studying our own posture, as well as that of our enemy, is as important to us in today's world as it was in Musashi's time.

In Black Science, "posture" includes how we sit, stand, fold our arms—all the subtle and subconscious twitches, tics, and "tells" of our body that unbeknownst to us all too often betray our true feelings and intent.

Other times we deliberately adopt a posture designed to disguise our true intent and feelings. More on such "posturing" in a minute.

So much about our body posture—from minor fidgeting, to flight or fight—is beyond our control, whether because we are unaware of these reactions or because we are too lazy to make the effort needed to master them.

Other body reactions we can learn to control, even activities we'd swear we have no conscious control over.

For example, Indian yogis can control their heart rates and Tibetan lamas use techniques called *tumo* to deliberately raise their body temperature, allowing them to endure extremes of cold.

Likewise deep cover spies have successfully used biofeedback and self-hypnosis to control body responses during intense interrogation—even to the point of successfully outwitting polygraph exams.

On a more mundane level, accomplished actors, conmen, and spoiled children can cry on cue.

Most of us can deliberately make our lips smile, even if our unsmiling eyes give away the fact we're faking it!

(Helpful mind-control hint #169: Always squint and "crinkle the crowsfeet" around your eyes when sporting a "genuine" fake smile.)

Fortunately, so far as our Black Science and mind control is concerned, natural reactions like sweating when anxious, blushing in embarrassment, and nervous laughter at funerals are beyond most people's ability to control.

Just by looking, most of us can easily tell if another person is in a good mood, a bad mood, nervous, or otherwise stressed out. (See Figure 18, on page 94.)

SPOTTING MOOD

	Good Mood	Stressed/Bad Mood	Deceptive
Mouth	Full smile (teeth visible)	Lips only smile. Quick smile if at all.	Nervous licking of lips, trembling, biting of lips.
Eyes	Wide and alert, good eye contact	Eyes narrowed, looks away. Conversely: Eyes may be wide and pupils dilated if frightened.	Eyes darting. Rubbing eyes with fingers. Avoids eye contact.
Hands	Hands open, fingers loose and expressive	Clenched. White knuckled.	Rubbing hands together. Playing with objects.
Arms	Loose. Wide "friendly" gestures.	Crossed. Closed off.	Hands in pocket (also denotes nervousness). Elbows close to body.
Sitting	Relaxed	On edge of seat.	Shifting
Feet	Wide stance, tipping back on heels. "Boxed" facing, shoulder-to-shoulder aligned.	Feet close together. Side toward you.	Shifting. Foot scraping floor. Tapping foot.
Breathing	Regular, deep, "belly breathing"	Irregular, short "chest" breaths.	Short "chest" breaths (facilitates "fast talking")
Muscles	Relaxed	Stiff	Stiff/twitching (i.e., "chomping at the bit")

Figure 18.

Professional "people readers"—from preachers to predators, psychic friends to police—concentrate on five of your areas when sizing you up: posture, face, eyes, hands, and feet.

When scanning another person for telltale signs of deception, pay special attention to the lower part of their body. That's because when trying to disguise their true feelings people pay more attention to their body from the waist up. Thus, their real feelings (e.g., tension, nervousness.) are all too often betrayed by their tightly crossed legs (deceptive, defensive) and by their feet (e.g., rigid, sticking straight up = tension. Shifting = nervousness).

In *Black Science* (Lung and Prowant, 2001) we revealed how people can be classified according to how they perceive the world: "Watchers" rely mostly on what they see, "Listeners" trust their ears to provide them with accurate information, and "Touchers" literally take a hands-on approach to life.

Here's a simple test to help you determine the other person's W-T-L (Watcher, Listener, or Toucher) orientation:

Approach your target with a pen and small writing pad in hand and ask them for directions to a location (preferably a spot you know they know the way to).

One type of person will quickly take the pad from you and start drawing you a map. In all likelihood he's a Toucher (with just a little Watcher tossed in for good measure).

Another type of person will ignore the pen and pad in favor of using his arms to gesture and his fingers to "point you in the right direction." He's probably a Watcher.

Still another type also ignores the pen and pad and instead gives you verbal directions. This person's probably a Listener—trusting more the spoken word than the written word—or map.

While we're on the subject, augment your initial suspicion as to the person's W-L-T orientation by listening for the types of verbal clues we taught you to look for in *Black Science* (Lung and Prowant, 2001).

> Frustrate Watchers by making them listen.
> Don't talk to Listeners. Torture them with silence.
> Frustrate Touchers by making them "sit on their hands."

Posturing

> *"Society runs on trust, and we ordinarily pay more attention to what someone says than to the accompanying nonverbal behavior— hand gestures, facial movements, smiles, eye contact. However, when the speaker is attractive and gives really impressive nonverbal performance, the effect can be reversed—we watch the show and pay little attention to what is said."*
> **—Hare**

From trying to get on and stay on the wife's good side, to convincing some suspicious-looking punk to stay on his side of the street (because our "walk" says we're a lot tougher than we look!), whether trying to get a promotion off the boss, or trying to talk the panties off that blonde over there, we all use "posturing."

Unlike our unconscious—mostly uncontrollable body language, posturing refers to physical mannerisms and patterns of speech we deliberately adopt to create an effect, to project a particular image of ourselves, especially when trying to make a false impression.

Anytime we adjust our tie, blow into our hand to check our breath, or stand a little straighter when the boss walks into the room, we're posturing.

Every time you deliberately force a friendly smile for a coworker you absolutely despise, every time you laugh at yet another "not the least bit funny" joke your boss tells, you're posturing.

Posturing falls somewhere between the ninja *Art of Disguise* . . . and kissin' deep ass.

Depending on our determination to accomplish our objective, we may need to master special skills: intelligence, mannerisms, and methods of speech that allow us to get closer to our intended target. Such skills can range from something as simple as learning what sports teams the boss roots for, to our acquiring complex skills of document/identification forgery, mastery of a foreign language, and the use of fake beards and elaborate disguise prosthesis, à la James Bond.

Other times, posturing is as simple as convincingly faking a "good ol' boy" Southern drawl in order to talk some yokel out of his prize-winning porker.

So what are the best—and easiest—posturing techniques we can use to manipulate others?

Three things: Make eye contact. Smile. And "walk the walk."

The eye of the storm. Fifth-century Zen founder Bodhidharma is always depicted with a fierce, unwavering (i.e., bug-eyed) stare, the result of his spending *nine years* staring at a wall to gain enlightenment.

Eastern masters, especially those of the Zen school, are often depicted in paintings sporting wild-eyed looks and crazy stares. For example, the eighth-century master Ma-tsu Tao-i (709–788) is described as "looking like a tiger, walking like the bull, with eyes that pierced to the heart of the matter."

In the West today, it's an unwritten rule: If you want to be a really diabolical mastermind manipulator like Rasputin, Hitler, or Manson (Charlie, not Marilyn), you need a pair of hypnotically penetrating (really creepy!) eyes.

But even if you've no immediate plans to start a cult or take over the world, you might be interested to know that recent studies have shown that we get more out of life—or at least out of other people—when we make eye contact:

- Salespeople sell more when they "connect" with the customer via eye contact.
- Parents and teachers are more effective when disciplining children when they make the child look them in the eye.
- Salvation Army Santas get more and bigger donations when they succeed in catching a passerby's eye—as do homeless people.
- Hitchhikers get more rides, even from complete strangers, when they make eye contact. (cf. study conducted by University of Utah, Salt Lake City)

(**Tip:** In order to make effective eye contact, don't actually stare directly into the other person's eyes, instead look between and slightly above the eyes. From the other person's perspective, you will appear to be looking directly into his or her eyes.)

> *"Things are not what they seem . . . nor are they otherwise."*
> **—Bodhidharma**

Fun time: Next time you see your rival talking to the boss, position yourself somewhere behind the boss (not too close!) and catch your rival's eye. *Without saying anything*, stare at his mouth and make the motions of him brushing an imaginary bread crumb off his face. As soon as he starts wiping one side of his mouth (and he will), feign impatience and begin brushing the imaginary crumb off the other side of your/his face. When he switches to the other side of his face (and he will), move your brushing hand a little farther up your cheek and his hand is sure to follow. In short order you will have him brushing furiously at the imaginary crumb.

Meanwhile, unaware of your "prompting," the boss thinks your rival is losing his mind.

Why a smile goes a mile. Body and mind are intricately connected. Mood influences behavior. Behavior, in turn, influences mood. Studies have shown that standing in front of a mirror and "forcing" yourself to smile when feeling depressed can help lift your mood. That's because your depressed brain associates you physically smiling with your feeling good and happy. So turn that frown upside down.

It's also no secret that a smile can be infectious. In one university influence study, electrodes were attached to subjects' facial muscles while they watched a speech given by then President Ronald Reagan. Even though the test subjects had expressed initial dislike for Reagan, when the image of Reagan smiled, test subjects still registered a small smile.

Big surprise: People are "disarmed" by smiling politicians (and other predators). A practiced smile paired with good eye contact can get you in almost any door.

And don't forget those sincere crinkles around your eyes that make your smile look genuine.

Walk the walk. Yagyu Munenori once said: "When walking, walk neither fast nor slow. Rather walk in a natural, flowing smooth way, unencumbered by superfluous thoughts. . . . You walk fast when alarmed and shaken, slower when held in check and afraid." We see a little old lady standing tall as she hurries down the street. What's wrong with this picture? Can you say "Narc!" disguised as a little old lady. As we all know, little old ladies are supposed to be bent over and walk excruciatingly slow (the same way they drive!).

We associate certain types of walking gaits with certain types of people and professions. Thus our walk gives us away, and is an important part of both posture and posturing.

Most often we don't pay any attention to our walk, but you can bet our enemies do. Police can spot a suspicious-acting criminal two blocks away just by their walk.

Likewise, street predators study how *you* walk: confident stride, head held high and alert? Versus head down and scurrying like a frightened rabbit hoping to be left alone. That tough guy's walk tells us he's looking for trouble.

Conversely, that normally belligerent street punk hurrying along—hands shoved deep into his pockets, head down, cap pulled low . . . he's definitely up to something.

Do you really think that super model walks down the street the same way she does when strutting down the catwalk?

Like our other deceptive posturings, we adopt saunters, struts, and strolls designed to create specific impressions. What message is your walk subconsciously—or deliberately—sending the world?

At the same time, we need to make ourselves aware of what our enemy's walk is telling us:

- His *long, purposeful stride* tells us he's in charge, a real go-getter, that he's a man on a mission . . . or at least trying to convince us he is.
- A *slow, careful walk*, perhaps bent slightly forward, gives us the impression he's goal-oriented and serious, a deep thinker . . . exactly the impression he's shooting for.
- A *quick step* shows us he's alert . . . and just a little impulsive.
- A *light step* tells us he doesn't have a care in the world, that he's a dreamer, and optimist . . . and not a threat to us. True . . . or truly deceptive?

The human touch. We all like our personal space, the distance at which we are most comfortable with others. This distance varies with our culture (or lack of). For most Westerners, three to five feet is considered a comfortable distance when talking to another person. Three feet and less is considered intimate distance and is reserved for close friends and family.

That being said, we connect better with people we touch, people we actually come into physical contact with.

> *"To pay attention to what someone does* not *do is often more important than noting what he does."*
> —*The Method of Zen*, **Eugen Herrigel, 1974**

When trying to establish a bond with (i.e., dominate) a man, lay your left hand on his shoulder when you shake his hand. Still gripping his hand, step closer, shoulder-to-shoulder facing in the same direction, as you slide the hand on his shoulder down to his seventh vertebra (between his shoulder blades). With your hand on this spot on his back, you can gently lead— propel—him where you want him to go.

Gently pressing on the spine at the level of the seventh vertebra stimulates spinal nerves responsible for both his breathing (calming him) and his lower body (getting his legs moving in the direction you want him to go). Ironically the spot between the shoulder blades we touch to accomplish this is the same perfect spot for figuratively—and literally—*stabbing him in the back!*

When trying to establish rapport with a woman, on the other hand, first touch her gently on the outside of her upper arm just above the elbow. If she tenses from your touch, withdraw immediately but *do not acknowledge her resistance* to your touch.

If you do not feel increased tension in her arm, confidently slide the hand touching her arm around to the small of her back as you move your shoulder next to her. (You're now standing beside her, shoulder-to-shoulder, both facing in the same direction, your hand at the small of her back.) From this position, with only gentle pressure on the small of her back, you can lead her anywhere.

I know what you're thinking: "Such a bold tactic would never work on me!" (Heh-heh-heh.)

Remember last week when you shook hands with that attentive used-car salesman? Before he led you around the lot, bet you'd never realized just how much you'd always wanted a previously owned but still mint condition ten-year-old SUV.

And what about last night at the club? Still trying to figure out how that suave gigolo had you turned around and back out on the dance floor before you knew what was happening?

Why does such a bold approach work?

When someone invades our personal space by stepping too close, we feel uncomfortable but seldom openly protest for fear of offending. This creates *cognitive dissonance* in our brain, where we find ourselves trapped between two contradictory desires (i.e., how to get back our personal space without offending the invader).

While our brain is temporarily in chaos and leaderless, conflicting with itself on how to respond, our *confident and commanding* invader steps up and takes charge, easily leading us where he wants us to go.

Here then begins the phenomenon of hypnosis: Timing is important in all endeavors. Just ask Sun Tzu and Musashi. Whenever you invade someone's personal space, you must be alert to their *responsive body language signals* that will indicate whether the person is "receptive" to your approach, falling for your line of "BS" . . . "Black Science", that is!

Thus, always accompany your physical invasion into their personal space with well-practiced smiles, eye contact, and of course a dazzling *verbal* assault designed to first befuddle and then overrun their defenses.

Perfecting Your Poker Face

Perfecting your "poker face" is an important part of posturing. Being able to adopt a deep and thoughtful look or an award-winning smile at the drop of a hat is what separates the great actors from the mediocre ones, the financial fluent from the convicted felon.

Never think for a moment that a poker face is always that stoic, non-expressive mask you quickly drop over your face the moment life deals you an opening pair. Such a sudden change from your normally animated demeanor is a dead giveaway.

A true poker face entails the ability to effectively disguise our feelings—excitement, disappointment—in order to lead our enemies—if only four Friday-night poker buddies—in another direction.

This entails two types of bluffing.

The two types of bluffing. Bluffing is all about *hiding.* Either you've got something you're trying to hide—like a winning hand, or else you're trying to hide the fact you got nothing—zilch, squat, *nada.*

In the same vein, you use a bluff when you really want something, but have to pretend you are indifferent—When you're really in favor of something but have to pretend you're against it. Obviously, bluffing and pretending are synonymous.

Most bluffers are easy to spot because they *overcompensate* in one direction or the other in order to create the opposite impression of how they really feel. Thus we spot them by noticing how they *try* to appear:

- Insecure, they erect a cavalier façade in an effort to appear confident.
- Confident, they pretend to hesitate, to be unsure if that "royal flush" they're holding is worth betting on.

Does the name Clark Kent ring a bell? Or how about the shy and timid persona Tony Curtis's normally confident character adopts in *Some Like It Hot* (1959) in order to get into Marilyn Monroe's . . . good graces.

To trap a bluffer, mention a person or an issue you know he has an emotional attachment to and then watch his reaction. He'll either show his real—true—reaction, which you can note for future reference, or else he'll pretend not to be interested at all, in which case his straining to hide his true feelings will give you valuable tells with which to read him like a comic book in future encounters.

Most often a bluffer tells on himself by protesting too loudly or, at the opposite extreme, by going out of his way to appear nonchalant and unconcerned.

Remember, loud proclamations of hate often mask secret attractions.

How to buff your bluff. The secret of effective bluffing is to *combine actions with words*. Just saying, "I'm not interested in the deal" (when you really are) isn't enough. Actually get up and start walking toward the door.

Likewise, when negotiations are stalled, sigh heavily and say with some finality, "All right then," as you make a final notation in your notepad before closing it. Or, make a show of calling your wife on the phone to tell her "I'll be home in a half hour . . . *maybe sooner.*" (See The Art of No-gotiation, later in this chapter.)

Stripping the luster from our enemy's already dull bluff game, while simultaneously buffing our own bluffing ability to blinding brilliance, means perfecting our own posturing skills while becoming more adept at spotting our enemy's pathetic attempts to put one over on us. (See Figure 19.)

Most people have no idea what they're really doing. Bluff like you do know and they'll follow you anywhere . . . or at least get out of your way!

SHADOW-TALKERS

"The words we use are strong, they make reality."
—Wang Chung

Introduction: Return of the Word Wizards

A study conducted by the psychologists Elizabeth Loftus and John Palmer found that the way in which people are asked to recall something affects what they recall.

Researchers showed subjects a film of two cars colliding. Asked a week later either "How fast were the cars going when they *smashed* into each other? or "How fast were the cars going when they bumped into each other?" Those asked the question primed by the word smashed remembered that the cars were going faster than those subjects who had been given the verb *bumped*.

The smashed test subjects also remembered having seen broken glass at the scene of the accident where there wasn't any. (cf. *USA Today Weekend*, Feb. 27–March 1, 1998:5)

Figure 19: PERFECTING YOUR POKER FACE

Signs of:

1. Openness: Arms spread wide, legs not crossed. Coat unbuttoned.

2. Cooperation: (negotiation)   Sitting on the edge of his chair, leaning forward, attentive. Unbuttoning his coat. Nodding. Rubbing chin in consideration.

3. Confidence: Hands and fingers "steepled." Fingers in pockets with thumbs exposed. Hands grasp lapels of coat. Back straight. Hands behind back, clasped (i.e., hiding an "ace in the hole").

4. Considering: (evaluating)   Rubbing chin (wise man stroking beard while he thinks about something). Cleaning glasses (so he can "see" more clearly). Finger tapping nose ("I like the way this smells.") Filling his pipe (He's already decided to take the offer and is preparing to "relax," or begins fiddling with a cigar, ready to "celebrate" the deal.)

5. Defensive: Arms and legs crosssed. Pointing fingers. "Karate-chop" gestures with stiff hand. Fast movements with hands (afraid slower movements will betray him).

6. Worry: (nervous)   Figeting. Playing with objects. Clearing throat repeatedly. Pulling on his ear. Wiping his nose (doesn't like the way this "smells").

7. Suspicion: Arms crossed protecting chest (heart). Sideways glances. Standing more than five feet away (out of arm's reach). Coat remains buttoned (for fast getaway). Rubbing eyes (to "clear" his vision and get a better look/keep an eye on you).

8. Insecurity: (lack of confidence)   Hands in pockets (afraid he'll accidentally "break" something). Playing with/chewing on pen, etc. (surrogate nipple). One thumb holds down (covers) the other (keeping "little brother" out of trouble). Jiggling money (ready to "pay" his way out of trouble). Playing with his keys (ready to start the car and go home, back to his "comfort zone").

9. Frustration: (irritation)	Hands keep making fists. Wringing hands (to relieve tension). Rubbing hands through hair (seeking to stimulate inspiration). Rubbing the back of his neck (to relieve tension). Taking short "noisy" sighing breaths. Making "tsk" sound and sucking in air through his teeth.
10. Fearful:	Quiver and hesitation in voice. He makes his silhouette "smaller" by slouching, putting his hands in his pocket, crossing his arms and legs (see Defensive). Avoids eye contact.

This study reaffirms what we learned in *Black Science* about how unscrupulous word wizards adroitly hold us in thrall with *word slavery*, both through the words they use, and through words they censor us from using.

In another study, when depressed subjects were read a list of depressing words, they showed a different response in the region of the brain called the *amygdala* than that displayed by normal, non-depressed subjects.

In the depressed subjects, the amygdala stayed active, humming away 150 percent longer (twenty-five seconds) after they heard a depressing word than the normal subjects whose amygdalas stopped showing activity after only ten seconds, suggesting that the depressed subjects continue to dwell on sad and depressing words long after the undepressed subjects had moved on (cf. *Biological Psychiatry*, May 2002).

On the same subject, the average person has more than 200 negative thoughts every day. These include worries, jealousies, insecurities, and forbidden desires. In comparison, routinely depressed people have more than 600 negative thoughts a day.

Already knowing that your enemy is prone to depression, now armed with this new knowledge that depressed people dwell on depressing words, it will be a simple matter for you to scatter seeds of sadness throughout your enemy's mental garden, encouraging his depression, until ultimately pushing him over the edge . . . figuratively, of course.

Here then is a perfect example of how word wizards attack us with spears of thought and daggers of the mind—*word weapons* that, without prior study, we are powerless to defend against.

We turn the tables on these unscrupulous word wizards by learning to use word slavery defensively, while adroitly wielding word weapons offensively.

Word Slavery

"The proper words can make people take actions. 'Sticks and stones can break my bones, but words . . . ?' Wrong. Words can do all sorts of things. For instance, words of praise can make you work harder, run faster, or behave in a jollier way. A word of criticism can do the opposite. Whether or not we believe the words, they do their work. 'Something always sticks' is the way the Romans put it. The word, being an exteriorization of a thought, is the key to our behavior."
—Holzer, *ESP and You*

Word wizards use a variety of word slavery ploys to manipulate us: from confusing our brain with "abstracts" and playing on the vanity we attach to our names, to their attempts at censoring what words and ideas can freely flow from our lips and pen.

Concrete versus abstract words. One way to spot wily word wizards is that these manipulators avoid concrete words, words with agreed upon, unambiguous meanings like "five hundred dollars, Friday morning at nine," instead preferring less restricting, more abstract words and phrases, words with different meanings for different people in different times and places.

Ask two people the meaning of "love," "patriotism," and "family values," and you'll get *three* different answers. Word wizards wallow and thrive in wavering vagaries, half-truths, and innuendo.

Any accomplished conman will tell you, the sweetest scheme, the most satisfying of scams, is one where greed makes the "mark" slip the noose around his own neck.

A word wizard's non-stop barrage of abstract images goes directly to the right intuitive side of the brain, setting the right side of the brain abuzz, avoiding the more analytical, reasoning left side of the brain responsible for dealing with more concrete images.

We trip up and trap agile word wizards by demanding they jump through specific hoops and over concrete hurdles. We make them produce a specific plan of action, and commit to specific dates, times, and amounts.

When someone offers you pie-in-the-sky, demand to see the recipe. When a politician tries to "pull your chain" with purposely evocative phrases like "morals" and "family values," make sure his idea of morals and family values is the same as yours.

The name game. It's a fact we love anything that reminds us of us. A recent study done at State University of New York at Buffalo concluded that when people feel good about themselves they also feel good about anything (associated) with themselves: a word that sounds like their name, numbers significant only to them (cf. *Popular Science*, July 2002).

This proclivity affects many of the choices we make. For example, a man named George or Geoffery is 40 percent more likely to become a *geo*logist than someone not named *Geo*rge. Likewise, a person named *Den*nis is more likely to become a *den*tist. This extends to numbers. Those born on March 3rd (3 + 3) are more likely to live in a town with a name like Six Forks.

> *"Most people would think this sort of thing happens only when you*
> *have trouble making a conscious decision. But actually, much of*
> *what you do is subconsciously decided."*
> **—De Schipper, "Blame the Name"**

This tendency may help explain the phenomenon of *synchronicity*, where events are connected by *meaning* rather than by any other discernible (physical) cause and effect.

This tendency also allows word wizards to get closer to their marks by seeding offers with words and phrases they know their mark will respond to—if not consciously, then subliminally.

For example, a man will be more susceptible to a woman named Jill if he'd once been dumped by another woman named Jill he never quite got over. Likewise, he will be more inclined to buy a policy from Puma Life Insurance simply because, "Hey! Pumas was the name of my old high school football team!"

A pair of tits. Tell the truth what's the first two things that come to mind when you read "a pair of tits"? (Heh-heh-heh.)

Wrong, "a pair of tits" is the proper term for two small plump long-tailed titmouse birds.

So how do words like "tits" become taboo?

> *"Language taboos, like all others, arise from our superstitious*
> *attitudes towards objects and ideas. A word represents a 'thing.'*
> *There is a ban on public recognition of a particular 'thing.' Hence*
> *the word may not be uttered for fear that if it were said out loud*
> *the forbidden 'thing' itself might show up. This explains the old*
> *phrase, 'Speak of the devil and he is sure to appear.'"*
> —**Funk,** *Word Origins*

Most of our "dirty" words are dirty because 1,000 years ago a bunch of Vikings-turned-Frenchmen known as the Normans beat the Hell out of the German Anglo-Saxons running England at that time. As a result, the French language of the conquerors was elevated in both court and in commerce, while the German-based language of the conquered was identified with the vulgar lower classes. The word *vulgar* itself originally meant "common people."

The best example of an innocuous word fallen into disrepute is the word *fuck*, which originally came from the Dutch *kokken* (lit. "to breed cattle").

Before the Norman Conquest of 1066, *fuck* was considered proper "English" (i.e., Anglo-ish).

To proper English-speaking people today, *fuck* is the bugaboo "F-word," though if you ask the average person "Why the fuck is *fuck* such a dirty word?" most would be hard-pressed to give you anything close to an adult answer.

In fact, you can stand face-to-face with a non-English-speaking Chinese man and—with a big smile—say, "Fuck you" and, *so long as you smile*, he will smile back at you because the word *fuck*—like all vulgar words—has only the meaning *we* give it. Funk said:

> The social rules governing such words are largely a matter of geography and of time. Centuries ago these improper words were quite proper and today at various geographic points the rules differ. . . .
> Of course the meanings of words are in your mind. Apart from that they are senseless hieroglyphics or empty sounds. If enough people think they are vulgar they are. (page 361)

In 2004, the FCC decided not to fine rock star Bono for declaring "This is *fucking* great!" at the January Golden Globe Awards, determining that the lead singer of U2 had used the offensive word as an *adjective* not as a *verb*.

Like the things we "see," everything we ultimately "hear" inside our head must first pass through any number of personal and social "filters." (See Figure 8, page 7.)

For example, you wouldn't normally consider the following list of words "dirty."

- pussy   a cat
- ass   a donkey
- bitch   female dog
- balls   sporting equipment
- Peter   a Saint
- cock   a rooster
- beaver   a dam builder
- pecker   a bird
- nuts   fruit fulla protein
- Dick   Nixon (who "Dicked" us all!)

Obviously, whether or not a word is obscene or even politically incorrect depends on *context*, where the word in question appears in connection with other words, and most importantly, how *we* interpret it.

Consider this classic poem:

> *Friends may come and friends may go*
> *and friends may peter out, you know.*
> *But I'll be your friend through thick or thin . . .*
> *peter out or peter in!*

Notice that the word *peter* takes on a completely different meaning in the last line. Why? What's changed? The spelling of the word is the same. The only thing that changes is how *you* "hear" (i.e., internally process) the word.

Consider the following story:

A mother drags her grumbling son out of bed at dawn to do his farm chores. Watching from the window, she sees him feed the chickens . . . and then *kick* one of the hens. She watches him slop the hogs . . . and then *kick* one of the pigs. Finally she watches him *kick* the cow when finished milking. His chores finished, the famished boy flops down at the breakfast table. He reaches for the eggs, but his mother slides them away. "No eggs for you, little mister man. You kicked the chicken."

The boy reaches for the plate of bacon, but his mother snatches it away. "Nope. You kicked the pig."

Sensing a disturbing pattern emerging, the boy makes a grab for the pitcher of milk but Mom beats him to it.

"No milk for you. I saw you kick the cow."

Just then, the father comes down the stairs. Nearly tripping over the cat, with a curse, the man's swift kick sends the cat sailing across the room!

The boy smirks at his mother, "You wanna tell him, or should I?"

Did you laugh at the joke? Why? There's not a single "dirty word" anywhere in the story. . . . So it must all be in your head!

We become slaves to words and don't know it, parroting popular words and slogans because they are socially or politically expedient, and even necessary for survival—*Sieg Heil!* while being equally fearful of using those words deemed insensitive, politically incorrect, and obscene by the reigning powers-that-be.

October 1972, New York radio station WBAI aired comedian George Carlin's—hilarious and *enlightening*—skit in which he mouthed "The seven words you're not allowed to say on the air": shit, piss, fuck, cunt, cocksucker, motherfucker, and tits.

The FCC was not amused. Nor were they the least bit enlightened. Created in 1934, the FCC is composed of five members appointed by the president (yeah, guys like George W.) to regulate all interstate communications, including the licensing of radio and television stations. Piss off the FCC and they'll jerk your license. No FCC license means kiss your radio or television station good-bye.

It is the FCC's job to decide what words are "too obscene" to say over the airwaves. In other words: "Five people determine what you cannot hear and see" (Hentoff, 1993).

The original "censors" were Roman census takers, magistrates in charge of taking a census of the Empire every five years. These censors doubled as spies, taking the pulse of the Empire, taking note of both morale and morals (e.g., celibacy, inhumane acts of cruelty against children, animals, and even slaves).

Fifteen hundred years after the collapse of the Roman Empire, the only thing that's changed is that today most censors are *self-appointed*.

Any time you can make a person think twice before they speak, write, or publish certain words, opinions, or knowledge—in effect controlling their actions, you're half way to controlling their thinking.

Remember the brainwasher's equation: Controlling a person's actions is the first step to controlling their thinking. Or as Lenny Bruce once put it: "If you can't say 'Fuck,' you can't say 'Fuck the government.'"

Word Weapons

> *"That's bold talk for a one-eyed fat man!"*
> —*True Grit*, 1969

In Sunday school they taught us the tale of how Jesus "made a rope of cords" that he then used to whop sacrilegious money-changers from the temple. Beyond the literal interpretation, cords in this instance can also be translated as "small words." Thus, rather than Jesus—a *pacifist*, remember?—physically thrashing evil-doers, he instead *spoke* a few short words—perhaps an admonishment from Scripture?—that so *shamed* the greedy bastards they quickly fled his presence (cf. *Unity Metaphysical Bible Dictionary*).

Just as words can be used to hold us in virtual slavery, so, too, our enemies stab at us—and all too often wound us!—with words. The technical term for this is *Dyshemism*, words used as weapons.

These "word weapons" fall into two basic types: "purr," words designed to attract, pacify, and placate us, and "slur," words that stab into us, hurtful and confusing words designed to repel and wound us.

Also known as "stroke or choke" words, "pushers and pullers," "attractors and detractors," these two types of word weapons can further be broken down into categories of black talk, white talk, and gray talk.

Black and white words, though apparent opposites, are both what Sun Tzu calls *cheng*: direct, both straightforward and concrete, purr compliments (white) or slur curse words (black), for or against.

Gray talk on the other hand is *ch'i*, less direct, more abstract, vague, more pliable, and thus better suited to the Black Science.

White talk. Shakespeare once said: "Yet words do well/When he that speaks them pleases those that hear." White talk is "positive" talk, words and phrases designed to draw another person to us, either because such talk makes us look so good or because we've used such talk to purposely make any alternative look so bad. White talk allows us to *associate* ourselves and/or our cause with something or someone our targeted subject already has good feelings about.

Thus, in order to get close to our mark, we adopt his hobbies, his persona, professional, and political likes and dislikes, all in order to *associate ourselves in his mind with something he already likes.*

One way to do this is to learn what trigger words he responds unthinkingly to, social, cultural, and religious words, and catch-phrases or words with more personal—perhaps even subconscious—meaning to him; words that make him feel safe on the one hand, words that galvanize him to action on the other hand. As soon as we find his particular trigger words, we can use these proverbial short hairs like marionette strings, making him dance where we choose.

This is where the time we've previously invested in gathering intelligence on an enemy and learning to read him, while disguising our own intent, comes in handy.

We talk to him on his level, *crafting mental images that make him remember or imagine pleasure.* His monkey-mind busy chasing after pleasurable images, his more suspicious analytical mind takes a backseat.

With our words and actions we make him associate us with everything good in his world: we unconditionally approve of him. We encourage his plans—the more unrealistic the better! We believe what he believes. We like what he likes. When he sees us coming . . . he drops his guard and holsters his suspicions because he associates us with pleasure.

Black Science (mind-control) hypnotists put this "association response" into practice using a technique known as "the anchor" to gain their subject's undivided attention. It works like this: Ask your subject a question that makes them remember something pleasant ("What's your favorite flavor of ice cream?"). When the person responds "strawberry," *immediately repeat their response*: "You like strawberry," while simultaneously making a gesture toward them with your hand, either with fingers splayed and dancing, or while holding a small (preferably shining) object in your hand.

This causes your subject to subconsciously associate (and replace) your voice for their own inner voice, the one that brings them pleasure by reminding them how much they love strawberry ice cream.

Pairing your words with a specific gesture/object also associates that gesture with your command voice, a pleasurable (confident and comforting) voice the subject will be all too willing to follow into deeper levels of relaxation and cooperation (i.e., hypnosis).

Now use this same "agreed upon" gesture every time your subject says something you approve of, further associating it in their mind with pleasure (i.e., being approved of).

Once you've linked (associated) both your voice and gesture with pleasure in the subject's mind, simply saying "strawberry" along with the specific gesture will be enough to place your subject into a light "hypnotic trance." (Review The Skinner School, in chapter 4.)

Black talk. Whereas white talk uses positive words designed to attract others to us, black talk is more negative and designed to repel, wound, and strike down our enemies. Shakespeare called this kind of talk "Ethiop words," dark words intended to do harm, to make an enemy stumble back, stunned, a sitting duck for your verbal (and physical?) coup de grace.

Black talk relies on bullying words: slurs, cuss words, and is not afraid to play "the race card" when prudent and profitable.

We use black talk in a direct attack against our enemy: either when engaged in direct conflict, or else when attacking his character and undermining him from afar.

"**Slur words**" are the most used form of black talk. These include everything from common "Fuck you!'s" to tried-n-true social (Jerry Springer trailer trash!); religious (devil-worshipping Pagan!); political (pinko Commie bastard!); sexual (faggot! bitch!); racial (honkey!); and ethnic (kike! chink!) insults.

Many common English slur words used today have origins both benign and revealing. Even some of our most despised racial and ethnic slurs:

- *Nigger* comes from the Latin niger, meaning simply "black." In fact, two nations in modern-day Africa, Niger and Nigeria, have the same origin.
- *Dago* is a corruption of the common Spanish family name "Diego" and

was originally applied as a slur against Hispanic peoples before becoming associated with Italians.

- *Wop* was a generic U.S. Immigration Department acronym meaning "without papers" before becoming specifically associated with Italians.
- *Gook* is a proper Korean noun meaning "person."

Whether for defensive or offensive purposes, it is worth taking the time and effort to familiarize ourselves with the origins of as many of these slur words as possible. *One*, so we can more effectively use them to discomfort and distract our enemy and, *two*, to turn the tide and gain advantage in a conversation/confrontation.

For example, you're at a party and somebody calls you a slur name and, instead of giving them the satisfaction of seeing you lose your cool, you smile it off by informing them (and the gathering crowd) of the actual—proper—meaning/use of the word; stifling his arrogance and showing your brilliance, both in a single stroke!

Some slur words came about, and survive to this day, as the result of powers-that-be promoting the propaganda that city dwellers are somehow superior to people who live in the countryside:

- *Civilized*, for "civitas," meaning "city." Thus the beginning of the myth that city dwellers are better than "un-civilized" country folk.
- *Savages*, simply "forest dwellers," another synonym for the uncivilized.
- *Heathen*: Back when feudal lords controlled all the good land (with the blessing of the pope, whose proclamations these land-barons in turn enforced with whip and sword) many landless folk fled into the bogs and swamps, worthless lands known as "the Heaths."
- *Villains*: From the root "villa," *villains* at first simply referred to poor serfs living in the "village" surrounding feudal *villa* (i.e., estates and castles). *Villain* became synonymous with *criminal* because, to make ends meet, the serfs—virtual slaves under the feudal system—had to resort to brigandage, stealing, and poaching just so their families would have enough to eat. Apropos, *danger* comes from a word meaning "dominated and ruled by a master."

Many present-day slur words developed their current meanings in Medieval times and were used as weapons to reinforce the dominance of the feudal system in general and the Catholic Church in particular.

How'd these words end up "slurs"? Simple: Church clergy and feudal royalty were the only ones who could (and in many instances *were allowed to*) read and write:

- *Profanity* means "outside the temple," that is, anything not approved by the Church. *Occult* means pretty much the same thing: "O" = "without," "cult" = "church."
- *Pagan*, from a root meaning "trees." This slur was applied to warrior tribesmen in Northern Europe who worshipped "the old Gods" outside in groves of trees, who refused to come inside a (Catholic) church to worship this strange new god who carried no sword and couldn't even outrun his enemies!
- *Heretic* comes from a root meaning "choice." Ironic, considering the only "choice" the Church gave "heretics" when burning them at the stake was "*regular* or *extra crispy*?"
- *Vandals* were bold Teutonic warriors, admired even by the Romans. Rhineland Vandals conquered Gaul (France), Spain, and then conquered Rome's old foe Carthage in North Africa. Their name didn't become synonymous with wanton destruction (and graffiti) until they sacked the "Holy City" of Rome in 455 CE.

Finally, here's a couple ironic ones:

- *Cretin*, originally meant "Christian."
- *Idiot* originally meant "those who *don't* hold public office." (Heh-heh-heh.) Use *that* piece of information the next time someone tries to tell you "Times haven't changed!"

And . . . next time someone tells you to "Go to Hell!" thank them. Our word *Hell* comes from the Scandinavian goddess Hel, ruler of the Viking underworld which was not nearly as bad as the later, less imaginative, less hospitable Christian version that stole her name.

"Cuss words" inserted into a "polite" conversation are always a shocker, and a good way to gain control of a situation. For best effect, don't scream the cuss word at the other person, instead, "mutter" the cuss word, making the other person pause in the midst of their diatribe to ask, "What did you say?" Seize on his hesitation to *repeat your initial argument*.

Cussing is also a good way to jump-start a stalled negotiation, "taking it up a notch," since most people will take your sudden use of "profanity" as a sign of *frustration* (i.e., you are at the end of your rope and about to "walk"), or they will see it as *potential physical violence*, since cussing is a form of verbal "violence." (see The Art of No-gotiation, later in this chapter.)

"Bully words" are used by some people to muscle and manipulate their way through life. (See The Art of Intimidation, later in this chapter.)

It's not beneath these bullies to use stereotypes, play the race card, and use other "control freak" tactics designed to get them the upper hand: Playing the "race card" is becoming more and more popular—and potentially more profitable.

The race card trumps every other card on the table because, even if the other players in the game suspect you're "full of it," they won't call your bluff for fear of being labeled "racist," "chauvinist/sexist," "insensitive," or "politically incorrect."

Generically, "playing the race card" means cashing in on anything you can make the other guy feel confused and uncomfortable about, and hopefully guilty enough to shell out some greenbacks. This includes:

- Getting paid for real, imagined, or manufactured ethnic and racial slights and slurs someone uses against you
- Collecting on your particular "disability" (*everybody's* got at least one these days!)
- Making the boss scared of firing you for fear of discriminating against any of the above, or against your "sexual orientation" (whether the one God gave you or the one that friendly priest pointed out to you that summer you volunteered as an altar boy)

According to one Heisman Trophy winner NFL/Hall-of-Famer, you can practically get away with murder if you know when to play the race card.

But most important, you can still play the race card to get better service at Denny's restaurant!

"Minority Manipulation" Rules Review:

- Minorities are never satisfied. (The moment they are "satisfied," they get swallowed up by the majority.)
- Every one of us is a minority *some place*.
- Stay away from *that* some place!

"Stereotypes" are easy to use, since they feed into expectations and images people already possess—about others and about themselves.

Not only can we "plant" a stereotype into one person's mind in order to poison them against another, but recent research shows that stereotypes can also be used directly against the targeted person themselves.

It seems people who are the object of stereotyping can adopt the negative traits attributed to them. In other words, "planting" (or triggering already existing) *images* of a stereotype in a person's mind reinforces that image, especially if they already hold the stereotype about themselves—whether consciously or subconsciously.

In a recent study, subjects' performance scores on a test of general knowledge decreased when the stereotype of "supermodel" (associated with "airhead" and "dumb blonde," etc.) was activated.

Conversely, subjects' performance scores rose when the stereotype "professor" (educated) was associated with them. In the same vein, when a stereotype of "elderly" was activated, subjects actually walked more slowly (reported in Psychology Today, Oct. 2001:28).

Simply put, when you "subtly remind" people of their shortcomings by making them associate themselves with stereotypes, they tend to take on the characteristics of that stereotype.

Gray talk. Where white talk sucks us in, and black talk repels us, gray talk's purpose is to confuse. The best defense is a *confusing* offense!

We plant confusion in enemy ranks by sowing "disinformation": revelations that *appear authentic* and are *exactly what our enemy wants to hear.*

We also encourage the spread of false information about our enemy via gossip, innuendo, and rumor designed to sway public opinion to our cause while effectively slandering our foe.

When the government does this, it's called "Public Service Announcements" . . . unless it's an enemy government doing it, in which case it's "propaganda." When the media does it, it's called "the Nightly News." But when you don't own your own television network, or a piece of the government, it's simply "gossip" and "rumor."

But don't despair, both gossip and rumor are respected tools in our mind-control black bag of tricks. (Just remember: Tricks well mastered are called "techniques." Techniques half-learned, merely "tricks.")

Consider: A masterful Merlin casually passes his hand through the air, scooping up unseen essence, which soon becomes visible to the eye as a pulsing ball of light. Under his attentive, unwavering eye, animated by his mental command, this orb of energy gradually coalesces into a tangible physical form befitting the will and whimsy of the magician.

In the same way, word wizards, using mind control, give life to their unseen thoughts, first as simple words and phrases that stir others to wonder, to speculate, to doubt, and to *gossip*—giving *voice* to what was merely thought.

Thus, through hints and innuendo, subtle suggestion, subliminal sway, and a myriad of mental maneuverings, these word wizards alchemize once intangible thought and ephemeral dream into physical effect.

History is full of examples of how fear, fueled by uncontrollable coincidence and happenstance becomes superstition becomes ritual becomes cult—which, if surviving long enough, grows into religion.

So, too, history is replete with examples of how the intangible dreams and desires of singular-minded men—tempered by trials, sharpened by a constant whetting of will—grow into the towering spires of empire.

What begins as thought, when fueled by emotion, positive or negative— Fear, Lust, Anger, Greed, Sympathy—all too soon becomes reality.

As natural a process as steam becoming water becoming ice, so, too, gossip—with just a little help—becomes rumor, becomes "truth," and manifests to measurable physical effect.

Robert Frost once said, "There are three great things in the world: There is religion, there is science, and there is gossip." Gossip has one aim: To get people talking and keep them talking . . . talking about what and who *we* want them to talk about. People are perpetually "hungry" for juicy gossip. Once the table is set, you can then freely offer up selected entrées designed to further excite their appetite for "news." Enquiring minds want to know.

Having gotten them talking, now drop hints about where they can find more information (information you plant, of course).

People appreciate things more when you make them work for it. Likewise, information (i.e., gossip and rumor) is somehow more real when you make them search and discover it themselves. Makes them feel smart. And their desire to tell everybody how smart they are for "tracking" down the information will make sure that information—*your* information—will be spread far and wide!

That's why the best way to get someone to use your idea is to make them think it's their idea. (See The Art of No-gotiation, this chapter.)

Never become the source for gossip. Always maintain plausible deniability. In others words, do not tell someone directly the "information" you want them to spread. Instead, point them in the right direction—to the person, file, or website—for "the real story" (i.e., where they'll "discover" the info *you planted*!).

You can do this by "casually" asking a coworker if they know anything about a disturbing piece of information you overheard while sitting in a toilet stall: "No, I didn't see the two men doing the talking—somebody from Accounting, I think. Anyway, they were saying someone who works *here* is listed on a website for sexual predators! No, I didn't catch who they were talking about, but the website address was slimeballs.com. I'm gonna have to look that up as soon as I get a chance. . . ."

What's the odds the first chance your coworker gets he's making a bee-line to that website . . . a website *you* set up, where they'll find the name of your enemy target prominently displayed.

These kinds of ploys are called "sidetalking," not talking directly to a person, rather allowing a person to "accidentally overhear" a snippet of conversation, or "find" a scandalous piece of information sure to spur them to go on a hunting expedition to discover more facts—gossip they will be sure to pass along to others in the course of bragging about how good a detective they are.

Shakespeare highlights sidetalking ploys in his *Much Ado about Nothing* (1598–99), where a group of friends scheme to finally get at-odds lovebirds Benedick and Beatrice together by allowing them to "accidentally overhear" how each secretly loves the other.

The "hypocrite's gambit" is another form of sidetalking, where you talk to someone about someone else who just happens to have the same type of attitude or behavior you're really trying to get the person you're talking to to change. Merely getting the person you're talking to to agree that the other somebody's attitude or actions need changing, puts your listener on the road to change.

This works because no one wants to be thought a hypocrite, especially to themselves. This cognitive dissonance spurs him toward change in order to bring his words in sync with his actions.

Sidetalking employs all the despicable tactics we've studied so far—slurs, stereotypes, cuss words—all of which we want others to associate with our enemy. Sidetalking also uses innuendo, implication, and the power of suggestion.

The "power of suggestion" is defined as "The process of inducing uncritical acceptance of an idea or course of action" (Goldenson, 1970:1274). Goldenson theorized that certain parts in the hypothalamus, at the very core of our brain, are activated by suggestion. Could this be the key to hypnosis?

Suggestion is at the heart of a ploy known as "lying through implying," or, as it is called in today's jargon "dropping lugs."

For example, say your goal is to undermine an office coworker. First, make friends with the biggest office gossip you can find. Shaking your head sadly, absentmindedly comment:

- "Too bad about Bob. Guess God's got a longer memory than the rest of us . . ."
- "Just because Bob's made *some* mistakes in the past . . ."
- "Darn! I was hoping Bob had put all that behind him . . ."
- "I really thought Bob had it under control *this time* . . ."

You'll know this ploy has taken root when the other person replies, "What do you mean?" Catching yourself, quickly shrug, "Oh, nothing. Forget I mentioned it. Nobody wants to reopen *that* can of worms again!" Exit immediately. Trust the office gossip to investigate and "fill in the blanks."

We all love to fill in the blanks," *and* we tend to fill in the blanks in *predictable* ways.

Fill in the following blank: Charlie's parents had three children: April, May, and————.

Did you answer "June"? The answer is "Charlie," but most people will answer "June" because, in the same way our brain makes three angled dots into a triangle, so, too, our thinking and thus our speech follows *predictable* patterns.

Our brain is lazy. When our brain hears several statements it accepts as true, chances are it will accept—unquestioningly—the next statement as true, too.

Example: "Bob's such a good worker. He's always on time, always willing to help others . . ." That's *three* true statements in a row. Now without missing a beat add, "Too bad about that incident with the kid." (Always hide a big lie inside a pack of little lies. See The Art of Lying, later.)

A single word can imply so much. For example, saying "really" in different ways:

- "Really!" with eyebrows raised implies *surprise and interest.*
- "Really." said in flat tone, with flat expression implies *disbelief.*
- "Really?" with sly smile and narrowed eyes implies *suspicion.*

"Don't think about a white elephant!" is another way of casting aspersions on any enemy. The old argument is that as soon as someone tells you "Don't think about a white elephant!" our mind latches onto this image and, try as we might, we can't get the image of the white elephant out of our mind.

Likewise, once we hear a slur or slander associated with a person—especially a sensational or emotional slander—it is almost impossible to get that image out of our mind.

Accomplished word wizards adroitly twist and weave words together, crafting unfathomable Gordian Knots with which to bind our minds.

Recall how during Desert Storm, President George H. W. Bush went out of his way to pronounce Saddam Hussein's name "Sodom" in order to associate the dictator with the forbidden act of sodomy (Lung and Prowant, 2001:103).

Once we accept such a name-play association in our mind, there's no getting it out. (Kinda like that song "Achey-Breaky Heart"!)

For example, did you ever think about how Nation of Islam cult leader Louis Farrakhan's name can be pronounced "Lucifer-a-con"? Bet you'll think about it from now on, every time you heard his name. (Heh-heh-heh.)

Got a ruthless plan you fear a needed confederate might object to because it will bother their conscience? Scoff at their concern and remind them that "conscience" is spelled *con*science.

Got a religious fanatic in your face, high on telling you what he believes? Point out to him that "You can't spell 'believe' without a *lie* in the middle."

While such ploys might seem simplistic and even childish at first glance, it is directly to the still childish part of our many layered mind that such ploys speak; that part of our minds least able to discern fact from fancy and defend itself.

Rumors are what fully blossom when you plant innuendo and gossip deep enough.

> *"If everyone who was told about a midnight murder told two*
> *other people within 2 minutes, everybody on Earth would know*
> *about it before morning."*
> —*Ripley's Believe It or Not!*

A "rumor" is defined by Goldenson (1970) as:

An unverified report or account that circulates primarily by word of mouth. . . . Rumors may be wholly false or may contain an element of truth that is usually distorted or exaggerated. Though they often circulate in the form of gossip and may be deliberately "planted" at any time, they tend to occur in greatest profusion during periods of public crisis when reliable information is hard to obtain. (page 1137)

And why do rumors spread? According to Getty (1966): "The predilection for accepting opinion or even rumor as fact is a fairly familiar and widespread human failing" (page 65).

The reason for this is most people are too busy (lazy) to check, let alone double-check, the facts of a rumor. Besides, most of us will choose an *interesting*, even if slightly implausible, rumor over the cold hard (boring) truth every time!

Three things help us start and spread effective rumors: -First, *disguising the source of the rumor*. In other words, take pains now (to avoid more pain later if caught!) to insure any rumor you start cannot be traced back to you.

The ideal, of course, is to allow a despicable rumor you start about one foe to be traced back to yet another of your foes! It's always a joy when you can maneuver your enemies into doing your dirty work for you!

Second, borrowing a page from rumor's big brother, propaganda, "3-D" your target. Make sure the "information" contained in your rumor demeans, dehumanizes, and ultimately demonizes your target—making him appear dangerous, perverted, a religious, social, and moral outcast.

(**Note:** Just making him look "foolish" won't cut it, since sympathy all too often transforms fools into "tragic figures" that people first pity . . . and then help.)

Finally, an emotional element must be included in your rumor to make your rumor stick in the listener's mind. Always construct your rumor around facts that evoke an emotional reaction from listeners, preferably one of the easily manipulated emotional FLAGS—Fear, Lust, Anger, Greed, or Sympathy.

Like urban legends, rumors survive best when you include this emotional element.

Studies on the phenomenon of urban legends show that these bizarre tales survive because they tap into basic emotions like fear and disgust (cf. *Psychology Today* March/April 2002:21).

Urban legends are like campfire ghost stories, strange anecdotes and cautionary tales passed from one person to another that people swear on a stack of Bibles are true, although no one can point to any specific place or time the actual event occurred.

Example: Live on stage, rocker Ozzy Osbourne once bit the head off a chicken . . . or was it a bat? . . . and drank its blood . . . or was that Alice Cooper . . . no, wait, KISS! Everyone "knows" this really happened—especially that guy you know who once dated this chick who was actually there, and saw the whole thing, Dude!

Must be the same girl who accidentally ate some watermelon seeds and nine months later gave birth to a watermelon . . . or was it an alien? Or was it an alien watermelon?

Rumors not only help us undermine foes, but can also be profitable. Prior to talking a potential community of suckers . . . uh, "investors," out of their hard-earned dollars, wily confidencemen "pre-plant" rumors slandering any competition while opposite rumors praising their get-rich-quick investment plan are likewise circulated throughout the targeted community.

Controversy swirled around the 2002 Academy Award's top contender *A Beautiful Mind*. Producers of the movie charged that rival producers were behind rumors that the Nobel Prize–winning physicist on whom the movie was based was both a bisexual and an anti-Semite.

Keep in mind that winning an Academy Award adds *millions* to your movie's video/DVD take. (How many rumors—okay, bald-faced lies—would *you* tell for a million dollars?)

The accused producers vehemently denied allegations they'd started such rumors and counterattacked, accusing the producers of the movie themselves of having initiated the rumors in order to garner the sympathy vote from Academy members.

Recall that Sympathy is one of the emotional FLAGS.

You can tell you've given birth to a good rumor when the little bastard shows up one day on your front porch full grown; when people start telling *you* the rumor *you* started!

As you've probably figured out by now, there's a very thin line dividing defensive word slavery, and wielding offensive word weapons.

It is said "A good blade cuts both ways" . . . so, too, well-chosen words!

DARK ARTS

Introduction: Lazy and Hazy

The key to mastering the Black Science (mind-control) "Dark Arts" of mind-manipulation is for us to stay "lazy" while keeping our foes "hazy."

"Staying lazy" means using the least amount of effort to accomplish the greatest amount of effect in order to obtain the greatest amount of gain.

Chinese martial arts students are taught the ideal: "Avoid rather than check. Check rather than block. Block rather than maim. Main rather than kill." Simply put, these students are admonished to use the least amount of violence necessary to defend themselves and to diffuse a foe's aggression.

As in the martial arts, so in the Dark Arts. Thus, we stay lazy, picking the simplest of ploys with which to bring about our foe's downfall.

Bruce Lee taught that to beat an opponent using a simple technique takes more skill than defeating an opponent using a complex technique. He also warned that the more complex a thing, the more easily that thing can be broken.

This simplicity principle applies whether we're trying to slip past a complicated alarm system, a complicated martial arts defense, or the convoluted excuses and other conscious and subconscious complexes our enemy uses to guard his mind.

"Keeping our foe hazy" means keeping him confused and spellbound and is a simple matter of giving him the "mushroom treatment."

Asked the best way to grow mushrooms, master cultivators tell you, "Keep 'em in the dark and feed 'em plenty of bullshit!"

To fulfill this twofold strategy, Black Science Dark Arts include arts of intimidation, ambush, no-gotiation, and Lying, as well as individual crafts of charisma, confusion, and conspiracy.

All these tactics and techniques meet the Dark Art criteria of being both easy for us to master, while simultaneously befuddling our foe.

The Art of Intimidation

> *"Love is preferred, but optional. Respect?* **Mandatory.** *Fear?*
> *Universal currency!"*
> —**Duke Falthor Metalstorm**

Niccolò Machiavelli understood the importance of keeping fear fixed in an enemy's heart. In chapter XVII of his masterpiece *The Prince* (1513), Machiavelli answers the question whether it is better to be loved or feared:

> And as to the question whether it is better to be loved rather than feared, or feared rather than loved: Some might answer that we should want both; but since love and fear can scarce exist together, forced to choose between the two, let us decide it is far *safer* to be feared than loved.
>
> For can we not agree that men are for the most part ungrateful, fickle and false? They study to avoid danger and are greedy for gain. Devoted to you while you hold position to heap benefits upon them. Eager to shed blood, sacrifice their lands and lives and their children in your cause, loud when danger is still distant, in your hour of need they turn from you.*

Twenty years did little to improve Machiavelli's overall assessment of man, nor change his conclusion that being feared was "safer" than depending on love. In 1531, in Book III of his *Discourses* he penned:

> Men are mainly motivated by two things: love or fear. Therefore a Prince either makes himself loved or makes himself feared. Ultimately, a man who makes himself feared is better served and obeyed than a man who believes himself loved.

Machiavelli's choice—fear over love—is sound if for no other reason than with a single *selfish* act love can be transformed into fear, yet many *selfless* acts are required to turn fear into love.

Remember: we've already established that "altruism" doesn't exist.

Intimidation, as used in mind control, does not necessarily mean keeping your enemies quaking in terror 24/7.

Intimidation as used in mind control is a tangible presence, an aura of both confidence and command we compose from craft and charisma.

Gerald W. Piaget, in his excellent *Control Freaks: Who They Are and How to Stop Them from Running Your Life* (1991) lists three factors necessary for being

---

*In their haste to paint Machiavelli the ruthless rogue, many writers neglect to mention that, also in *The Prince*, Machiavelli draws a distinction between being feared and being *hated*.

an effective intimidator: a reputation, a set of intimidating moves, and a willingness to actually squash people who get in your way.

First, you need a reputation. This means creating an image of invincibility that makes an enemy think twice about raising a hand against you.

Such reputation comes about as a result of effective public relations, that is making sure everybody knows what a bad-ass you are, whether in the boardroom or on the battlefield. This can be actual accounts of your past conquests (ruthlessness) or completely fabricated tales strategically designed to terrorize the competition.

Remember: Reputation spills less blood.

Watch the movie *The Usual Suspects* (1995). The character Kaiser Sose knows the value of good PR.

Second, to be intimidating you need a set of intimidating moves. Once you decide on intimidation as your overall strategy, you must acquire tactics and techniques—"the walk and the talk"—that makes others "see" just how competent (dangerous) you are.

Recall how untrustworthy our perceptions can be? Perception, no matter how screwed-up, *is* reality. If your enemies "see" you as a force to be reckoned with, they will act (cower!) accordingly.

Finally, in order to be truly intimidating, every now and then you have to utterly crush someone like a bug!

In the same way you must always reward loyalty and efficiency within the pride, so, too, occasionally you have to snatch one of the indolent and infirm from the herd, making a glaring example of them, just to keep the rest of the herd stepping lively.

This, in turn, reinforces your reputation for ruthlessness, dissuading other predators from testing the temper of your tooth and nail.

When this is your decided course, adhere to Machiavelli's admonishment from *The Prince*: "Men are either to be treated kindly, or else utterly crushed. . . ."*

People are overpowered (intimidated) by another's social status, rank, or position (their power to socially ostracize us), by specific knowledge they possess about us, by their education, by their enthusiasm and emotional intensity over an issue, their show of anger (and cussing), their reputation for

---

*Machiavelli feels so strongly about this point he mentions it twice, in chapter III and again in chapter VII.

past violence, and by actual threats of violence. Sometimes these are attributes and accomplishments the intimidators actually possess.

Just as often, such "intimidating factors" are unrealistic fears (false perceptions) of the person being intimidated, or a false image expertly crafted and deliberately projected by the intimidators themselves.

The "no" blow. Nothing is more intimidating to others than our having the power to say "no." Except perhaps, our willingness to ruthlessly wield that power!

We don't ask questions, we don't make requests, we bite our tongue all too often, all because we don't want to hear that terrible, dream-crushing, four-letter word "no."

A frigid, flat "no" is the ultimate sign of dominance (and disrespect), that one word one finger that leaves no doubt: "I'm in charge, I don't have to explain my decisions to peons." "You don't deserve an explanation." "You're too stupid to understand if I did lower myself to explain!"

In the unlikely event they can deep-throat their fear long enough to spit out a request for clarification, you meet them with the condescending (bored) look you generally reserve for a puppy with a bladder-control problem. And silence. Silence is *very* intimidating.

Other times, when you don't want to completely burn your bridges, you may decide to explain your reason for saying "no". In which case, soften your "no" blow by giving well-prepared excuses. (See The Art of Lying, later.)

Always make it abundantly clear to the person "how hard it was" for you to have "had no other choice" than to say "no"; how your decision was (one) made "under extreme duress" or "only after much soul-searching," and (two) how your "no" will somehow benefit them in the long run.

In other words, when you say "no", you're actually doing them *a favor*. (Heh-heh-heh.)

For especially bothersome souls (e.g., gun-collecting postal workers), soften them up (distract them and diffuse potential violence) with humor and flattery (See The Art of No-gotiation, later.)

According to David Lieberman, in his *Get Anyone to Do Anything and Never Feel Powerless Again* (2000), if you ask for a favor immediately after saying "no" to a person's request they are more likely to grant *your* request. Lieberman advises we include the word "because" in all our requests *because* it triggers unconscious acceptance (page 135).

Name game. Control the name and you control the person. Folks at one time superstitiously guarded their names for fear witches would use their "Christian names" to conjure foul spirits. No less today, when word wizards all too easily use our names, and our coveted titles, to possess us.

Conspiracy buffs worry. "We're all becoming just numbers!" but when it comes to face-to-face encounters, name games still hold sway. From the prettiest of pet names reserved for loved ones, to the ugliest of racial slurs, the names—and titles—*we identify with* still have power to motivate and manipulate us.

When first introduced to a person:

- Repeat their name back to them.
- Encourage them to talk about themselves.
- Start a conversation with them about their name.

People love it when we talk about them. Ask about the origin of their name, where their family is from.

Immediately mention—and praise—any famous people or notable historic sites sharing a same or similar name.

Take time to study the origins of names in general and particularly the names of anyone you plan on "accidentally" bumping into. People love it when you tell them something interesting and/or exciting about their name.

Use this information to ingratiate yourself with the person you've zeroed in on, to show you're sincerely interested in them.

On the flip side, you can also use such trivia against your enemy, casually pointing out the fact his name means "duplicitous bastard" in some obscure Patagonian dialect.

Remembering a person's name is important, both as a tool and as a weapon, whether used to get closer to that person, or in order to denigrate them.

To help you better remember names:

- Take an interest because it's in your best interest.
- Really look at the person. Note any unique facial characteristics, mannerisms, and traits that will help you more easily associate their face with their name.

For example: "Bill Monroe" has a long nose so picture him *rowing* a boat shaped like his long nose across a lake filled with *money bills* instead of water. The more colorful, "silly," and action-filled you can make your mental image, the easier it will be to remember the person's name.

Depending on whatever role you want your new "friend" to adopt, create a fictitious person you once knew with the same name as your new friend, giving this made-up person the positive attributes (e.g., generosity, open-mindedness) your new friend with the same name will want to identify with or live up to.

You can also invoke the names of actual famous people sharing a same or similar name as your target, casually mentioning obscure and little known "facts" about them as suits your game plan.

Your enemy comes to the party with a game plan. He comes armed with rehearsed dialogue, practiced mannerisms, a carefully crafted reputation, and enough titles, rank, and positions to choke a horse. He's also well-studied in the "rules of etiquette" and feels insulated by decorum and social decency, secure enough to be rude.

He plays by the rules, so the only way to beat him is:

- Know the rules better than he does (allowing you to cash in on loopholes and trap him with "technicalities"),

   and

- Break the rules!

Deliberately mispronounce his name. Say, "That's a foreign name, isn't it?" with suspicion in your tone. Later, should he dare challenge you on a fact or point of order, remind listeners that he's a foreigner by asking, "Is a question/tone/behavior like that considered appropriate where you come from?"

Better yet, *ignore* his titles. Titles are a very effective form of word slavery.

Whether we belong to a particular religion or not, whether we voted for the present regime or not, we are still expected to start kissin' rings and kissin' ass any time anyone puts on a uniform or flashes a commanding title—no matter how arbitrary.

We all do it. Who among us would dare refer to the pope as "Mister"? Calling a nun "Miss"? There's a damned good reason Catholic priests are called "Father."

What about calling the president of the United States by his first name? (Remember, Secret Service can shoot to kill!) Think calling a Louisiana state highway patrolman or your Paris Island drill sergeant "Mister" would be a wise career move?

During the infamous *Chicago Seven* trial, hippie activist Abbie Hoffman continually disrupted the proceedings by calling the Judge by his first name and by "Mister," rather than "Your Honor."

Don't mistake being famous for having power. Being *famous* is to have your name on everyone's lips. To have power, on the other hand, is to make people zip their lips with just a whisper of your name!

To get the upper hand in any theological argument with a Christian (or a Muslim for that matter), simply insert the pronoun "she" or "her" when speaking about God. Doesn't matter what the initial argument was about, they will instantly forget it, in favor of smiting your "sacrilege."

Hindus and most other Easterners won't blink an eye if you add an "S" to the end of "God", but monotheistic Westerners will go ballistic, and be instantly distracted from their original theological argument.

Using such disruptive ploys to unbalance an enemy is known as "knocking them out of the box." The "box" is accepted and expected social behavior in general, as well as the specific behaviors demanded of us because of our particular place in the food chain: our socioeconomic status, position, rank and uniform, or our gender.

The walls of the box are constructed from names and titles, those social kowtows and taboos we are all taught to respect (fear) from birth.

Society then uses these to manipulate us beginning in childhood, putting us in the box by telling us to: "Act like a little gentleman . . ." "Behave like a proper little lady . . ."

Later we're told to "Stay in your place" (the box), and "Remember your station in life. . . ."

From amateur manipulators to media masters, we're constantly being told how a real man should scratch, how a proper lady should sit. And always we're taught how to show proper respect by genuflecting to the powers-that-be by helping polish that gold nameplate on their desk.

From politicians to the Promise Keepers, would-be word wizards know they can pull our strings by using evocative terms like: "Act like a *man*!" and "A *true* patriot wouldn't hesitate!" to make us follow them anywhere.

Of course we can (and already do) use these same ploys on others, freely using words, names, titles, and nicknames dreaded or coveted to bend others to our will:

- You gonna put up with that? What are you, a *man* or a mouse?"
- "Do you think that's how a *true* (man/Christian/patriot) would act?"
- What *kind* of mother are you!

Few of us have *cojones* big enough to challenge the status quo, to step "outside the box."

Thus anytime some rebel or malcontent does trespass social norms by challenging procedure and protocol, by questioning what it means to be a man or where a woman's place really is, those depending on such fickle social glue to hold their fragile world together are knocked out of the box.

The amount of freedom in any society is directly proportionate to how many farts and "Fucks you's" you hear.

The three types of "craft." In his *Discourses*, Machiavelli speaks of a quality called "astutia", from the Latin *astutus*, "adroitness" and "cunning." Astutia is a synonym for the type of craft that means shrewd and wily.

> **"Balance is the key: Balance in training; balance in life."**
> **—The Ninja Craft**

All told, there are three definitions of "craft":

- *Craft as vehicle*—like a boat, something that takes you where you want to go.

In India, the suffix *-yana* means "vehicle," for example, Mahayana ("great/bigger vehicle," a branch of Buddhism). In Japan, the suffix *-michi* and *-Do* have similar use. Meaning both "way" and "art," mystically they imply a vehicle that can carry us across a sea of troubles toward enlightenment.

In Black Science, *craft as vehicle* is our overall *strategy* we adopt to take us where we want to go, to accomplish what we set out to accomplish—be it poetry or plunder!

- *Craft as skill and Art*—the actual hands-on attitudes, abilities, and actions we use to accomplish our goal.

In Black Science (mind control), craft as skill and art corresponds to *tactics*.

- *Craft as cunning*—slyness, guile, and the use of both innate and gathered intelligence.

In mind control, this definition of "craft" applies to specific *techniques* we employ (cf. Lung, 1997a:15).

In developing and deploying their craft, students of the Black Science make sure their strategies, tactics, and techniques correspond to and compliment these three definitions of craft:

1. A "vehicle" designed to carry you where you want to go, i.e., a comprehensive *strategy* cognizant of all pertinent factors;
2. "Skills" and "arts" appropriate to the job at hand, i.e., realistic *tactics*; and
3. "Cunning" *techniques* designed to quickly and efficiently get the job done.

In choosing which Black Science craft is appropriate to a situation, when crafting our individual mind control craft, we must be sure our craft is versatile (adaptable) enough to meet these three criteria.

The craft of charisma. Charisma is the art of selling yourself. Think of life as a commercial for yourself. Most people have no idea what they're really selling.

Accomplished salesmen wink, "People pay more for the sizzle than for the steak."

"Charisma" *is* that sizzle. Before you can sell a product, you have to sell yourself.

> *"For I must tell you friendly in your ear, Sell when you can,*
> *you are not for all markets."*
> —**Shakespeare,** *As You Like It*

The art of charisma has gone by many names down through the ages. Ancient Celts called it *glamour*, a presence so overpowering, so magickal, as to dazzle the mind, hence our modern usage of "glamor" as a synonym for beauty and style.

The French call it *je ne sais quoi* (lit. "I know not what"), an attractive aura and ability to make others feel important and blessed just for being in our presence. In Yiddish it's *chutzpah*, bold self-confidence and daring. And any complete definition of charisma would have to include a dose of *panache*, a flamboyance in both style and action.

When we make people like us *and* like themselves for liking us . . . *that's charisma!*

In baseball it's "Three strikes, you're out." When it comes to the art of charisma, it's "Three *likes* and you're in!"

One, we like people to like us, so it is worth our while to put a little time and effort into *helping* people like us.

Two, we like people who are like us. A certain amount of xenophobia is built into our DNA, a logical survival mechanism that makes us suspicious of strangers. This is why such ploys as mirroring and matching, imitating our target's patterns of speech and their mannerisms, is so effective—helping assure others we're just like them. Anna Nicole Smith aside, opposites *don't* attract. Studies show that we tend to associate with and marry within our same race, ethno-religious group, our socioeconomic class, and within our general education level. (So if you don't share the likes and dislikes, or naturally move in the same social circles as your target, add *study* and *skulduggery* to your course curriculum at the Black Science Institute.)

(FYI: Nietzsche advised that one must choose a wife for her conversation rather than for her beauty since, when you both grow old and her beauty fades, you will still have something to talk about.)

Three, and most important, we like people who like us.

Conversely, people *dislike* you because:

- They think *you* dislike *them*.
- They are intimidated by you.
- You're rivals, for the same lover or for the same parking space.
- You've given them a real reason to hate you, i.e., you've beat them out or beat them up sometime in the past.
- They *think* you've given them a reason to hate you. (Can you say "psycho-delusional disgruntled coworker"!)
- They hate everybody and you're stuck being part of "everybody."

So what can you do to *make* people like you more?

- *Project strength and confidence* without being overpowering.

Confidence and power are both attractive and intoxicating. Offer to let them "share" your strength and confidence. Convince them "We're stronger together."

- *Be "vulnerable"* without being weak. Nobody likes a wimp. (We equate weakness with *need*, and "need" means you want something from *me!*)

- *Be approachable.*
- *Make eye contract*, without being rude. Eye contact links us with others. Remember to smile with your eyes.
- *Ask others for help.* Asking others to help you, and for their opinion, shows you respect and value them.

Make people *feel* useful, and they'll be useful.

- *Make them feel good about themselves* (which in turn makes them feel good about *you*).
- *Speak positive*, about yourself (without bragging), and about your plans (that they can be a part of—*if* they're smart enough).

Most important, speak positive about *them*, without sounding condescending.

- *Keep the emphasis on them*, even when shamelessly promoting yourself and your agenda. At least make them *think* you are still talking about them.
- *Use matching and mirroring*, i.e., imitating and mirroring their actions and speech patterns (without mocking), in order to further establish rapport with them.

The Art of Ambush

Our word *ambush* is from the French *embushchier* ("to sit in the woods"). But whether crouched in some southeast Asian jungle waiting for Charlie to slink down the trail, or busy scattering psychological bread crumbs along an enemy's mental pathways to entice and trap him, the same "rules" of ambush apply.

And the consequences for getting caught at either ambush site can be just as disastrous.

The four principles. Whether a physical ambush or one played out on a psychological battlefield, carrying out a successful ambush requires four things:

First, intelligence, both the common sense variety and the scuttlebutt you gather on your target. (see The Two Types of Intelligence, in chapter 4.)

Second, preparation and patience. An ambush must be set up in secret. This is not as simple as it sounds, especially if your plan requires the help of others.

Successfully plot out your ambush with a diligence to detail. It's always the things you forget to pack that you live to regret . . . if you're lucky . . . if you live.

Once all your pieces are on the board, your players in place, patience is now required—whether the patience to hunker down, unmoving in muck and monsoon waiting for your prey to materialize out of the mist on some dark jungle trail, or the patience or nerve to nonchalantly continue working side-by-side with coworkers who never suspect the other shoe is about to fall.

Third, execution of your ambush must be both swift and merciless. Your target must be down for the count before he realizes he's even in the ring. Your blow must be telling, a single strike intended to take him out of the fight for good—for your good!

Most important, make certain your ambush leaves no survivors, no one who can regroup and counterattack (or testify!), no one who can flee "into the hills" to carry on a "guerrilla" campaign against you.*

Finally, escape and evasion: It's no fun unless you get away with it.

A vital part of the preparation stage of any "Black Op" infiltration is setting up your *two* "exit strategies."

Note I say "two."

As a covert team penetrates deeper into enemy territory, they set up booby traps and trip-wires behind them, traps anyone attempting to follow them will stumble over; traps that, after completion of the mission, in the event a hasty withdrawal is called for, pursuing troops can be led into.

When it comes to mental combat, planting booby traps for your enemy to stumble over is called "banking," that is, "money in the bank," information held back until needed.

Work one of these simple banking questions into your conversation:

- Give him the "Count the F's" test from part I, but don't immediately correct him when he answers only three.
- Ask him "How many sides a pyramid has?" When he answers "three," bank this mistake for later use.
- Ask him which of the fifty states is the farthest south. When he answers "Florida" just let it go. Later, when needed, embarrass him by pointing out the correct answer is "Hawaii."

---

*In some *rare* instances you might decide to leave *one* enemy "alive" in order to carry the tale of "terror" back to his tribe! (see *Theatre of Hell*, Lung and Prowant, 2003)

Get him to commit to a certain fact, when possible, encourage him to expound on this fact—digging his own grave all the deeper!

Remember, don't call him on his mistake then and there. Only later, when he is vehemently arguing a different case, ask him if he's 100 percent certain of the point he's trying to make. Of course he'll answer "yes."

Now play your ace, the info you've banked.

And as he stands there stunned, finally at a loss for words, shake your head sadly, "So, Bob if you were so 100 percent certain about that, yet so obviously wrong about something as simple as that, how can we know you know what the Hell you're talking about now!"

Depending on Bob's claimed area of expertise, there's no telling how much obscure trivia you might turn up to trip up ol' Bob.

Nothing is so satisfying as beating a man at his own game.

In the movie *Ronin* (1998), Robert De Niro plays an out-of-work CIA agent concentrating on making himself a cup of coffee while his less-experienced, loud-mouthed rival tries to convince the other agents assembled in the room that he, and not De Niro, should lead an upcoming ambush.

Casually De Niro sits his steaming cup of coffee down on the edge of the table, before unexpectedly turning to confront the loudmouth. Startled by De Niro's sudden change in demeanor and his verbal assault, the loud-mouth hurriedly back-pedals several steps . . . right into the table, spilling the hot coffee onto his leg.

In an instant, De Niro is on him like white on rice! "And *that*," quietly explains DeNiro, "is how you set up an ambush!"

When caught in a verbal ambush yourself, or when realizing the tide of a conversation/negotiation has turned, sometimes you counterattack with doubled ferocity in an attempt to rattle your attacker(s).

Other times, you need to run like Hell . . . uh, *strategically retreat*.

When Verbally Ambushed Yourself:

- *Don't get defensive.* Don't say things like "What did *I* do"? "Why are you picking on *me*?"
- *Keep the spotlight on him.* Say things like, "What's really bothering *you*? I thought we agreed to focus on you and *your problems*."

Now he's on the defensive, trying to keep control of his ambush while simultaneously his mind is racing, asking itself questions like: "When did we agree to that?" and "Oh God! What *problems* is he talking about?"

"Walkaways" are your emergency exit strategy, words and actions you can use when "trapped" in a conversation, when you've painted (*talked*) yourself into a corner, or when you're just bored to tears by the other guy's line of bull—which is nowhere near as entertaining and imaginative as *your* mesmerizing mix of mental marmalade and malarkey!

Exit stage left *immediately* after you:

- Point your finger like a pistol, click your tongue loudly twice, and wink, "I was hoping you'd say that."
- Say, "That makes sense . . . *this* time around."
- Nod and say, "No."
- Shrug, "Things are different down South."
- Say, "If what I hear happened to you, had happened to me, I'd probably feel the same way."
- Say, "I see you don't read your Bible much." Shake your head and "tsk" when saying this.
- Say, "I see someone's not been reading their Nietzsche (or Machiavelli, or Sun Tzu)!" Say this with a chuckle of condescending amazement.
- Say, "I could tell you . . . but then I'd have to kill you." Say the first half of this with a broad smile, which suddenly—and menacingly—disappears when you hiss the second half.
- Tell him, "Ben Franklin said, 'Three can keep a secret, if *two are dead*.'" Lean in menacingly and wink when whispering this last part. Emphasize "two are dead" as if you actually know where the bodies are buried!

> *"He who is prudent and lies in wait for an enemy who is not likewise prudent, that man will know victory."*
> —Sun Tzu, *Art of War*

The consummate literary example of a successful ambush is Edgar Allan Poe's *The Cask of the Amontillado* (1846) in which the "hero" of the story meets all four criteria:

First, he *gathers intelligence* about his hated enemy, who doesn't suspect he's been targeted. Our hero learns his enemy fancies himself a connoisseur of fine wine.

Second, *he prepares the ambush site beforehand*, baiting the trap with the perfect enticement: An entire barrel of the rare wine his enemy covets has just been discovered! The only catch is it's located in some out-of-the-way catacombs.

Next, *patiently* he lures his still unsuspecting prey *literally* deeper and deeper into his doom.

Finally, when the time finally comes to spring the trap—his enemy totally taken in, still distracted by greed and lust—our hero pounces!—executing his ambush *swiftly and surely*.

Having trapped his enemy with no hope of escape, our hero begins methodically—again *literally*—sealing his enemy's fate . . . by sealing him up inside a wall!

And, most important, our hero comes away from his successful ambush *unscathed* . . . and *unindicted*.

(**FYI:** Poe's tale also gives us the two rules of revenge: First, your enemy has to know it's *you* who's brought about his downfall. Second, you have to get away with it!)

The craft of confusion. The craft of confusion hinges on our ability to deny our enemy accurate information. This means we must *disguise* our intent to do him harm, while providing him with plenty of disinformation.

> *"If you come across someone you are not sure of while walking on a road at night, quickly speak to him. Talk in such a way that the stranger may not really understand you as you stride up to him. While this is happening, you should be able to find out who he is. Someone with a nefarious intent is sure to be taken aback by this approach and lose heart."*
> —**Munenori, in Sato,** *The Sword and the Mind*

Sun Tzu: "All warfare is based on deception."

Deception = disguise and disinformation.

Disguise and disinformation create confusion, which leads to doubt, which leads to defeat.

Disguising your intent to do your enemy harm comes first and foremost:

> *"A swindler's greatest tool of the trade is his ability to camouflage his identity and true intent."*
> —**Whitlock,** *Chuck Whitlock's Scam School*

We hold the upper hand when our enemy doesn't see us coming or, better yet, when he counts us his confidant . . . right up to the moment we strike the telling blow.

Nature punishes the predictable.

Watch a magic trick enough times and, sooner or later, you figure it out. Likewise, it's harder to hit a moving target. That's why boxers train to stick and move, stick and move. Disguising your intent and plans means going about your business as if nothing is happening beforehand; afterward, as if nothing has happened.

When planning an operation, never draw attention to yourself by suddenly changing your routine. Instead, begin varying your routine and habits incrementally, far in advance. The further in advance of your target date, the better.

On the other hand, sometimes deliberately going out of your way to act strange, activity outside your normal routine, is a good way to distract an enemy away from your true objective. This is an especially good ploy when helping draw attention away from the activities of a co-conspirator. Whitlock (1997) said: "Until we all develop ESP, we will never be able to say with certainty just what the intentions are of the other people in our lives" (page 203).

Disinformation throws a monkey wrench into our decision-making machinery. We (should!) make decisions based on all available information. However, if your intelligence gathering procedures (e.g., personal perceptions, agents) are flawed or if someone *deliberately* feeds us false information, our decisions cannot but lead to disaster.

In this "age of information" it's becoming increasingly difficult to keep information out of the hands of our foe, so the next best thing is to supply him with plenty of disinformation.

Thus, we prepare for battle while helping our enemy *un*-prepare. Again, to quote Sun Tzu: "Long ago warriors knew to make themselves invulnerable while patiently anticipating the enemy's moment of vulnerability."

We accomplish this by feeding him spurious information and skewed facts—either firsthand, because he still trusts us, via a third party he trusts, or by planting revelations for him to brag about discovering.

The goal of disinformation is to get your enemy to show up at a gunfight with only a knife. The classic: your office rival shows up at the boss's formal dress birthday party in a toga because somehow he was fed erroneous information that it was a masquerade party!

Other ploys for sowing confusion in a foe's mind include deliberate

Freudian slips, "zoner" words and phrases, and false praise, as well as making them think we're agreeing with them when we're not.

Deliberate Freudian slips confuse your enemy with quickly rattled-off phrases, guaranteed to interrupt any diatribe:

- "Wipe your ask'n me for?" ("Why are you asking me?")
- "Cow shit I know?" ("How should I know?")
- "Ex-squeeze me?" ("Excuse me?")
- "I bake your powder?" ("I beg your pardon?").
- Say, "No" while shaking your head "Yes."

Zoners are words and phrases that confuse us by giving our brain contradictory images to process. As the name implies, zoners cause us to lose concentration and "zone out."

Luckily, zoners have the same effect on our foes. Causing your enemy's train of thought to pull out of the station without him accomplishes two purposes:

First, he stumbles in both thought and narrative, opening a gap into which you thrust your own agenda.

Second, his hesitation will be seen by others as a lapse in concentration, as his being indecisive. And they will question his ability.

When we hear an abstract word like *think, suppose, pretend, imagine,* or *believe,* especially at the beginning of a sentence, we access a different part of our consciousness than when a sentence begins with a concrete word like *rock* or *dog.*

Therefore, begin your sentence(s) with short but effective hypnotic commands intended to activate the right imaginative side of your enemy's brain, leading his thoughts away from the left logical and more verbal side of his brain.

Make eye contact and, when possible, actually touch your subject with your hand as you open your sentence with a firm suggestion:

- "*Imagine* this . . ."
- "*Picture* this . . ."
- "*Suppose* that . . ."
- "*Think* about this *picture* . . ."
- "*Believe* what I'm about to tell you . . ."

Believe is by far the best example of a zoner word. After all, the right side of the brain is where we store all the hoodoo and hobgoblins we "believe" in. Facts tend to land in the left hemisphere.

Undermine your enemy's belief in the power of the word *believe* by reminding him (and any audience assembled) that you can't write "believe" without writing "lie" in the middle.*

With a look of disbelief on your face challenge him:

"Do you believe what you just said is a true belief or a false belief?"

"It's a *true* belief!" he'll immediately protest.

"So you admit it's *only* a *belief.*"

Note the obvious confusion on his face . . . and *pounce!*

Another challenge: "Who here do you actually believe believes what you obviously can't convince yourself to actually believe?"

By the way, never be foolish enough to imagine that any science-based argument can ever get the upper hand against an argument based on belief.

Science, which by its very charter must rely on bothersome points like logic and evidence, all too soon becomes frustrated and fatigued when faced with belief, which literally plucks *its* "facts" from thin air!

False praise allows you to confuse an enemy by sending glowing messages of praise and encouragement . . . with strings attached.

- You say, "You must be working out. You don't look nearly as big as you used to." They hear, *"You're still a fat bastard no matter how much you exercise!"*
- You say, "Is that a new dress? I really admire a woman who's not afraid to thumb her nose at convention!" She hears, *"Something's wrong with the way you're dressed!"*
- You say, "Who cares what other people think, right?" They panic, *"What do other people think!?!"*
- You say, "I admire a rebel. I wish I had your guts!" They hear, *"You're gonna be fired as soon as the Boss sees you!"*

False tells, ticks, clearing the throat, obvious hand gestures, and other bogus physical clues, can be "pre-planted" in your enemy's mind for use at a strategic moment.

Part and parcel of being a good poker player is being able to read the

---

*Simplistic word play? Sure. But it's the "simple things" that really stick in your mind. For example, from now on, every time *you* hear *believe you* will think about the *lie* in the middle! (Heh-heh-heh.)

tells of other players—that shifting in your seat, that scratching of nose or ass that alerts everyone at the table that you've got another good hand.

Ah, but what if every time you get a relatively "good hand" you treat the other players to *an obvious tell*—a *false* tell.

Then, when Lady Luck stops PMSing and finally deals you that royal flush, and the tell you've trained the other players to expect from you is nowhere to be seen, they bet big. You win big.

More Agreeing without agreeing: No matter how much the other guy disagrees with you, keep nodding, smiling, and keep saying, "So you agree with me," and "I see you see what I'm saying."

More of this in The Art of No-gotiation, later.

> *"Uproar and confusion appear to call the battle, but fixed*
> *rules still carry the day."*
> **—Li Quan, 818–906 CE**

The Art of Seduction

> *"When a rogue kisses you, count your teeth."*
> **—Hebrew proverb**

Whether trying to ferret your way into someone's panties, or weasel your way into their pocketbook, whether looking for a lover for life or just looking to lift someone's life savings, the tactics and techniques of seduction are the same.

At best, the word *seduction* conjures the image of a suave renaissance Don Juan, a gaggle of giggling girls melting in the palm of his caress. Worst-case scenario, seduction evokes the image of a 24-caret gold-toothed, velvet-wrapped, '70s pimp whipping the hard-sell on some wide-eyed Iowa runaway fresh off the long dog.

But most times seduction simply means getting someone to sit still long enough for you to give them your best sales pitch—whether peddling a piece of the Brooklyn Bridge or stalking a hot piece of . . . passion.

Don't be intimidated. Don't think you have it in you to be a seducer? (Heh-heh-heh.) Keep reading . . . we'll put it in you!

In the end, the art of seduction comes down to the art of talking. Add to that a couple of smooth "intimidating" moves, and some little known facts about Mother Nature, and you could be well on your way to buying your first lavender Cadillac—or at least getting your first gold tooth!

Seduction is simply *charisma* wrapped in cashmere.

Men. Don't be intimidated just because you're not Sir Lancelot. *Relax*, women outnumber men three to one. Pretty good odds you'll "get lucky" sooner or later.

Of course, take a little time to internalize the following insights and you just might increase your odds.

You women on the other, just be patient—and *look* available—men will come to you. Just think: Pavlov's pups!

Reading the fine print. If you've gotten this far into studying the Black Science (mind control), you've undoubtedly gotten a little better at reading people, picking up on their nervous tics and tells; matching their body language; mirroring their speech patterns; and employing whether they're watchers, listeners, or touchers to your advantage.

These Black Science observations apply to both men and women. Thus we can read men and women in the same way, with only slight variations between them.

However, when it comes to the art of seduction, you must become adept at perceiving her subtle signals—her nuance of both motion and emotion.

In other words, you gotta learn to "read the fine print."

To accomplish this, you have to look at more than her chest! Take time to *really* look at her. After all, this might be the woman you end up spending the rest of your life with . . . or at least the next ninety minutes down at the nearest Motel 6.

Don't mistake *her* showing interest for your *being* interesting. You might just have something stuck in your teeth.

Also, don't get cocky (no pun intended). Many a time a man thinks he's the puppet master only to discover he's the one being stringed along.

Mrs. Robinson aside, when we hear the word "seduction" we generally think of men "seducing" women. Sexist bastards!*

Truth be known, women play the controlling role in many a seduction

---

*Since men have to try harder, this section speaks from a decidedly male perspective. Still, there is much women can learn from this section . . . if only how to get men to try harder!

scenario . . . they're just more subtle when they seduce. (Men, on the other hand, usually give themselves away by salivating too much. Again, Pavlov.)

For example, studies bear out what men have suspected since time began, that women do not send clear rejection signals. In fact, women often send "encouraging" sexually explicit signals even when they have little actual interest in the man. Such signals can be either conscious ploys or unconscious behavior, but both are designed to get men to reveal more about themselves. For example, women use such things as nodding to encourage and direct the flow of conversation (cf. *Psychology Today* Oct. 2001:26).

She'll also hit you with batting eyelashes, a quick smile you're not sure you actually saw, and other subtle movements you've no idea how to "read."

Don't panic! All this is simply "operant conditioning." (See The Skinner School, in chapter 4.)

In other words, it's simply feedback: You tell a joke. She laughs. Encouraged, you keep telling jokes until she becomes convinced you're a blithering idiot!

But that's not wholly unexpected since men just naturally make more noise around women. And women make less noise when men are around. Dare we say, they "clam up." (Heh-heh-heh.)

It's a Darwin thing. Such behavior is found throughout nature, where males—from birds to apes—make displays—songs, calls, and howls; ritual mating dances; posturings against, and fighting of, other males—all designed to attract the attention of the female.

Females, for the most part, tend to preen and pretend not to notice the males' display. Sound familiar?

Of course you want her to notice you, but only your good points. "You only get one chance to make a first impression" still holds sway. Opening a conversation with your potential baby's mamma isn't as terrifying as you first might think. Provided you *do* first think.

What's the worst that can happen? All right: total rejection, public humiliation, and emotional emasculation so severe it scars you for life. Who of us hasn't "been there, done that."

Breaking the ice successfully depends on your *actions* and your *attitude*.

Action-wise:

• *Make eye contact*, but don't stare. When/if she says something flattering about you, smile and look away/down at the floor as if embarrassed by her compliment. (This shows you're both "humble" and just "shy" enough to be adorable.)

• *Avoid crude come-on lines.* Safest bet: Just say, "Hi." Guess who gets no respect when you try too hard to impress her with your practiced Rodney Dangerfield one-liners. Don't invade her intimate space. Give her at least three feet, unless in a crowded venue where pressing in close is unavoidable, or when sitting next to her at a bar. Always ask permission to sit next to her, even on a bar stool or in a crowded theater.

(**FYI:** Make the first word(s) she says to you "yes." Her saying yes to your sitting next to her sets the stage for future Yes's you'll elicit from her. Therefore, don't ask, "Is this seat taken." To which she'll say "No"; instead phrase it "Am I correct this seat isn't taken?" to which she'll reply "Yes, you're correct.")

• *Don't touch her . . . too soon.* Unless brushing up against her is unavoidable, time permitting, let her touch you first. Her taking the initiative to touch you (e.g., while laughing at your joke) is a good sign . . . not a *sure* sign. (The only sure sign is that Do Not Disturb sign you hang on the motel door!)

Introduce yourself, but only offer your hand to shake *after she introduces herself.*

(**Clue:** She's more interested in you if she tells you both her first and last names when introducing herself.)

• *Be aware* of the shadow-walk and shadow-talk going on; hers, as well as the signals you're giving off consciously and unconsciously.

Attitude-wise:

• *Don't get too personal too soon.* Pick a neutral, non-threatening topic to talk about, for example, how good the band is. (**FYI:** Three good reasons to go out of your way to make friends with any bar band you run into. One, knowing the band is a great conversation starter between you and the babes in the bar. Second, babes love bands. The guitar gets her hot and, since she can't get to the guitar player, she's soon singing your tune. Finally, the band just might become famous some day, and who couldn't use Bruce Springsteen—and all the babes *he* knows!—as a pal!)

Or you could harken to John Cougar's advice for scoring with chicks, "Forget all about that macho shit and learn how to play guitar!"

• *Show vulnerability* by asking for help. Ask her for the time, if she knows the bartender's name. If you're cruising the grocery store, ask her which of these two products is "healthier."

Thanking her for her help, confide to her that you know you should eat healthy but sometimes your sweet tooth gets the better of you. Chances are she can identify with that.

In a clothing store or jewelry store, obviously lost and confused, you ask her "which one of these" does she think your beloved grandmother would like. (Talking about your mother makes you a "mamma's boy." Talking about your sainted "grammie" makes you caring.)

Thank her profusely for her help. Studies show that people are more likely to agree to additional "favors" after having done us an initial favor.

Hitting her E-spot. Fuggitaboutit! You're never gonna get close enough to even sniff around her G-spot unless you first learn how to hit her E-spot. That's "E" as in "emotions."

> *"Successful con artists know how to relate to their marks*
> *on an individual level. They are very intuitive about a mark's*
> *weaknesses and insecurities."*
> **—Whitlock, 1997:20**

Recall that 90 percent of all human decisions are based on emotion. Therefore her decision to continue listening to your line of BS or take you home and jump dem bones will be made based on her emotional reaction to you.

Reactions come from actions. And her emotional reactions—emotional decisions—will come from your actions . . . so, for better or worse, richer or poorer, you're the one running the show.

And if you want to keep running the show you better learn to cater to her emotions. This means adding two new words to your seduction vocabulary. . . . No, not "restraining order"! The two words are *empathy* and *validation*.

Empathy means convincing her "I *feel* you" (as opposed to "I want to feel you up!"). This means expressing the same kinds of thoughts and feelings she has.

For example, you understand her feeling(s) of hesitation to talk to a stranger. Just like her, you were hesitant about coming to a bar (etc.) to meet people.

Mirror her trepidation, "It's okay to be nervous, I'm nervous too." And "I'm not comfortable in bars either. Would you like to go get a cup of coffee or . . ."

She's just come off a bad breakup. . . . You've been there, done that. You know just how she feels.

Empathy is emotional mirroring. In the same way Black Science (Lung and Prowant, 2001) taught you to "mirror" a person physically in order to more easily establish rapport, empathy brings you into emotional synch with her.

Don't just empathize with her feelings, thank her for making you feel comfortable enough to express your own feelings.

Have you picked up on the key word feelings yet?

(**FYI:** Don't just tell her you empathize, show her you share her feelings about life in general, and about sunsets, puppies, mom and apple pie in particular by literally showing her a picture of your dearly departed *grand*mother cuddling your lost puppy while she stands—better yet, sits in a wheelchair—in front of a beautiful sunset.)

In fact, a photo of your adorable lost puppy—the puppy Grammie gave you right before she died—is a great way to strike up a conversation with a woman anywhere.

Validation means making her believe you truly believe in what she claims to truly believe in.

Validation consists of two parts: First, you validate *the person she is*. This means acknowledging *her total person*. (Didn't I tell you to stop looking at her hooters?)

She has to feel understood. (There's that word feel again.)

She has to feel safe and secure and relaxed enough to express herself around you. That means you can't be judgmental.

Let her have her say—no matter the topic, no matter how scatter-brained her opinion—and then go out of your way to find some truth, (validity) in her outlook . . . no matter how hard you have to look!

Sincerely praise her opinions and accomplishments, no matter how paltry. Just don't get *caught* being "sincere" (condescending).

Second, you have to validate *the person she wants to be*. This means allowing her to rationalize the goals and roles she's chosen for herself and for you.

Basically, validation means *giving her an excuse to act on her fantasies*.

Goals. Think of her goals as the basic plot of a movie she's writing in her head. Roles are then played out by the actors in her movie—you and her.

The basic theme of her movie is already fixed in her mind: She's looking for an Oscar-winning love story while you'll be satisfied (hopefully several times in a row!) with an XXX video.

In other words, she sees herself starring in a feature-length epic, but might end up settling for a bit part in an all-too-short (!) featurette.

It is a woman's oldest dilemma: "Mr. Right" or "Mr. Right-now!"

Her goal(s) can be a complex mixture of natural curiosity, flirting with decadence and danger, and challenge (e.g., seducing a virgin, enticing away a married man).

She's motivated by both conscious and subconscious feelings somewhere between her innate nesting urge and her—just as natural—animal lust. Simply put, she's torn between settling down and gettin' down!

Your goal? Getting some. But then again, you might luck out and find someone willing to put up with you past next Tuesday. So your real goal(s), reframed are:

- Finding out *what she wants*.
- Finding out *what she'll settle for*.

Find out what her goals are and help her achieve them.

Of course someone with a Ph.D. in Black Science (mind control) will be able to make her aware of "goals" she didn't know she wanted! (Ph.D. = "play on her desires")

Roles. Bonnie Tyler had a hit with the '80s refrain "I'm holding out for a hero!" If all women were holding out for a hero, life would be so much simpler, at least for me.

But until we get that cloning thing perfected, assume all women are unique. And how do you get close to a unique woman? *You*-nique up on her! (Heh-heh-heh.)

Instead of scoffing at and resisting the role she's chosen for herself (as so many men would do), take a unique approach and *reinforce her role*. Follow her lead. Figure out the "roles" she's already picked out for herself and for you. Help her establish her role, her identity—then hold her to it.

Remember cognitive dissonance, the need human beings have for consistency, the need to balance our internal view with our external actions.

No one wants to be caught being a hypocrite. In other words, make her put her mouth where your . . . money is . . . or something like that.

For example, instead of trying to convince her to have sex with you, encourage her "independent woman/feminist" role by convincing her you also sincerely believe in women's rights. This leads to you both agreeing that women have "needs" (i.e., they get horny, too!) the same as men and should be allowed to act just as stupid and licentious as men.

You then casually challenge her with the idea that most women wouldn't be strong and daring enough to take advantage of such equality. You also lament (heavy sigh) how refreshing it would be to run up against such a free-spirited and *truly* independent woman.

(Now don't be surprised when she makes you her *bitch*, screws you silly all night like the slut you are, and leaves you—literally!—limp at dawn with only a vague, "Yeah, sure, I'll phone you, Stud.") You will feel *sooo* used! (Heh-heh-heh.)

Of course, some women do want to play the damsel in distress role and be swept off their feet. But just as many women long to take charge, to figuratively and literally be on top.

What's her preferred role? Naughty girl? Free spirit? Or cool, detached observer—above it all? Princess in peril, waiting to be rescued by that knight packing a lot-o-lance? Or Lady Jane in charge of teaching an uncivilized half-naked ape-man how to properly sup tea . . . in exchange for his introducing her to the fine art of long vine monkey love!

And how do you determine *your role* in her mind-movie? Figuring out her role tells you your role.

Back to our "movie" analogy: She arrives on "the set" all decked out like Princess Di—eagerly awaiting the arrival of her princely costar. Unfortunately, because of a mix-up in the props department, you show up beating on your chest, sporting only Tarzan's loincloth!

The key is to employ all the mind-control skills you've acquired so far to listen to what she's saying—verbal *and* nonverbal—and to what she's not saying.

Is she really looking for a chivalrous knight in shining armor to jimmy her chastity belt, or a raucous Hell's Angel to rock her world? A long tall drink of water in a Stetson who'll rope her in and slap a brand to her behind, or a shy, slightly insecure "nerd" the dominatrix in her is just dying to "deflower"?

Once you figure out what hat (or loincloth) she wants you to wear, once again you can use cognitive dissonance to see she sticks to "the script."

For instance, she's assigned you the role of "swashbuckling Cavalier," so you turn the tables by playing the role of the sword hilt, reminding her that "A gentleman would feel honor-bound to see a lady such as yourself makes it to her door safe and sound."

Having played your assigned role to the tee, try to *act surprised* when she asks you in—all the way in!

A bad boy biker, on the other hand, will be expected to challenge her—to convince her!—to take a chance.

Depending on the role she's chosen for you, be ready and willing to:

- Take the blame.
- Take control.
- Take a hike!

The "value" of flattery. There's an old adage: "All talk between men and women is foreplay." If you think "flattery won't get you anywhere," one, you obviously need to get out more often and, two, you've obviously never heard of Giacomo Casanova de Seingalt, Don Juan Tenorio, or read the *Kama Sutra*, all of which praised and pandered the power of flattery.

When we're talking about flattery, we're talking about *talking*—inserting just the right compliment, morale booster, and motivator at just the right juncture in our negotiation for nookie.

Ever notice that men and women talk differently? And that they talk differently to one another? Ironically, studies show that men and women both want to talk about the same things up to a point.

The top five things both men and women like talking about—in order of importance—are:

1. Home life, especially their kids. (Always ask to see the pictures.)
2. Health (theirs, not yours. Be sure to *empathize!*)
3. Job (specifically, how much they hate theirs. Again, *empathize.*)
4. Professional growth (their hopes for promotion, plans for advancement)
5. Personal growth (what they plan to get around to doing just as soon as the world stops plotting against them!)

This is the point at which priorities diverge for men and women. Beyond these, men and women still talk about some of the same things, for example, recreation and travel, the opposite sex, but these vary in order of importance and are offset by the inclusion of clothing and shopping on the women's list and sports and politics on the men's list.

Deliberately flatter someone by talking to them about things you know they're interested in, whether male or female. We flatter others with our attention, especially when we compliment them on their insight, eloquence, and expertise.

When you flatter, be specific. Don't compliment her with generics like "pretty" and "smart," instead pick specific parts of her physique (eyes, laugh, etc.) and personality (attitude, sense of humor, etc.).

When talking to women in particular, remember the value of flattery. Also remember this "VALUE" when talking to women:

- *Vulnerability*: Showing someone is always more effective than just telling them. Show her you're emotionally approachable, you have feelings and you're secure enough in your manhood to show those emotions. Tell her how you cried like a baby when . . . you saw the injured puppy, or the ending of *Sleepless in Seattle* (1993), *The Piano* (1993), and *The Notebook* (2005). (**Note:** Go easy on the blubbering. There's a thin line between being sensitive and being a wimp.)
- *Altruism*: I know, we told you, "There's no such thing as altruism." Which still holds true. That means you gotta practice sincerely faking it, showing her how you go out of your way to help everything from kids and charities to stranded motorists.
- *Loving*: Whip out those feelings again. Show her how you care for Grammie, and kids, and lost puppies.
- *Uniqueness*: She's one of a kind. You've never met another woman like her. She has a unique way of looking at that boring subject. Yada-yada-yada. You get the idea.
- *Empathy*: You feel her pain. You value her incredible insight and you'll defend her right to bitch-bitch-bitch! Remember: hit her E-spot and that won't be the only thing you'll be hittin'!

Conversation killers. These "killers" include religion and politics (for both genders) and sports (with women). It's been said, "It's better to remain silent and have people wonder if you're a fool than to speak . . . and leave no doubt!"

A few suggestions to keep you from putting your foot in your mouth and leaving no doubt in people's mind just how lame your seduction technique really is:

- Avoid personal pronouns. Don't start every one of your sentences with "I" and go easy on "me" and "mine." Likewise avoid beginning sentences with an accusatory "You . . ." or with commands like "Let's . . ." or a premature "We."
- Avoid absolutes, words and opinions that close off avenues of expression . . . and alleys of escape!
- Avoid "always" and "never." Instead try, "Up till now . . ." and "In the past . . ."
- Avoid voicing absolute judgments like "That movie *sucked!*" Instead, ask her opinion and sincerely pretend to listen. (**FYI:** If your self-respect won't allow you to agree with her hare-brained opinion—in effect kissing her ass just so you can . . . well, kiss her ass—instead compliment her on how well she expresses her opinion rather than on the merits of the opinion itself.)
- *Avoid*: coulda, shoulda, woulda, ought to, must, and don't. Instead try can, might, and perhaps.
- Avoid sentences that begin with "Why?"

Tricks of the trade. You gotta learn to think on your feet if you want to get her on her back. That's why every man on this planet has at least one foolproof seduction trick up their sleeve.

The truth is, when it comes to seduction, everything works. But everything doesn't work all the time.

- Use The Anchor Plot we taught you in White Talk, earlier in this chapter.
- Use humor. When it comes to getting a woman to open up, humor is the best lubricant. After that, K-Y Jelly.
- Make people laugh. Use self-deprecating humor to show them you're not stuck on yourself.
- Give them the gift of laughter. They'll feel obligated to give you something back in return, like their time and attention. Besides, laughter makes them feel good. Things that make us feel good we do twice.
- Avoid ethnic and sexist jokes—unless it's a sexist joke where the woman wins.

- Give her a chance to tell her jokes. Practice your sincere laugh. And don't forget to include "smiling" with the eyes.
- Hand her your keys and tell her "Give these back to me the minute I begin to bore you."
- Do one magic trick to catch her attention. But like jokes, don't overdo it. One magic trick shows her you're good with your fingers. A dozen magic tricks just makes you David Blaine creepy.
- Use chemical warfare. No, not that mad scientist cocktail of Rupies, alcohol, and Viagra! Human pheromones for both men and women can now be bought off the shelf.
- Don't take "no" for an answer. Just because she says no today, doesn't automatically mean she'll say no tomorrow or next week. Persistence still counts for something. (**FYI:** Experience is what you get when you don't get what you wanted. One man's persistence is another man's stalking!)
- Use future phrasing. If she won't agree to go on a date with you this weekend, get her to agree to meet you next Fourth of July, or when Hell freezes over, and work backward to today. Studies have shown that getting someone to agree to anything, no matter how farfetched or far away, makes them more likely to agree again. The further in the future and the more farfetched, the safer people feel talking and agreeing about a subject.
- A change of background. There's a big difference between talking to a woman in a quiet laundromat and trying to make yourself heard in a crowded nightclub. Setting matters.

"The bedroom is the room in which most people tell a lie."
—Bearden, "100 Mighty Sex Facts"

- Separate her from the herd. There's a big difference between talking to a single individual and talking to a crowd. You don't stand a chance of getting her to roll in the hay so long as she's insulated by a barnyard full of cackling hens. Your odds increase the further you can pull her away from her posse . . . I said "posse."

Whenever possible, get to know one person, win them over, and then allow them the honor of introducing you to their friends and associates.

(**Note:** Would-be cult leaders use this ploy. Rather than try to win over a whole congregation, all you have to do is convince/convert one dedicated follower. That follower brings another into the fold. Those two then entice two others to join. And so on: two becomes four becomes eight, becomes sixteen, and so on until you're cutting the ribbon on your new compound in Waco, Texas.)

So how do you know your line of seduction B.S. ("Black Science," that is) is working?

Experts point to:

- A glow or flush on her skin.
- The air suddenly smells thicker (actually, you're subconsciously picking up on her increase of sexual pheromones, the same way you can smell rain coming).
- She moves or leans in closer to you.
- Her eyes soften or get moist.
- Her voice lowers and gets deeper.
- She starts breathing deeper (a subconscious effort on her part to suck up more of your pheromones).

And the number one sign you're still in the running?

- She isn't screaming "No!" at the top of her lungs while drowning you in pepper spray!

By the way, men might be from Mars and women from Venus, still the plottings and ploys outlined in this section can—with minor variations—just as easily be applied to the seduction of men.

Mister Man will, of course balk at the very idea he could be susceptible to sweet talk, 100 percent certain the art of seduction could *never* work on him. (Heh-heh-heh.)

> *"Even in present-day man purely reasonable motive can effect*
> *little against passionate impulse."*
> **—Sigmund Freud**

The Art of NO-gotiation

*"We sit at the bargaining table for one reason—the other side
has something we want."*
—Shapiro, "How to Negotiate"

An old business adage warns against trying to negotiate with the kind of
man who, in a fifty-fifty proposition, insists on his getting the *hyphen*! Be
one of those men!

Humbly settling for second place sounds like the oh-so-politically correct thing to do until we remind ourselves that in a race to the finish the lion
gets the laurels and the antelope gets to be lunch!

Diplomat has been defined as a man (or woman) who can tell you to
"Go to Hell" in such a way that you look forward to the trip! Likewise, so
much of the Black Science and mind control comes down to telling others
no in such a way that they think you've done them a favor.

There are two skills to acquire—two goals to accomplish—toward mastering the art of No-gotiation:

* *Know* what you want.
* *No!* what he wants.

Two power rules to power. Rule one: *Whoever picks the battlefield has the power.*
Gettysburg. July 1, 1863: Confederate General Robert E. Lee (1807–1870)
has boldly struck deep into Union territory, into Pennsylvania, where he
finds himself confronting well-entrenched Union forces who've taken the
high ground and placed a wide-open deadly field of fire between themselves
and Lee's forces.

Lee's second-in-command, General James Longstreet (1821–1904) begs
his mentor not to attack the Union lines, correctly pointing out that if Lee
feigns retreat, Union forces would have no choice but to abandon their
advantageous positions and give chase. At any point then along the way, at a
battlefield of his choosing, Lee can then turn and make a stand. Longstreet's
sound strategy falls on deaf ears.

Two days and 20,000 dead Johnny Reb's later, under cover of rain and
night, what was left of Lee's forces tucks tail and retreats in earnest. It was
the beginning of the end for the Stars-n-Bars, the turning point in the Civil
War, all because Lee ignored that most basic of military dictums—ironically

an ironclad rule Lee himself drilled into students (like Longstreet) while superintendent at West Point: *Never let your enemy choose the battlefield.*

Consider the big difference between negotiating in his office as opposed to in *your* office; his penthouse versus your soundproofed basement?

This is why, when fishing, police always ask, "Would you mind coming down to the station?" Home court advantage.

When you can't pick the battlefield, the next best thing is picking apart the battlefield.

In an actual war zone, this entails seizing control of bridges and other vital avenues needed to facilitate your maneuvering and logistics, while simultaneously laying land mines and destroying lines of communication in order to deny the enemy reinforcement.

As on the battlefield, so in the ruthless boardroom, the smoke-filled backroom, and the lust-filled bedroom. Take the fish out of the water, attack his comfort zone.

For example, once you peg your adversary as a Watcher, a Listener, or a Toucher, manipulate rooms and rendezvous so as to keep him guessing and make him uncomfortable:

- Touch and otherwise crowd Listeners and Watchers, invading their space.
- Make Listeners sweat over visual images (e.g., a pile of dull, incomprehensible graphs, photos).
- Make a Watcher listen to a lecture so mind-numbing that when you finally whip out your brightly colored graphs and fast-paced videos, he'll see you as the Second Coming.

Uncomfortable chairs, poor lighting, someone continually buzzing his private pager number, as well as other distractions can all throw him off his game.

If nothing else, raise the temperature of the meeting room. Research shows the human brain works best in a cool room, around 65 degrees.

(**FYI:** While the No-gotiation rule is "never give up home court advantage," there is one very notable historical exception. Read on.)

In 1938, Stalin agreed to a non-aggression pact with Hitler, which allowed them the following year to divide Poland between them. This was a win-win deal for Stalin.

Unlike so many in the West, Stalin had actually taken time to read Hitler's *Mein Kampf*, but even if he hadn't, it didn't take a military mastermind to see Hitler was planning to winter in Moscow.

Realizing it was only a matter of time before the red bear and the black eagle would be tearing at each others' throats—again, Stalin reasoned why fight the Hun on Russian soil, when he could just as easily fight them on Polish soil . . . with the added bonus that, once Hitler was beaten back, Poland would be given the dubious honor of becoming the newest Soviet satellite.

When it comes time to "get down to business" in negotiating, the key words are defer, demand, delay, and discipline.

- *Defer*: Whenever possible, let the other side make the initial offer in any negotiation. They just might surprise you with an offer that exceeds your wildest expectations.
- *Demand*: Ask for the outrageous in order to get what you really want. If you'll settle for ten, demand twenty. Give the impression your demands are not negotiable. This gives your enemy a false sense of accomplishment when they think they've convinced you to stay and negotiate.
- *Delay*: No matter how much you like their opening bid, never accept it immediately. Take time to think: Is their offer too good to be true? If I hold out, will they up their offer? Probably. Your delaying will give them time to stew—to worry. Beware, however, lest they purposely delay negotiations to their advantage, in their attempt to rattle. Turnabout being fair play and all.
- *Discipline* is measured by what you can do without. Never enter into any negotiation when you're desperate, afraid, or hungry.

Learn to say no to your weaknesses, of which impatience is the most deadly.

No-gotiation rule two: *The person asking the questions has the power.*

The police. Your boss. Your wife. They ask the questions while you stutter and sputter trying desperately to figure out what they want you to say. When trapped in such a situation, use stall tactics: Act confused (which you probably are anyway!) and buy time by repeating the last thing they said.

We ask questions for two reasons: First, we need information, and sometimes people just give it to us. Second, we use unexpected and unusual questioning to disorient and get the upper hand over our competition.

But all the questioning in the world comes to naught until we take the time to master the craft of listening.

The craft of listening. When applied to listening, craft has at least three meanings: First, really listening to others shows you have craft, another name for "wisdom." In other words, it's smart to listen. Smarter still to actually hear what people are saying (especially when you don't realize they're saying it!). Old adage: "We're born with two ears and only one mouth, which means we're meant to listen twice as much as we talk."

Second, just pretending to listen is, in and of itself, "crafty," sly, and puts us at an advantage. When people think you care enough to listen, when they think you're listening, they talk more and more openly. And the more they talk, the more they spill the beans.

Third, "craft" refers to actual techniques we've learned so far for discerning and deciphering an enemy's shadow-talk and shadow-walk.

> **"The best place to get information about the other side is from the other side."**
> —Shapiro, 2001:11

Most people don't really take the time to listen. Most people just wait for their turn to talk. *How* we listen, like our other perceptions, is filtered through our prejudices. Are you listening with your ego or your pocketbook? Your ambition or your pecker?

Listening requires us to switch off our ego and switch on our empathy in order to feel what he's really saying. Is he defending his argument or defending himself? Or just showing off—playing to the audience?

Does he truly believe in the "cause" or simply using the cause to promote himself? If the latter, make him your agent and ally. Remember there's no such thing as altruism. Show him what's in it for him and turn him.

(**FYI:** Study chapter XIII of Sun Tzu's *The Art of War*, on how to turn his agents into your agents, and how to entice him to embrace your point of view. And, Book Three, chapter II in Machiavelli's *Discourses*.)

Get the other guy talking (digging his own grave!) and keep him talking—answering all your questions, providing you with invaluable intelligence. The more he talks, the more you know.

This technique is a variation of boxer Muhammed Ali's "Rope-a-dope" ploy; getting an opponent to exhaust himself before launching your counterattack.

Once you've got him talking, keep him talking but don't *interrogate* (or at least don't let him realize he's being interrogated).

It's been said the only difference between an interview and an interrogation . . . is how many volts you use! (See Lung and Prowant, 2003. Review the Interrogation Character Types.)

Sometimes all it takes is silence and a look of impatience or disbelief to keep them talking.

Other facial expressions that will encourage them to spill their guts include: shaking your head, pursing your lips, loudly sucking air through your teeth, rolling your eyes toward the heavens, and arching a single eyebrow. (This latter technique works well for Mr. Spock and the Rock!)

Repeat his last point, adding a question mark at the end, to encourage him to continue, or in order to seize control of the conversation by using the last part of his sentence as the first part of your sentence. This also gives you an opportunity to paraphrase (twist his words).

Prodders are words, phrases, and gestures that encourage conversation. A show of hands. Who remembers that snappy Saturday morning cartoon *Conjunction Junction* . . . "What's your function?" If you do, then you remember that a conjunction is a word that ties together two thoughts (e.g., "I went to the store *and* to the park." "I want to go to the park, *but* I have to work").

But what about *Conjunction Junctions's* "evil" function?

Adding a conjunction to the end of someone's statement will cause them to keep talking. Immediately as he finishes a statement, add:

"And . . . ?	"Because . . . ?"
"But . . . ?"	"Now what?"
"However . . . ?"	"So . . . ?"
"Meanwhile . . . ?"	"Consequently . . . ?"
"Meaning what?"	"Or . . . ?"

Include accompanying gestures (e.g., rolling hand movements, palms spreading up and out) which, by themselves, will often be enough to keep him talking.

(**FYI:** Such leading words are similar to the flow words used in hypnosis, words that blend hypnotic suggestions and commands together seamlessly—"as . . . while . . . and . . .")

Offering anonymity is another way to encourage people to say things they wouldn't normally think of uttering. You'd be surprised what revealing and outrageous things people will say—even police and politicians, who ought to know better!—when speaking confidentially and off the record.

Being anonymous lessens inhibitions. Big surprise: People act differently when they think no one is watching or listening. As a result they become indiscreet and start passing insider information out like candy. (Think "Deep Throat" . . . No, *not* Linda Lovelace. That Watergate informant who remained anonymous for thirty plus years.)

In one study, disguised test subjects gave other test subjects electric shocks twice as long as did another group of subjects whose identities were not concealed. Ah! What we would get by with, if we know what we could get by with!

Successfully interrupting another speaker is easy. As he completes a sentence:

- Say his name, firmly, as if scolding a child.
- Say a ridiculous or foreign word. When attention turns to you, use your definition of the word to launch your own diatribe.

The second ploy works even better when the word sounds dirty. Example: In the middle of his ramblings absentmindedly (but loud enough for all present to hear) proclaim "Cock-a-hoop!" "Cock-crow!" or "Cock-shy!"

When everybody stops listening to him and turns to you, you nonchalantly begin your diatribe by providing the definition of your dirty word:

"Cock-a-hoop!" Then explain, "How exulting it is to hear such talk . . ."

"Cock-crow!" Definition: "The dawn of new ideas. Like this one . . ."

"Cock-shy!" Sympathize: "I was just thinking I don't envy you being the target of criticism. Because of that, I'm willing to make you a counter-offer . . ."

Other interruption ploys include:

- Look past him, pretend someone has just arrived. When he turns to look, seize control of the conversation.
- Draw a word or symbol on your hand prior to the meeting. Suddenly flash the decorated palm of your hand into his line of sight will make him stumble.
- Do a sudden sleight-of-hand trick to distract him or draw away the attention of his audience. (See Figure 12.)

(**FYI:** End conversations with a downward inflection of voice. Immediately leap into a completely unrelated topic. Move on. Don't chew your cud twice.)

Types of "no." There are two types of "no": Your enemy's no and your no.

Your no of course is carved in stone and means "Hell, no!" (or at least that's what you want him to believe).

His no, on the other hand, is just a temporary inconvenience on your way to your getting what you want.

Before turning down someone's request, repeat their request so they'll know you understand what they're asking and won't feel obliged to keep repeating their request—and further waste your time. Immediately after turning down his request, boldly ask him for a favor. Believe it or not, he's likely to say, "Yes."

The psychology behind this seems to be that he'll be eager to show you (and himself) that he's a good human being who knows how to do someone a favor, that he's the bigger man, that is, he's not as big a prick as you!

Saying no is a reflex designed to keep us out of trouble. By the way, doing nothing is not the same as saying no. Like acquiescing yes, doing nothing is passive.

Firmly declaring, "no," on the other hand, is active, aggressive.

Sometimes, however, strategy requires we say no hesitantly and reluctantly. So it's all about how you say no.

Black Science Ph.D. candidates can always convince the person they say no to that they're actually doing the person a favor:

"I could give you that manager's job in Hawaii, Bob. But I'm not going to. And do you know why? Because I like you too damn much! A job like that—all that sun and surf, that unlimited expense account—all that would just make a real go-getter like yourself go soft. Hell, Bob old buddy, you'd die from boredom within a week! So by saying no to Hawaii, I'm really saying yes! to *Bob*, the Bob we just can't do without around here!"

Or how about:

"That kind of thing's not for a guy like you, not with your (high moral standards, ambition, positive attitude, patriotism?) . . ."

Or how about:

"I'd feel like I was betraying your trust in me if I gave you that (loan, promotion, business contract, etc.), Bob. And do you want to know why? Because I know you trust me to do right by you. And because of what I'd have to ask for in return for it. I just wouldn't feel right asking you to make such a (sacrifice, commitment) . . . no matter how noble that (sacrifice, commitment)!"

Right about now, Bob—in tears—will be begging you to let him make that noble sacrifice, take that radical pay-cut, bear your love-child!

Types of "no" include:

- The "no, because": Like the line you just fed Bob.
- The "I'd Love to" no: "I'd love to do that, but . . . ," "I'd love to just as soon as . . .," "I'd love to if it wasn't for . . ."
- The "no" ignore: You say "no" sans explanation because the person you're saying "no" to isn't worthy of an explanation. (This ploy has double devastating effect when used to minimize a person in front of his coworkers and friends. One, it marks him a non-entity in the eyes of onlookers. Two, it strikes terror into their hearts for fear they might be treated the same.)
- The "no indictment": Say, "No. And you know why." Then walk away. Of course he doesn't know why, so he's confused, worried you've discovered some heinous secret about him. And of course, anyone overhearing you tell him this won't believe him when he assures them he has no idea what you're talking about.
- The "no" future: Make it clear that "no" is your answer . . . for *now* . . . "But if this changes . . ."
- The witch's broom "no": Remember *The Wizard of Oz*? Nobody was gettin' nothin' off the man behind the curtain until they brought him the witch's broom. Think: Strings attached.
- The big picture "no": He's crying for a raise until you start hinting that the company is about to go out of business. (See *Making Mountains Out of Molehills*, next)

Making mountains out of molehills. Hindus tell the tale of a farmer who one day found a beautiful horse wandering his property.

"Oh, what very good luck!" claps his neighbor.

"Who can see far enough into the future to say what is truly good luck?" replied the farmer.

True enough, the farmer's son no sooner mounts the horse than the horse bucks the young man to the ground, breaking the young man's leg.

"Oh, what very bad luck!" laments the neighbor.

"Who can see far enough into the future to say what is truly bad luck?" sighs the farmer tending his injured son.

Later that day, a tyrant and his army marches through the area, taking what they want from the farmers and forcing all the able-bodied young men in the area to enlist. But they leave the farmer's son behind because of his broken leg.

The next day the tyrant and all his host are slaughtered in a horrific battle.

"What good luck your son was spared!" declares the neighbor.

The farmer only smiles.

This tale tells us two things: First, it's not what happens to you in life, it's all in how you look at it—your perspective. Second, it's how you look at something compared to something else.

Or maybe the real lesson is "Things can always get worse!" Einstein called this the Law of Relativity. We call it the Law of Contrasts.

The Law of Contrasts says that we don't see things and happenings as they really are, but rather in their relationship to other things and happenings. To a warm hand, tepid water feels cool. To a cold hand, the same water feels warm.

Fringe political organizations often use this principle to their advantage. When the powers-that-be refuse to negotiate with them because of their radical views, another more threatening splinter group, breakaway faction, or military wing (that the parent organization claims to have no control over) pops up out of nowhere and begins wreaking havoc.

Suddenly that radical parent organization doesn't look all that bad in comparison to the new terrorists on the block. Do Sinn Fein/IRA, or PLO/Black September ring a bell? In other words, "Feed me or feed that bigger, uglier dog down the block!"

Can you say, "Lesser of two evils"?

This kind of ploy is one of the oldest examples of the protection racket.

Medieval Samurai daimyo, finding themselves targeted for assassination by a ninja clan would often hire bodyguards from a rival ninja clan to protect them . . . only to later discover the two rival groups were actually one and the same clan—with one faction drumming up business by being threatening, until the other faction steps in, offering protection for a price (Lung, 1997a).

The Middle Eastern *Hashishin* cult threatened and thrived for centuries, masters of just this extortion ploy (Lung, 1997b).

Other variations of this ploy include police using good cop/bad cop and opportunist politicians creating convenient enemies for us via wag-the-dog scenarios.

To successfully negotiate, or *No*-gotiate, we need data. Data is both our weapon and our ammunition. (Take time to review the section in chapter 4 on gathering intelligence . . . on second thought, this *whole book* is about gathering intelligence!)

All human conflict—be it bloody war or equally merciless boardroom negotiation—comes down to Information versus Dis-information.

Dis-information is as simple as distorting facts and figures and then force-feeding them to your foes.

Any time you can further distend and distort your enemy's perception of reality, the further you hinder and incapacitate him, preventing him from getting the upper hand in life in general and negotiations in particular.

To create dis-information we freely use hints, innuendo, rumor, and bald-faced lies, planting doubt in his mind to increase his anxiety, exaggerating and amplifying his problem(s), in effect, turning his molehills into mountains.

We can also use the opposite approach to upset his apple cart by downplaying any concerns (suspicions) he might have about us or our offer. In this instance, turning his mountains into molehills. (See Figure 20.)

This latter approach can also be used to make him drop his guard, leaving him vulnerable to our real attack.

MOUNTAINS AND MOLEHILLS

Mountains	Molehills
Permanent	Temporary
Significant	Insignificant
Critical	Marginal
All-consuming	Isolated (incident)
Impossible	Possible (doable)
Never	Soon (eventually)
Mandatory	Optional
Now or never!	Chill. It can wait.

Figure 20.

Think of this as emotional Ju-jitsu. As in the martial art: When he pushes, you pull. When he pulls, you push, turning his own force and momentum against him. When he starts complaining about how bad and unfair life is—agree! And then convince him things are even worse than he suspects.

Or, he's optimistic. Things are definitely looking up! Again, agree with him. Point out all the good things in his life (just be sure to take your humble portion of credit for things getting better!).

In *Black Science* (Lung and Prowant, 2001), we discussed The Art of Agreement, actually, the art of agreeing without agreeing: "No matter how different another person's argument is, the mind-slayer agrees with them, or at least appears to" (page 96).

When agreeing with someone, make eye contact. Keep nodding. Raise your eyebrows to show interest. The more you agree with them, the more they will begin agreeing with you. It's called give and take. (To be more specific, in Black Science it's: *they* give, *you* take!)

Keep agreeing with them, gradually leading them to their conclusion (which just happens to be your agenda). Just make sure they think it's their own idea and never let them realize you've been herding them in one direction by slowly but surely limiting their options.

Fewer and Faster is the key. Limit his choices and give him only "limited time offers."

Continuously thank them for clarifying the issue for you and for setting you straight. Sincerely fake this.

Make them think they've already done/are doing you a favor. Studies show they'll be less quick to object and more likely to agree and to do other things for you, if they think they've already done you a first favor.

This approach is called the Law of Inertia: Objects in motion tend to stay in motion.

No matter how different your opinion is from his, no matter how adamant he is in his disagreement with you, keep saying, "So you agree with me. So you see my point."

First, this will stifle the flow of his diatribe when he has to stop in mid-rant to clarify or protest that he doesn't agree with you.

Second, the more you force him to openly disagree with you, the more you make him look like the bad guy.

When in a group setting, whether true or not, tell him "All of us agree, why are you so Hell-bent on ruining your career by being the odd man out?"

"Ruin my career?" "Odd man out?" He's not gonna like the sound of either of those (even when he has no idea what the Hell you're talking about!). He'll stumble. He'll sputter. And the floor will be yours.

The more time you force him to spend defending himself, the less time he'll have to defend his position.

The big payoff. The big payoff is what negotiating is all about. There are two kinds of payoffs in life:

1. Tangible payoffs are the kind of stuff you can stuff in your wallet, drive, live in, and screw.
2. Intangible payoffs are hugs and handshakes, and things of the heart; things that, for the most part, you can't trade for tangible payoffs.

On the positive side, intangible payoffs satisfy our honor and make us feel good about ourselves. Love and respect top this list. Toxic intangible payoffs are what pimps and politicians (is that redundant?) deal in.

Cults also deal in intangibles, selling invisible products. That's why they have to convince us "the next world" (the one they're selling tickets for) is more real than this world . . . because they have nary jot nor tittle tangible to show us in this world.

Which one is your foe looking for? A tangible payoff or an intangible payoff? If he's expecting a tangible ("Put the balm in my palm!") payoff, there's little chance he'll be satisfied with only a hearty handshake and your undying gratitude.

Conversely, if he's motivated by dreams of some intangible payoff (e.g., power or fame) or if he's morally driven, will you be able to tempt him away with tangible payoffs like dead presidents and live hookers? (Read: *Winning through Intimidation* by Robert J. Ringer, 1993.)

The final word when it comes to *No*-gotiating is: *Open-to-close, Close-to-open.*

When one door closes, another always opens . . . if it doesn't, kick it in! Don't pick fights you can't win. Don't enter into any negotiation until you're sure you have the upper hand—not if you can help it.

Wait until you're ready to follow through and do what has to be done to win. Nothing is more dangerous than impatience. Unless it's half-assin'.

Winning is still the name of the game. Anyone who tries to tell you different is either secretly afraid they don't have what it takes to compete, or else they've read *Black Science* or *Mind Control* and are trying to get you to drop your guard in order to thin the playing field!

Embrace ruthlessness like a too-long-denied lover. *Ruthlessness* is just another name for *determination*. If you're not ready to turn the heat up in the kitchen . . . stay the Hell out of the chef's way!

If trapped in a no-win situation—walk away. The difference between an amateur and a professional is that a professional knows when to walk away. If the other guy doesn't play fair, take his balls and go home.

Just like any movie needs a good beginning, it also needs a good ending. So *Close-to-open*. When you complete one deal, don't walk out the door, don't even think about putting down that phone, until you lay the groundwork for your next deal:

> **"An effective negotiator makes deals and builds relationships**
> **that lead to more deals."**
> **—Shapiro, 2001:11**

Ask yourself: If it's such a dog-eat-dog world, why do I always end up eating crow!

> **"In order to succeed in this, we must use great cunning and**
> **penetration during negotiations and agreements, but, as regards**
> **what is called the 'official language,' we shall keep to the opposite**
> **tactics and assume the mask of honesty and compliancy."**
> **—so-called *Protocols of the Wise Men of Zion***

The Art of Lying

> **"The lie is an essential social lubricant. We're not supposed to lie,**
> **and we do, which in some biologically determined way probably**
> **means we're supposed to."**
> **—Scott Mowbray, *Popular Science*, August, 2002**

Lies have a habit of getting out of hand. For example, in our book *Black Science*, we discussed lying as a craft. In *Mind Control*, it's already been elevated to an art. Children grow up so fast these days!

Winston Churchill warned: "Once you tell one lie, you need to create a whole bodyguard of lies to protect it." That ol' British bulldog was right. Lies are not just words. Like aging rock stars, lies drag an entourage around behind them. This entourage includes the context and tone in which the lie is told, the subconscious shadow-talk body language that accompanies the lie, and the believability of the lie itself.

For example, a liar often overemphasizes the very word he needs to complete the lie: "I did *not* do it!" "I was *not* there!" "I did *not* have sexual relations with that woman!"

In addition, his words will be saying one thing but his body tells will be telling you another.

And, finally, his facts just don't fit reality.

Not only is lying an art, in today's world, it's a vital survival skill. So is being able to spot a liar. Contrary to what you might have heard, their pants are not always on fire. (Bill Clinton being the exception!)

From hot coals to hypnotism. Shulman (2002) says: "The ability to distinguish truth from lie, to tell the guilty from the innocent, is one of the most basic challenges in all human interactions. Everyone lies, and everyone tries to spot a liar. No one is consistently successful at either" (page 56).

Down through the ages a fantastic array of methods have been used in the quest for what has been called "the Pinocchio response," that one perfect, unbeatable way to tell when a person is lying. These methods, ranging from the mystical to the mechanical, from holy hot coals to hypnotism, have met with varying degrees of success.

- Ancient Shamans used portents and potions and communed with the spirits to discern truth from a lie. The more savvy of these medicine men could tell if a person was lying by reading the blush on their face, the darting of their eyes, and by feeling the person's pulse (at wrist or throat) without the person being aware of what was going on. (See Lung and Prowant, 2001:137).

- In ancient Egypt it was believed God Osiris balanced the ka (soul) of a dead person against the weight of a feather. In many cultures, threat of punishment in the next life was expected to keep people from lying in *this* world. (Yeah. Like that works.)

- In ancient China a person suspected of lying was forced to put rice powder in his mouth. The theory being that a dry-mouthed liar would be unable to speak.

- Japanese ninja were said to have refined a technique (originally derived from their Chinese "ninja" cousins, the dreaded *Moshuh Nanren*) whereby, through the use of strategically placed acupuncture needles, not only would a victim be unable to move, they would also be unable to tell a lie.

- The Old Testament treats lying at least by patriarchs and prophets, as acceptable strategy (Genesis 27:18, 29:27, 3:13; Judges 16:10; 1 Samuel 20:6; and Matthew 26:69, New Testament).
- King Solomon used psychology to determine the true mother of the disputed child from the liar.
- The Romans were big fans of truth and so employed everything from seers to torture and trial-by-gladiator.*
- In Medieval Europe it was trial-by-combat for nobles, and trial-by-fire for the rest of us not-so-nobles.
- *The Inquisition* began raging across Europe officially in 1232 and had achieved ultimate efficiency (terror!) by the fifteenth century with the infamous Spanish Inquisition (as if the *regular* Inquisition was already infamous enough!).

The Spanish Inquisition itself officially lasted up till 1834. But blessing for the Inquisition (i.e., trial-by-torture) has yet to be officially repealed by the Roman Catholic Church. (See Lung and Prowant, 2003.)

Like the Romans, members of the Inquisition were also big fans of the truth, at least *their* truth. Their basic belief was that—as long as you were being truthful—God would protect you . . . from the mallets crushing your bones, and the white-hot pincers squeezing your testicles, and the hooks ripping pieces of flesh from your body and . . . well, you get the idea.

Ironically, Inquisition torturers were forbidden to shed blood: *Ecclesia non novit sanquinem* ("The Church is untainted with blood."). As a result, they developed some really inventive ways to hurt you sans having to clean up too much of a mess. This is also why heretics and other liars were ultimately burned at the stake.**

---

*Our word *testimony* comes from the fact that since pre-Christian Romans didn't (yet) have a stack of Bibles to swear on, when a Roman was called before the Senate (which doubled as their Supreme Court) the witness was made to grasp his *testicles* in his hand, to swear by his (Lt.) *testis*, hence "testis-mony," with the clear understanding that were he caught lying to the Senate, he'd soon be singing *soprano*!

**Compare the Inquisition's aversion to shedding blood to yet another religious prohibition against shedding of blood: the oath binding members of the *Thuggee* cult of India who ritualistically strangled their sacrificial victims, since shedding of blood was forbidden by Goddess Kali, whom they worshipped (Lung, 1995).

• Muslim law has always considered torture to be the only infallible lie detector, down to and including modern times (Lung and Prowant, 2003).

• The Salem Witch Trials (1692), which ended in nineteen "witches" being hanged, was the culmination of a long history of witch hunts that began in Europe with the Inquisition. Suspected witches were subjected to various tortures: drowned in dunking chairs, crushed beneath tons of weight, all in a righteous effort to get at the truth.

• In 1734 the development of *mesmerism* opens the door to getting at the truth through the use of *hypnotism*. (**Note:** In modern times, the use of hypnotism as a lie detector has given rise to concerns that, rather than uncovering truth, hypnotists may actually be encouraging or implanting false memories.)

• In 1895 the Italian criminologist Cesare Lombroso (credited with coining the term "born criminal") is the first to use a lie detection test.

• During the 1920s, John Larson gets the credit for inventing the first polygraph machine. Kudos for helping develop and perfect the lie detector go to Doctor Leonarde Keeler, Doctor Chester Darrow (the founder of "Psychphysiology"), and William M. Marston.

(**FYI:** Marston is better known by his nom de plume "Charles Moulton," under which guise he created the comic book character *Wonder Woman* who, curiously enough wielded a "magic lasso" that when placed over a criminal forced the evildoer to tell the truth.)

The basic concept of this 1920s polygraph changed little in the following decades. Modern polygraphs still measure body responses like respiration and cardiovascular activity.

The fact there has been little actual improvement in the polygraph led to the American Psychology Association declaring in 1986 that the polygraph does not yield "definitive information."

• During the 1950s, in the wake of the brainwashing scare that followed the repatriation of American POWs from North Korea, government agencies like the CIA (created 1947) and NSA (created 1952) began funneling funds into MK (mind control) research that included the quest for foolproof methods of (1) lie detection and (2) a better way of concealing their own lies.

• Throughout the 1960s, government agencies continued spending your tax dollars on numerous experiments to facilitate lie detection. These ranged from the mechanical and electronic (e.g., "Wiggle seats" designed to measure unconscious movement, Infrared beams designed to measure heat on a liar's upper lip) to so-called truth serums, to even employing psychics to read minds.

• In 1975 CVSA (computer voice-stress analyzer) was developed by the CIA. Though its viability and reliability is still in dispute, the technology has continued to increase in popularity and is now commercially available: the *Handytruster Portable Lie Detector*, a three-by-three-inch device with LCD screen that registers a person's stress level by analyzing that person's voice.

New methods for lie detection (mostly machines and drugs) continue to be tested. The latest, most promising (or threatening!) being "brain finger-printing," using a Magnetic Resonance Imaging-like process that scans blood flow to areas of the brain associated with imagination (lying) and true memory storage (being truthful) (*Psychology Today*, Jan/Feb 2002:15).

You can't beat a lie detector, but you can beat the man who gives you the test. (See *the Killer "B's,"* chapter 3.)

Shakespeare's seven types of lies. A line from the movie *State and Main* (2000) said, "It's not a lie, it's a gift for fiction."

Any time you discover twenty-three out of twenty-four lawyers counsel their clients to perjure themselves (*Psychology Today*, March/April 2002:73), then you can understand why Shakespeare advised we "first kill all the lawyers."

The immortal bard also gave us, via the voice of his character Touch-stone in *As You Like It* (1599), the seven types of lies:

1. *The retort courteous.* This is when you tell someone they're wrong (even if you know they're right), but you tell them oh-so-politely something on the order of "I fear you are mistaken, sir," that they begin to doubt themselves.

Replying courteously buys you time to get your alibi or counterattack in order (something you really should do beforehand). Replying courteously also makes you appear *unconcerned* by any of his allegations (no matter how star-tling).

In addition, your nonchalant reply marks you as a gentleman (or a lady, as the case may be) by virtue of your patience, restraint, and eloquence in replying. (Hint: Allow your tone to hover just shy of patronizing.)

Tell him, "Perhaps you require more time to double-check your facts?"

When you know for certain he's got the goods on you, make a show of bowing out (or otherwise dismissing him with a distracting flourish of your hand). Giving him no time to counter, fire off your Parthian shot, "If you can't contribute something positive, why burden us all with something so obviously distasteful?"

You just made him the bad guy for "daring" to bring up such a negative subject (see *The reply churlish*, below).

2. *The quip modest.* This small witticism or humorous comment is designed to distract listeners from the truth of the bombshell accusation he's just dropped with your name on it.

He might have just announced to everybody in the room that he's got proof positive you're a card-carrying Communist, but the only thing "red" they'll be talking about around the water cooler tomorrow morning is how red faced he got when you responded with that witty joke about the red thong he got caught wearing!

People will trade the truth for an entertaining story anytime.

3. *The reply churlish.* This reply allows you to devalue his opinion and downplay his allegation by dismissing his dubious information.

You also counter by seizing the moral highground, attacking his (lack of) morals/honor for the underhanded way he came by his information.

Convince listeners that his information (no matter how damaging to you) was obtained by despicable and deceitful methods. Shocked and chagrined, his listeners will turn on him, forgetting the message (at least temporarily) in favor of chastising the messenger.

Your line: "I'll not dignify such a base allegation—nor would I presume to insult all these good people here—with a response." (**FYI:** This is similar to the *argumentum ad hominem* (argument to the man) attack used in politics, i.e., when you can't successfully counter the obvious truth of a candidate's message, you attack the candidate himself.)

4. *The reproof valiant.* This reproof directly dismisses any evidence an enemy attacks you with as simply not being true. No matter how overwhelming his evidence, no matter how compelling his proof or how convincing his witnesses are, deny-deny-deny.

It seems no amount of bothersome facts are enough to sway you. This keeps the burden of proof on him. (**FYI:** Any time you have to stop in mid-rant to let the other side take their good sweet time to nit-pick over your evidence, it slows your momentum and messes with your natural flow.)

"Confusion" might not be the horse you rode in on but, when the deal is all Aces-n-Eights and it's time to skedaddle, "Confusion" kicks up the most dust!

Example: He pulls out a picture of you caught in the act, pants down, hand in the cookie jar. Your nonchalant response: "Well, there it is then. Guess that finally solves the debate over whether or not they really have Walt Disney cryogenically preserved."

You should be halfway out of Dodge before the dust kicked up by good ol' dependable "confusion" settles!

5. *The countercheck.* Say that *he* lies when he claims *you* lie. Often called "the countercheck quarrelsome," this kind of response also puts him at a deficit, making him produce evidence to back up his claim (see *the Reproof Valiant*).

6. *The lie circumstantial.* This lie is a lie by omission, that is, when you leave out a vital piece of information. Women favor this type of lying.

7. *The lie direct.* On the other hand, the lie direct is a lie by commission, deliberately adding false facts. Men favor this approach. (See *The Ten Commandments of Lying*, below.)

How did the immortal bard put it: "All the world's a stage, And all the men and women merely players; They have their exits and their entrances, And one man in his time plays many parts . . ."

And don't be surprised if some of those parts you're asked to play before that final black curtain descends requires you to lie your ass off!

(**FYI:** William Shakespeare (1564–1616), himself an adept at playing many parts, is required reading for any serious student of the Black Science or mind control.)

Shakespeare's intuitive insights into the schemings and skulduggery of the human mind marked him as a Master of Observational Psychology long before that science came into its own.

Still today, we know so little of this mysterious playwright who had such a profound influence, not just on the world of literature, but on the world at large.

Many suspect the real Shakespeare of being Francis Bacon (1561–1626), that (in)famous freebooter and Freemason who, as a member of the "invisible college," helped draft and craft the King James Version of the Bible in 1611—taking careful pains to infuse that text with esoteric Masonic references and ritual, not the least of which was the inclusion of his nom de plume "Shakespeare," in Psalms chapter 46.*

Perhaps Shakespeare considered a well-executed "masquerade" as the *eighth* type of lie?

Who, how, and what about. Who lies? Everybody lies. It only varies from person to person *what* we lie about, and *how* we go about weaving our wicked webs.

It's estimated only 5 percent of people are "natural liars." That means the rest of you have to work at it. (Heh-heh-heh.) The good news is, by the time we're adults, we've had plenty of time to practice.

Age influences how we lie. We begin lying in childhood. Young kids lie, but kids younger than eight lack sophisticated lying strategies. For the most part, these kids lie about actions: "I didn't break it . . . a big gorilla came in through the window and did it!" Kids at this age are concrete (literal) thinkers and so aren't very good at hiding their feelings.

Between ages eight and ten, having developed abstract thinking, kids become better liars, as they acquire more sophisticated lying techniques.

By puberty, they're accomplished liars, often telling lies just for the thrill and power of fooling adults.

Parents of little liars, take heart, children who are imaginative enough to be good liars, also tend to have the best social skills and, consequently, often grow into the most popular teenagers and adults.

Most adults themselves have no idea how often they lie every day. The average adult lies twenty-five times a day, roughly one to six times an hour. Factors ranging from gender and stress and individual motivations and goals influence how and what adults lie about.

Stress influences how adults lie because people handle stress differently. (See Figure 14, p. 70.) The more stress in your life, the better the odds you'll be willing to lie (just a little . . . at first) to try and relieve a little of that stress. The tighter you squeeze a rat, the more he squeals.

Gender influence also affects how we lie. No surprise, men and women lie differently:

---

*Count forty-six words in from the beginning and then forty-six words in from the end and see if you still have any doubt "Shakespeare" helped write the Bible!

MEN	WOMEN
Lies of Commission (Adding information)	Lies of Omission (Withholding information)
Key: Listen to what he says.	Key: Listen to what she *doesn't* say
Men lie to promote themselves.	Women lie to make others feel better.
Men lean in toward you when lying.	Women lean away from you when lying.

Our Motivations and Goals also influence both how we lie and what we lie about. Most people will knowingly and willingly lie if they have a good enough cause, for example, helping a friend out of a jam.

Curiously, even when they won't lie to save themselves, most people will lie to help a friend, if only to save that friend from embarrassment.

Protest all you want but, when it comes to lying, each of us has our price—that line, the other side of which, "the end *does* justify the means."

> *"The result justifies the means. Let us, however, in our plans, direct our attention not so much to what is good and moral as to what is necessary and useful."*
> —so-called *Protocols of the Wise Men of Zion*

If we think hard enough, we can pretty much justify any action. Of course, it helps if we have some half-assed religious or cock-eyed political agenda behind which to cloak our lack of honor and integrity.

Setting out on this serpentine path of perfidy, perjury, plagiarism, and prevarication, we have plenty of role models from which to choose. The Oliver Norths and tobacco executives of the world think nothing of lying to Congress. Why should we?

And, tell the truth now, weren't we all just a little relieved when that Executive Order came down from the Oval Office declaring that oral sex didn't qualify as "sexual relations"!

Likewise, religious people are forever digging through scripture for that twisted verse that will give blessing to their latest indiscretion or atrocity.

(**Note:** Lest you begin to think ill of Dr. Lung, please note that he made much distinction between being religious and being spiritual. In the Lungian definition, *spiritual* is when you boldly look into the abyss . . . and not flinch when you realize the abyss is looking back! *Religious*, on the other hand, is just some dusty book you carry, or that ridiculous hat you wear.)

For example, cults like the Jehovah's Witnesses are permitted to lie as long as it is for a good cause (*their cause!*):

> Lying generally involves saying something false to a person who is *entitled* to know the truth . . . While malicious lying is definitely condemned in the Bible, this does not mean that a person is under obligation to divulge truthful information to people who are not entitled to it. (*Aid to Bible Understanding*, Watchtower Society publications, reported in MacGregor, 1998:5)

Thus, unless we're certifiable born liars, we find it easier (i.e., easier to justify) lying about things that are important to us. Example, one in four people lie when applying for a job (*London Financial Times*, July 2002).

In his book *Lies We Live By* (2000), Carl Hausman teaches us there are three ways to lie: with words, with numbers, and with images.

Lying with words is pretty much self-explanatory. Pretty much what 90 percent of the Black Science is all about!

Lying with numbers works because, as someone once pointed out, if you torture numbers long enough, they'll confess to anything.

Author and statesman Benjamin Disraeli (1804–1881) got even more specific when he declared there are three (that magic number again) types of lies: lies, damn lies, and statistics.

(**Note:** While on the subject of lies and "threes," don't forget Fritz Perls "Three Types of Shit" [Lung and Prowant, 2001:72].)

The U.S. government spends more than three *billion* of your tax dollars every year gathering and analyzing statistics. Sometimes this accidentally results in realistic statistics that can actually help in predicting trends and helping decide where best to direct limited resources. Just as often however, such statistics become ammunition for self-promoting politicians and special interest groups.

For example, suppose a "get tough on crime" candidate from North Dakota pointed out that the 2003 homicide rate in his state had jumped a whopping *150 percent over the previous year*. Holy Cow! 150 percent? Sounds like North Dakota is in the grip of a major crime wave and we should thankfully vote for any politician perceptive enough to point this out to us . . .

but, what if you then found out North Dakota only had 2 homicides in all of 2002. A "150 percent rise" in 2003 then means North Dakota *only had a total of 5 homicides in 2003!* Hardly the crime wave we were first led to believe.

Lying with images including bombarding us with images (conscious and subliminal) on TV, billboards, computers, in magazines, and even on those free T-shirts and drink-mugs handed out at sporting events and rock concerts. Look in your closet right now and I'll bet you'll find at least one T-shirt advertising either a rock star or a soft drink or else a rock star hawking a soft drink.

Of course, it's still a free country (heh-heh-heh) so anyone and everyone everywhere—from Madison Avenue to Pennsylvania Avenue, Wall Street to Waco—are free to mix and match these three lying mediums anytime they care to try influencing our mind.

In other words, if you don't stay on your toes, someone with a twisted agenda is sure to try stomping on them.

The Ten Commandments of Lying

I. *Lie as little as possible.* Don't just lie for practice or for the thrill of getting away with it. Have a reason. We lie better when we're motivated—a gun to our head, a warm hand on our thigh.

Preferably, use lies of omission rather than commission. It's easier to "fill in the blanks" when pressed than it is to defend some big fat lie you've already committed yourself to (see Commandment VIII).

II. *Respect nature and number.* Keep your lies within the realm of possibility, within the bounds of "reality" as most people recognize it.

Don't overinflate your numbers into the astronomical—not your salary, golf handicap, or how long and hard your best . . . putt was. Mother Nature only makes fish . . . and other things, only so long. Lie "too big" and, sooner or later, some listener is going to call your bluff and then you'll be forced to reach into your pants and whip out . . . those snapshots from your fishing trip. (Good thinking, borrowing those from your co worker's desk!)

The bigger and more bald-faced your lie, the more you need to blend in elements of real truth.

It's okay to "bend" credulity and the Laws of Nature, just don't blatantly "break" them.

III. *The devil is in the details.* Bad liars tend to be vague. And when you don't supply your listeners with enough detail, they start asking questions. Never a good thing.

Be sure to provide plenty of *entertaining* detail (see Commandments IV and V).

Instead of risking your listeners stopping you in mid-lie to ask where in the world you got a particular piece of information, when you begin your lie, always invoke some unimpeachable authority and source like *Nova*, the Discovery Channel, or the *National Enquirer*. (Heh-heh-heh.)

IV. *The telling is in the telling.* Be confident, but not cocky. Believe in your ability to tell the lie and people will believe the lie.

Craft your words, tone, and slang—reverent or ribald—to suit your audience. Always tell your audience what they want to hear (see Commandment X).

Master the art of implication and innuendo.

V. *Be hard on yourself.* Use self-deprecating asides and humor to keep them off your scent. Humbly laughing about how lucky you are to have succeeded, almost in spite of yourself, makes people identify with you and like you and the people we like we don't question as hard.

Most of an amateur's lies are meant to make him look like a big man. Everyone knows braggarts and liars are cut from the same black curtain.

VI. *Put your ass into it.* Make sure your body language matches the lies pouring out your pie-hole.

VII. *Put your heart into it.* Emotion is the fuel for any really good lie— both your emotion and the emotion you squeeze out of your audience.

Get animated when lying. Be excited, sad, mad . . . *something*, anything but bland and boring. Get your audience caught up in your emotion. Remember, most human decisions are emotional decisions, not necessarily logical decisions. When you touch your audiences' emotions they forget all about thinking logically (which most people aren't all that good at anyway).

When telling a lie, facts are never as important as feelings—both the ones you successfully fake and ones you make your listeners feel.

Make them laugh, cry, get them pissed off (but not at you!)—get their emotions involved, get them caught up in your story, and watch their reactions. Get feedback and then adjust your lies accordingly.

VIII. *Stick to your guns.* Stay the course. Pick a lie and stick with it. No matter what, refuse to confess.

When they catch you with your hand on the knife still sticking in his throat, swear to God you were only trying to give him a tracheotomy to save his life!

Always have supporting evidence ready, just in case.

IX. *Keep track of your lies.* Abraham Lincoln warned that no man has a good enough memory to be a convincing liar. When it comes to lying, follow the KISS rule: *Keep it simple, Stupid!*

X. *People believe what they want to believe.* No matter how overwhelming the evidence, bottom line, people pretty much pick and choose what they want to believe—usually anything that reinforces what they already believe. If you doubt me, just ask O.J.

Remember: You can't spell "believe" without a *lie* in the middle.*

Remember too: People will choose an entertaining line of BS over the boring truth any day. So don't imagine you have to have lots of "evidence" and "facts" to prove your case. All you have to do is *be entertaining* and *tell people what they want to hear*. Lieberman (1998) said:

> The easiest person to lie to is someone who wants to be deceived. While several factors get in the way of our getting to the truth, the worst offenders are usually ourselves. If you don't want to see the truth, you often will not . . . Only the exceptional person is willing to look at what he doesn't want to see, listen to what he doesn't want to hear, and believe that which he wishes would not exist. (page 183)

How to trap a liar. The rules for trapping a liar (sans a handy polygraph) are the same your mother taught you to do before you crossed the street: Stop, look, and listen.

- Stop, or at least slow down, a fast-talking liar so you can have time to "consider his offer," i.e., pick apart his line of BS.

Science will never beat out religion. Oh sure Science gave us medicine and MTV, but religion gives us the one thing science's cold, hard, proven and double-checked facts of life can't . . . *a warm hug.*

- Look into his eyes and watch his "shadow-walk." Body language betrays all but the most accomplished of liars. Even when liars consciously will themselves to believe their own lies, subconsciously they know they're lying and this bleeds through in the form of tells and twitches.
- Listen, not just to the words he's rattling off but to the tone as well. Listen for words he emphasizes and especially for the words (and details) he tries to hide. Hint: If he uses contractions like "don't" and "didn't" instead of "do not" and "did not", odds are 60-40 in favor of his being truthful.

Keep asking questions. This will force him to come up with other lies in order to bolster his initial lie. Besides, asking questions stifles his flow, forcing him to start over.

Pretend you missed something, ask him to start his story over. Ask him to repeat questionable points and passages.

So what do you do with a liar once you've succeeded in trapping him, once you have proof positive he's lying? You can spend it or you can bank it.

You can confront him with proof of his lying, go for that instant gratification by completely humiliating your lyin'-assed enemy in front of his girlfriend and peers.

Or you can opt for delayed gratification by "banking" the proof you have of his deceit and dishonesty till later; a rabid rabbit you can pull out of your top hat any time you need it.

A third option also has you not exposing his lying immediately. Instead, *let him know you know*, that you hold information that could be the end of him. You now have the option of using this information to blackmail him. . . .

Or you can agree to keep his secret between the two of you, thus gaining an ally . . . or at least a co-conspirator.

> *"The truth must be falsehood unless it be the whole truth; and the whole truth is partly inaccessible, partly unintelligible, partly incredible and partly unpublishable—that is, in any country where truth in itself is recognized as a dangerous explosive."*
> —The Confessions of Aleister Crowley, 1929

Part III

MASTERMINDS AND MADMEN

*"I have said nothing which other and better men
have not said before me in a much more complete,
forceful and impressive manner."*

—Sigmund Freud

 ## *Introduction*

"The Blood-Pulse"

In ancient times, when a student of the Eastern martial arts had learned all his master had to teach him, his Shihan presented him with a scroll, the equivalent of today's diploma. But when the graduate unrolled the scroll, rather than finding it emblazoned with fanciful calligraphy and adorned with his master's signature, to his amazement he discovers the scroll to be completely blank!

The meaning behind his blank scroll was as simple as it was symbolic: Whereas, prior to this, the student had spent years hanging on his master's every word, imitating the master's least nuance of method and movement, the graduating student was now free to—literally—write his own destiny on the blank scroll.

More important, to honor his master and in gratitude to the school, the graduate was also expected—through his actions and attitude—to write the next chapter in the history of the art, continuing the lineage of his alma mater.

In Japan, this blank certificate is called *ketchimyaku*, "the blood-pulse," and symbolizes undiluted teachings passed from Master to student down through the ages. Chuck Norris (1998) said:

Awareness of the credentials and lineage behind almost every teacher should be of great comfort to us all, for it reflects the fact that at one time or another everyone was nothing more than a beginner and that learning continues throughout a lifetime, from pre-school years on. . . . Because of this handing on from teacher to student to teacher, behind every art is a row of masters, a succession of teachers and students, that leads back, in many cases, to the very beginning of the art in question. (page 117)

The present learns from the past or it never survives long enough to become the future. Those who would be the masters of tomorrow must spend today learning from the masters of yesterday.

To accomplish this, we must be able to put aside our prejudice long enough to learn from both the saint *and* the sinner, gleaning the wit and wisdom of the worldly, the wily, and, yes, even the wicked.

Especially the wicked:

> **"Good, as has been pointed out, is capable of being appreciated fully only when viewed alongside Evil."**
> **—Marquis de Sade,** *Juliette,* **1797**

We must not be so quick to judge the masters of past ages by today's standards (or lack thereof).

A man is molded by his times. Yet this fact must never be used to excuse him from individual responsibility.

Modern censors have already dismissed as tainted, beneath our notice, and otherwise unworthy of an honest man's study, the cunning and counsel of so many of these past masters of the Black Science.

But rest assured—or rather *rest uneasy!*—our enemy has no qualms when it comes to doing whatever it takes to bring us low. He will not hesitate to dig for and dust off the most "forbidden" of texts, nor temper his already-forked tongue from freely voicing Endorian vowels intended to resurrect the restless—and ruthless!—spirits of these past masterminds.

It goes without saying that not every would-be mind manipulator and penny-ante philanderer merits mention. But, by the same token, just because a man decides to dedicate his life to "looking out for number one," and then spends that life deliberately amassing means mystical and monetary to accomplish that end, that hardly suggests we should dismiss him out-of-hand, arbitrarily deciding there is nothing we can learn from such a scoundrel.

Quite the contrary. The world has learned so much more from scoundrels than it ever has from Sunday school teachers.

From Sun Tzu to Shakespeare, Machiavelli to Mao, East and West, there have been some who've sought to fill the future with possibilities . . . others simply want to fill their pockets. Where some seek to advance the whole of our species . . . others merely seek to advance self.

Yet if each man concentrates on advancing self first and foremost, making himself healthy, wealthy, and wise, in the end will not the whole of humanity ultimately be the better for his "selfishness"?

Nothing is guaranteed in life except death . . . and that only until the vigorous hand of Science finally breaks free from the arthritic grip of superstition!

Thus, we have no guarantee where our path of study will ultimately lead . . . nor with much certainly down which path—straight and smooth, crooked and rock-strewn—strode the patriarchs and the past masters of our particular "blood-pulse."

"The quest for hidden knowledge may end with initiation into
divine truths or into dark and abominable cults."
—Webster

And there are indeed dark lineages, with masters as cunning and as capable as the malleable minds of their wide-eyed neophytes are rapeable. The blade is only evil by the hand that wields it.

Thus, if our education is to be complete, in our time we must expect to walk not just the sunlit avenues of accepted academia, but also those neglected back alleys of the mind that even shadows fear to frequent.

As for those masters of "questionable character"—past and present— we are free to ally ourselves with them or else arm ourselves against them.

Either way, in modern parlance: We don't have to like these guys to learn from them:

"So long as a cat can catch mice, it is a good cat no matter
whether it is white or black."
—Deng Xiaoping

Thus, rather than making a habit of making snap, sophomoric judgments about the "good" or "evil" of these past masters, let us instead concentrate our energies on acquiring the insights and, when necessary, understanding the insanities of these masters.

Nothing grows in a vacuum. Even accounting for a rabid strain of DNA, psychopathic genes still need a house to grow up in, peers to pick on, and a school to play hooky from.

Thus, when looking at past masters of the Black Science, indeed when looking at any historical person—saint or sinner, publican or plebeian, great emancipator or the slyest of slaver—we must examine not just the attitude of the man but also the attitude of his times; times that either or alternately encouraged or incarcerated him, either nurturing him or making every effort to neuter him; tender or tumultuous time and clime in which he practiced his craft, preached his cult, and pandered his politics.

From Sun Tzu and Musashi in the Far East, Machiavelli in the West, and Rasputin somewhere in the middle, we must study how these past masters—a few mighty of spirit, a few too many megalomaniacs—expertly molded and marauded the malleable minds of persons, pacts, and even empires.

The first rule to stealing their thunder is found in our seeking out how these masters are similar in method and madness, rather than allowing detractors to distract us by harping on their seeming differences.

For the ways of the masters *are* similar; East and West, ancient or modern, cloaked in royal purple or shrouded in wizards' pitch, draped in virginal white or adorned in whore's scarlet.

From conmen to cult leader, from getting their foot in the door to slipping their hand in our back pocket (hopefully only looking to lift our wallet!), the ways and wiles of mind-slayers are ever the same, with more similarities than differences.

In the end, does not the Chinaman bleed like the Hun? Does he not hold his children tight and his gold tighter when a stranger smiles? Of like blood, of like mind.

So, whether we journey to the East or from the East, or remain with feet firmly planted on Western soil, diligent study that lends itself to deliberate design is the key to unlocking the mysteries of the mind—both mundane and magical, no matter if that mind be "inscrutable" Eastern or "ingenious" Western.

And no matter the particular lineage(s) to which we seriously or spuriously lay claim, what matters most is that the blood-pulse continues pumping strong.

For in the end what tale will all our study tell? That we are the penultimate product of a lineage insightful or insidious, or that we set ourselves to becoming the patriarchs of a new blood-pulse, one even more benevolent . . . or blackhearted than those of Masters past? Lieberman (2000) said:

> Whether it's a battle of the mind or of the flesh, the strategies are almost identical. This is because all battles are first waged within the mind; it is there where you win or lose and then the outcome is manifested into the material world. Whether it's a tennis match, a spelling bee, or two men vying for the attention of a woman, *competition is competition. Attack the mind of your opponent* and you will divide him against himself and then he will fall before you, without a single touch. (page 105)

6

The Art of Shapeshifting

Those well-studied in the Black Science make it a habit to adapt to changing circumstance and flux. The world is a cold place and the wise and the wily dress accordingly. Never is a wise man's cane (replete with hidden rapier) nor his reversible overcoat far from reach. If that wise man also just happens to be an accomplished conman . . . or a wily Nazi war criminal like Martin Bormann, he also keeps his *suitcase* within arm's length . . . and he packs light!*

Adapt or die is the most unforgiving rule of nature. We adjust ourselves to changing realities . . . or those changing realities "adjust" us.

That's why the Art of Disguise is one of the Nine Training Halls of *Ninjutsu* (Lung, 1995).

Leopards can change their spots . . . just connect the dots vertically and you get a pretty convincing tiger.

Of course it helps if you can convincingly fake a roar and if the person you're trying to sell the tiger to really needs a tiger!

---

*Martin Ludwig Bormann (born 1900) was Hitler's Nazi Party deputy and wielded extraordinary power until his prudent disappearance during the fall of Berlin. Sentenced to death in absentia at Nuremburg, he has since been rumored still livin' large (off Nazi gold and stolen art treasures), in Argentina, Russia, and that secret Nazi UFO base in Antarctica.

BLOOD OF ABRAHAM

*"Evil men with minds like sword blades may seem to be pacified
and contained, but in the end, they will show their ferocious nature.
Therefore, kill them. Or train them soothingly."*
—Tshe Ring Dbang Rgyal (1697–1763)

When it comes to strategy, patriarch Abraham was as wily as they come.

His guerrilla force was well trained enough to defeat larger, more conventional armies (see Genesis, chapter 1).

Black Science also played a major role in Abraham's world. For example, when necessary, encouraging your wife to prostitute herself was permitted. Lying was also okay . . . but only when the truth didn't fit. (Genesis, chapter 20).

(**Note:** Like father like son. Abraham's son Isaac gets caught using this same ploy with *his* wife in Genesis 26.)

At one point, Abraham even tries talking God out of nuking Sodom and Gomorrah (Genesis 18). Luckily God got the upper hand in that negotiation, otherwise we'd have all been screwed in the end.

Speaking of fruits not falling far from the tree. . . . Abraham's two nieces would have fit right in on *Jerry Springer.*

Finding themselves without the prospect of husbands, the two young girls conspire to get Lot, their conveniently gullible father, drunk before "raping" him two nights in a row! Both daughters subsequently become pregnant.

Of course, poor, deceived Lot was "too drunk" or unconscious to realize what was going on . . . *two nights in a row* (Genesis, chapter 19)?

Evidently they hadn't yet invented the saying: Fool me once, shame on *you.* Fool me *twice,* shame on *me!*

The Bible says Abraham lived 175 years. Guess that means he literally outlived his enemies. During that time, Abraham had two sons, Isaac and Ishmael, who went on to found the tribes of the Jews and the tribes of the Arabs, respectively. (Though they've hardly respected each other since!)

Thus, Abraham fathered two distinct bloodlines. Emphasis on the word *blood,* since one line of Abraham's loins gave the world the word *zealot,* while the other cursed us with the word *assassin.*

Bible Black Science

"Keep yourself far from your enemies, and be on guard
toward your friends."
—Jesus, Son of Sirach

The Old Testament is pretty much one long chronicle of war. From Abraham's guerrilla raids against the "Five Kings of the North," the Canaanite conquests of the warlord Joshua, the exploits of Samson and Kings Saul and David, down to the successful guerrilla strategy of the Macabbees in their second and first centuries' fight for independence from Syria, the whole of the Old Testament is written in blood on scrolls of tortured flesh.

The arrival of the Romans in Palestine in 63 BCE saw the addendum of yet another bloody chapter, one that coined the word *zealot*.

A *zealot* is defined as an unstoppable, suicidal religious-political fanatic. The word comes from a Jewish cult who thought nothing of using assassination to further their religious-political agenda.

The Romans called them "terrorists," by the way.

Founded by Judas of Gamala in the early years of the first century, Zealots led both a terror campaign against Roman occupation forces and against any Jew deemed to be a collaborator.

Barabbas, whom the Jewish crowd chose to pardon, was a popular Zealot (Luke, chapter 23).

Zealots "worked the crowd"—a sharp whisper in this ear, the prod of a keen dagger in those ribs—and the mob was more than happy to vote to free the Zealot murderer rather than that bothersome carpenter from Nazareth.

Zealots fought . . . "zealously" during the failed Jewish rebellion that led to the destruction of Jerusalem by the Romans in 70 CE.

The Zealot cult (but not the zealot mentality—such energies can never be destroyed, remember) ended when the Zealots all killed themselves, their wives and their children—970 people in all—at the siege of Hasada. (**Note:** Coincidentally, the same number of cultists who committed suicide with Jim Jones's People's Temple in 1979 in Guyana.)

While a strong sword arm was praised in Old Testament times, Black Science was also well respected and well documented in the Bible.

From talking your brother out of his birthright and tricking your aged, blind father out of his blessing (Genesis, chapter 27), to convincing a whole tribe of your enemies into circumcising themselves so you can then slaughter them "On the third, when they were sore" . . . dah (Genesis, chapter 34)!

Then there's Samson. An accomplished guerrilla fighter who used unexpected tactics (burning enemy crops) and even more unconventional weapons. (Hey, that "jawbone of an ass" thing caught everybody by surprise!)

Black Science—wise, Samson's riddles screwed with his enemies' heads. And they weren't too keen on his screwing their women, either.

But it wasn't until mighty Samson made the mistake of letting his "little head" do his thinking for him, succumbing to Delilah's sighs and thighs, that the roof literally fell in on him (Judges, 15).

And what about King David's son Absolom smiling in his brother Amnon's face for two years, all the while plotting, before eventually successfully carrying out Amnon's murder for his having raped their sister Tamar (2 Samuel, chapter 13)?*

The Old Testament is full of such tales of the sons (and daughters) of Abraham outwitting their enemies time and again. Of course, the *victors* are the ones who write the history books . . . and the Bibles.

Jesus, Son of Sirach

> *"The root of wisdom—to whom has it been revealed? Her clever devices—who knows them?"*
> —Jesus, son of Sirach

The Apocrypha are the "lost books" of the Bible written in the two centuries before Jesus of Nazareth, sandwiched between the Old and the New Testaments.

Though a respected part of the Catholic Bible for the 1,000 years previous, Shakespeare and his Masonic "Invisible College" brethren left the Apocrypha out of their King James Version of the Bible in 1611. Consequently, these books have been ignored by Protestants ever since.

A pity, since these eighteen books contain a wealth of practical worldly wisdom: from the primer on guerrilla warfare in the first and second books of the Maccabees (see especially, 2 Maccabees, chapter 8), to the astute insights into human intercourse catalogued by Jesus, son of Sirach.

---

*Do you think the fact first-born Amnon was next in line to become King might have influenced Prince Absolom in any way?

The Wisdom of Jesus the son of Sirach (aka Ecclesiasticus) is the only book of the Apocrypha whose author is known for certain. (**Note:** This fact in and of itself does not justify Protestants washing their hands of the Apocrypha since the actual authors of the majority of books in both the Old and the New Testaments are *unknown*.)

Jesus, son of Sirach (Hb. Joshua ben Sira), was a Jewish scribe and teacher of Old Testament law who ran an academy in Jerusalem around 180 BCE.

Thanks to his place in time and to his chosen profession, Jesus, son of Sirach, inherited both the wisdom and wiles of what we today think of as the "Old Testament," while his words undoubtedly helped inspire at least some "New Testament" thinking:

> *"Behold, I send you out as sheep into the midst of wolves. Be wise*
> *as serpents and an innocent as doves."*
> **—Matthew 10:16**

Far from having his head stuck in the clouds, Jesus, son of Sirach, spoke on practical strategy, not otherworldly pie-in-the-sky strategy you can't actually use.

His observations and advice range from insights on family, to finding out who your real friends are, to how best to take revenge against your foes.

Jesus was keenly aware of how to "read" another's body language and speech patterns, as well as how to use an enemies' "FLAGS" weaknesses against him while jealously guarding your own.

His understanding of strategy and psychology (i.e., Black Science or mind control) was up to par with Sun Tzu and other Asian Masters. Compare Jesus' "Presents and gifts blind the eyes of the wise" (20:29) to the strategy of twelfth-century Chinese Master *Ch'en Hoa*: "Give the enemy young boys and women to infatuate him, and jades and silks to excite his ambitions."

According to Jesus, there are "Nine things that gladden a man's heart":

His children. Says Jesus: "He who teaches his son will make his enemies envious, and will glory in him in the presence of friends." (30:3)

Do not mistake this for the "unconventional love" people tout today: "It is a disgrace to be the father of an undisciplined son, and the birth of a daughter is a loss." (22:3)

Living to see the downfall of his foes. Jesus, son of Sirach, lived before that whole "Turn the other cheek" thing had been invented. Back in the day, even when it was over . . . it still wasn't over. This is where having strong children comes in handy: "The father may die, and yet he is not dead, for he has left behind him one like himself; while alive he saw and rejoiced, and when he died he was not grieved; he has left behind him an avenger against his enemies, and one to repay the kindness of his friends." (30:4)

Living with an intelligent wife. "I would rather dwell with a lion and a dragon than dwell with an evil wife." (25:16)

"Do not deprive yourself of a wise and good wife, for her charm is worth more than gold." (7:19)

Not making a slip of the tongue. "A slip on the pavement is better than a slip of the tongue." (20:18)

Not serving a man inferior to yourself. "When a man looks to the table of another, his existence cannot be considered as life." (40:29)

Having gained good sense. "Do not praise a man before you hear his reason, for this is the test of a man." (27:7)

Good sense is the shell, while wisdom is both our whey and our yoke.

Speaking to attentive listeners

Having gained wisdom. "Pursue wisdom like a hunger. Lie in wait on her paths." (14:22)

"Wine and music gladden the heart, but the love of wisdom is better than both." (40:20)

Knowing that no one is superior to he who serves his lord. Consequently, Jesus' nine thoughts that gladden a man's heart also give us nine goads with which to prod our enemy in the direction we want him to go; that is, weaknesses we can exploit: More wisdom of Jesus, son of Sirach:

Friends

"What fellowship has a wolf with a lamb?" (13:17)

"Who will pity a snake charmer bitten by a serpent?" (12:13)

"Every friend will say, 'I too am a friend.' But some friends are friends only in name." (37:1)

"Do not forget a friend in your heart, and be not unmindful of him in your wealth." (37:6)

Enemies

"A man's enemies are grieved when he prospers." (12:9)

Shapeshifters and Shadow Warriors

"Curse the whisperer and deceiver, for he has destroyed many who were at peace." (28:13)

"Do not bring every man into your home, for many are the wiles of the crafty." (11:29)

"An enemy will speak sweetly with his lips, but in his mind he has plans to throw you into the pit. He weeps with his eyes, but when he finds the opportunity, his thirst for blood will not be satisfied." (12:16–18)

"A man will kiss another's hands until he gets a loan, and will lower his voice in speaking of his neighbor's money; but when the time comes for repayment he will delay, and will pay in words of unconcern, and will find fault with the time." (29:5)

Shadow-Walk

"A man's dress, his open-mouthed laughter, and his manner of walking, all show what he is." (19:30)

"Whoever winks his eye plans evil deeds . . ." (27:22)

Shadow-Talk

"In your presence his mouth is all sweetness, and he admires your words, but later he will twist his speech and with your own words he will give offense." (27:23)

"The mind of fools is in their mouths, but the mouth of the wise men is in their mind." (21:26)

Education vs. Experience

"An educated man knows many things, and one with much experience may speak with understanding. He that is inexperienced knows few things, but he that has traveled acquires much cleverness. I have seen many things in my travels, and I understand more than I can express. I have often been in danger of death, but have escaped because of those experiences." (34:9)

"Do nothing without deliberation and when you have acted, do not regret it." (32:19)

Allah's Daggers

Abraham's first bloodline left us the word *zealot*, but his second bloodline left us in fear of an even more dreaded word . . . *assassin!*

The English word *assassin* is a corruption of *hashishin*, "one who uses hashish," itself a European corruption of the term *Hashimite*, ironically an honored title in Islam meaning one who can trace his lineage back to the sixth-century founder of Islam, Muhammed Koresh.*

"Corruption" being the operative word here, since corruption—extortion, mind control, and murder—was the stock and trade of the sanguine "Assassin" cult founded in Persia in 1090 by Hasan ibn Sabbah (aka "The Old Man of the Mountain").

From his impregnable "Eagle's Nest" castle hidden in the mountains of Persia (now Iran), Hasan loosed wave after wave of suicidal agents—spies and assassins—upon the world.

The tale of how Hasan acquired his Eagle's Nest mountain fortress is classic Black Science:

One day a caravan carrying the original princely owner of the Eagle's Nest was attacked by bandits. Just in the nick of time (heh-heh-heh), Hasan and some of his men appear out of nowhere and save the endangered prince.

In gratitude, the prince insists Hasan accept a reward. A chest of gold, perhaps? Finally, after much cajoling, Hasan agrees, but "Only so the prince's honor will be satisfied."

Hasan then explained to the prince that he had swore an oath to Allah to set up a monument like the world had never seen before and so would accept only as much land from the prince as could be encompassed by the green cloak he wears, the same cloak, he assures the awed prince, that the prophet himself—Peace be upon him!—used to lift the sacred black stone back into place when rebuilding the Kaaba shrine in Mecca.

---

*Would-be prophet David Koresh, whose own short-lived cult went up in smoke in Waco, Texas, in 1993, once claimed descent from the same Koresh clan as Muhammed.

The prince pledged himself to such a noble endeavor. Besides, it wouldn't cost him much, only the small patch of land that could be surrounded by Hasan's cloak. Hasan agreed to reveal to the prince the patch of land he had chosen at dawn.

The next morning, the prince was flabbergasted to find that during the night Hasan and his men had unraveled the green cloak, tying all the threads together until their length wrapped completely around the Eagle's Nest castle!

The prince was forced to honor his pledge and turn his castle over to Hasan.

And, true to Hasan's word, the Eagle's Nest did stand as a "monument" for the next two centuries . . . a monument to terror!

Hasan's assassin cult was the template for all secret societies, spy networks, and terrorist groups that followed—down to the present day.

This was the original *al Qaeda*!

In his time, Hasan used every conceivable tactic, torture, and tool, from magic to murder, hashish and harlots, to dazzle and dirk enemy and initiate alike into doing his bidding. For Hasan and his assassins, the end justified the means. The means are terror and treachery and the end was power.

Master shapeshifters, whenever expedient, the Assassins made unholy covenants with heathen Hindus and allied themselves with infidel Christian crusaders against their Muslim brethren.

For Hasan, and the Assassin Grandmasters who continued his lethal legacy, Islam was but a convenient black curtain behind which to hide. Hasan's assassins ruled by subterfuge and slaughter for over two centuries, until invading Mongols broke the cult's back in Persia in 1273.

But remember, "energy can't be destroyed."

After the destruction of their Persian HQ, the Assassins continued to survive and thrive from India to Syria, spawning "spin-off" groups and imitators, some as far-flung as Europe. More on this European connection in a minute.*

---

*For a complete history of the cult of the Assassins, their terror tactics, and fighting technique, see: *Assassin! Secrets of the Cult of Assassins* by Dr. Haha Lung, Paladin Press, 1997.

7

Masters of the East

*"And in that inscrutable East, the cradle of all the mysteries, the
profoundest European adept of secret society intrigue may find
himself outdistanced by past masters in the art in which he believed
himself proficient."*
—**Webster**

When studying past masters, we must try to suspend any prejudices and
preferences we have. Any prejudice can cause us to dismiss potential teachers out of hand because of their race, religion, gender, or culture. A truly
wise man learns from both friend and foe.

Prior to 9/11, how many Americans knew much about Islam? Sadder
still, how many Americans even today really know anything about Islam? No
one trains your sons as well as your enemies.

Just as dangerous, our preconceptions may cause us to seek out "masters" from a particular time or clime, thinking that one race, region, or religion has a monopoly on knowledge. (Would-be cult leaders *love* this kind of
thinking!)

We've failed already if we allow ourselves to be dazzled and distracted by
the differences rather than straightaway seeking out the similarities between
East and West.

Any snake-oil salesman worth his spiel knows all you have to do is add
the prefix "Oriental" or "Chinese" to anything and it instantly becomes more

"mysterious" . . . and more expensive. It seems the West has always looked "to the East" for wisdom. Is not the mythical Garden of Paradise situated somewhere "east in Eden" (Genesis 2)?

We're told the three Wisemen (*Magi*) came from the East. Ask a dyed in the wool Freemason or International Finder.

Didn't everyone from Aleister Crowley to the Beatles take Hermann Hesse's advice to "*Journey to the East*"?

And, be honest, wouldn't you rather buy a book on martial arts and other "mysteries" of the East written by someone with an Asian-sounding name . . . like "Dr. Haha Lung" from exotic Katmandu, Nepal, than an "Ed Walsh" from Cleveland, Ohio?

It's human nature. "The grass (or in this case, bamboo) is always greener" . . . anywhere but *here*.

Perhaps ancient Westerners saw the East as the cradle of wisdom because that's where the sun is "born" each morning. The original Chinese word for Japan literally meant "the place where the sun rises."

While it's true there is much the Western mind can learn by opening itself to the mysteries of the East, lest we give in to our preconceptions, or worse still fall prey to a deliberate ploy that wisdom is only to be found "in the East," ask yourself: When seekers in China and Japan "look east," out across the Pacific, what lands do they see?

A JOURNEY TO THE EAST

"The past is studied for the sake of the present."
—Mao Tse-tung

China takes credit for inventing everything from paper to spaghetti, gunpowder to the crossbow. However, other accounts have the crossbow being invented by indigenous people of what is now Vietnam. This illustrates how blind admiration (preference) for an admittedly great land like China can skew both individual perception and historical perspective.

In the same vein, China is today synonymous with Kung-fu-style martial arts. Yet the Indian Buddhist patriarch Bvodhidharma (whom the Chinese call *Tamo*, and the Japanese *daruma*) is credited with bringing martial arts and *Zen* meditation from India to China and with founding the *Shaolin* monastery in Hunan, from which nearly all today's Eastern martial arts lineages trace themselves.

In the same way, Japan is acknowledged for birthing two of history's fiercest fighting forces, the Samurai and their dread nemesis, the Ninja.

Yet it's no secret both these killer cadre finagled and forced many of their deadliest—and darkest—tactics and techniques from foreign "friends" . . . and foes.

Thus, if we only make landfall at China and Japan during our Black Science junket to the East it will mean depriving ourselves of so many other just as exotic, just as educational—just as potentially exploitable—Asian ports of call.

For example, did not mysterious Tibet already arm us with its knowledge of *Nam She Tsog Gye*, "The Eight Minds"? (See chapter 4.)

Indian Insights

India, "the Mother of all civilizations," was crafted from a curious mixture of indigenous matriarchal culture and the patriarchal Indo-Aryan invaders who swept across the subcontinent around 1500 BCE.

We in the West today have a tendency (inherited from the days of British colonialism) to still think of India as the land of little half-naked holy men, adept only at mesmerizing cobras and sleeping on beds of nails. We forget they now have nukes.

According to S. Radhakrishnan, translator and editor of *The Principal Upanishads*, the Upanishads (the primary socio-religious "bible" of Hindu India) recognizes two distinct types of wisdom:

- *Para vidya*, "Higher wisdom" concerned with "spiritual" matters . . . like how to get right with the Gods, and
- *Apara vidya*, "lower wisdom" that concentrates on more mundane, practical matters . . . like how to get back at your enemies.

The wise ancients recognized that a totally "religious" person can have their head so far up in the clouds as to be no earthly good. Hence, the ideal was for a Hindu man to first go through stages of his life as a student, warrior, and householder, executing his filial and societal dharma (lit. duty), before giving it all up to become a monk in his later years.

We in the West are most comfortable thinking of India as the land of an incredible lineage of spiritual teachers, from Buddha to Gandhi.

This shows in the fact so many Western seekers—from Burton and Blavatsky to the Beatles—have wondered and wandered the length and breadth of India in search of magical formula and fakir.

This can also be seen in Indian words adopted in English: *yoga, guru, swami, ashram*, and *mantra*. But India also gave us *thug* and *mugger*.

India's notable sons include not only mendicants and magicians but also master strategists and martial artists, from the *Kshatriya* warriors of the epic *Mahabharata*, to the *Sikhs*.

Indeed, Mother India has also birthed a brood of ruthless *Rajas* and scheming king-makers, none more adept than the fourth-century "Machiavelli of India," *Kautilya* (see Lung and Prowant, 2001:136).

Down through the centuries, alongside 10,000 temples built to honor 10,000 gods, India has also produced 10,000 secret societies, Tantric sex cults, and sanguineous sects, not the least of which are the devotees of the fierce black-faced bitch-Goddess *Kali* whose *Thuggee* stranglers preyed upon the subcontinent until finally (?) suppressed in the mid-nineteenth century by the British. (See Lung, 1995.)*

Following the destruction of their Persian stronghold in the thirteenth century, surviving members of the Muslim cult of the *Hashishins* (Assassins) relocated to India, adding their sharp insights and sharper incisors to India's already complicated political scene. (See Lung, 1997.)

Craft of the Hircarrah. India's history is one of constant intrigue, stimulating perpetual internecine political and religious strife, punctuated by the occasional rise and fall of empire and dynasty, and further encouraged by foreign invasions (e.g., tenth-century Muslims).

By the 1520s the *Mogul* empire had been established just in time to meet, but not defeat, invading Europeans: the Portuguese, Dutch, the French, and ultimately the British.

Thanks to this volatile "tradition" of vacillating and violent politics throughout India's history—down to the present day, it's not surprising that every ambitious militarist and merchant, every suspicious *Raja*, and every ruthless religious leader felt it necessary, if only for self-defense, to field their own spies and, when need be, assassins.

Most of the British in India, high on newfound colonial wealth and power, remained blissfully ignorant to the Hircarrah's ages-old system of sophisticated skulduggery swirling right under their stiff upper lips.

---

*The cult of *Kali* gave us the words *thug* and *mugger*; the former shortened from *thuggee*, while the latter is an English corruption of the Hindi *magar*, British slang for Thuggee since these killers struck with the speed and ferocity of a "crocodile."

But not all Europeans were so naive. While serving in India, the "Iron Duke" of Wellington (1769–1852) co-opted the Hircarrah network for much of his military intelligence. Wellington would later use these same spying tactics and techniques in successful campaigns up and down the Iberian Peninsula and against Napoleon at Waterloo (Keegan, 1987:135).

While in India working for the East India Company, that (in)famous freebooter Sir Richard Francis Burton (1821–1890) was initiated into the craft of the Hircarrah. Burton later used Hircarrah disguise techniques to successfully penetrate the so-called holy shrine at Mecca in 1853, the only "infidel" to ever do so.

Occult author Helena Petrovna Blavatsky (1831–1891) also sought out the craft of the Hircarrah while in India—*mind-manipulation techniques:* this intrepid adventuress used to facilitate her extensive, expensive—and often perilous—travels throughout Asia, and disguise techniques she successfully used when dressing as a man to penetrate the "forbidden" Tibetan capital of Lhasa.

(**FYI:** In 1875, H. P. Blavatsky founded the Theosophical Society. Occult oriented, this international organization borrows freely from fakir and Freemason alike.)

Still another noted author, also part-time spy and full-time Freemason, Rudyard Kipling (1865–1936), understood the potential of Hircarrah tactics.

Kipling's successes spying in northern India and Afghanistan, along with the difficult—bloody!—lessons they'd learned suppressing the secretive cult of *Thuggee*, helped convince British military authorities of the value of forming more "special forces" units: "commandos" adept at thuggee infiltration and assassination technique, as well as specialized intelligence operatives (Lung, 1995).

(**FYI:** Kipling's life bears closer scrutiny. Born in India, he acted as a journalist-cum-spy in India from 1882–89, during which time he somehow found time to become both a Freemason and a *Hircarrah* adept. Kipling journeyed throughout the Kasmir, reportedly spying on Russian intentions. However, some sources maintain that Kipling was obsessed with Masonic legends of a fabled lost city hidden somewhere between India and Afghanistan. Founded by Alexander the Great, this Shangri La was said to be the repository of the forbidden knowledge of the *Roshaniya*, the "Illuminated Ones," mystical adepts from whose lineage so many subsequent secret societies, including the Freemasons, lay claim.

Some of Kipling's adventures, thinly veiled, subsequently appeared in his novel *The Man Who Would Be King* (1891)—the tale of two ex-British soldiers who, after an arduous search, finally succeed in discovering just such a hidden city somewhere in the Kasmir. The heroes of Kipling's story are both Freemasons, a fact that not only saves their lives but ultimately proves to be the key to their gaining riches and power. The 1975 movie starred Sean Connery.

Auyurveda. Like *ninja* everywhere, Hircarrah were always looking for the "Edge," that one vital piece of information, or deft incision of dirk, guaranteed to turn gross speculation into glowing success.

Given this atmosphere of political dog-eat-dog, it's no surprise even the (in)famous Indian love manual The *Kama Sutra* describes how to win the "perfect" (i.e., rich and influential) mate in the same way one would carry out a ruthless military campaign (Lung and Prowant, 2001:46).

Other Indian strategists also borrowed freely and often from age-old *para vidya* texts, finding more mundane *apara vidya* uses for this ancient wisdom; weaving techniques originally meant for the enlightenment of self into tactics for putting out another's lights!

For example, we've already seen now easily the Indian science of *Chakras*, "The Seven Wheels of Power," originally intended for the enlightenment of self, can give us invaluable insight into others (see chapter 4).

The time-honored practice of the *Hatha* and *Kundalini* types of Indian *Yoga*, both of which concentrate on stimulating the flow of healthful energies in the body, were soon corrupted into techniques designed to interfere with and even stop the flow of positive energies, helping give birth to the Chinese art of *Dim Mak*, the "Death Touch." (See "Ninja Death Touch: The Fact and the Fiction" by Ralf Dean Omar, *Blackbelt* magazine, September, 1989. Also, Lung, 1997a.)

Another *para vidya* system that easily lends itself to practical (i.e., Black Science or mind control) use is *Auyurveda*, an ancient system of mind and body medicine, now at least 5,000 years old.

At first glance, Auyurveda somewhat resembles the discarded Western psychology theory of "Somatotypes." (See Lung & Prowant, 2001:65.)

Auyurveda maintains there are three basic principles known as *Doshas* that control us: *Vata*, *Pitta*, and *Kapna*. These Doshas correspond to everything from our body type and size, to our mental attitude—strengths and weaknesses.

Most people are a combination of two types of Dosha, with one Dosha predominating.

Identifying which Doshas dominate our enemy helps us better plot out our approach strategy (see Figure 21).

INDIAN AYURVEDA

	Vata	Pitta	Kapha
Build	Thin	Medium	Solidly built
Metabolism	Fast	Methodical	Slow
Orientation	Loves excitement and change	Likes challenges, an innate drive	Likes status quo, but needs stimulus of new sights, sounds and people
Nature	Cheerful, enthusiastic	Enterprising, energetic	Tranquil, relaxed
Temptation	Tempt with novelty	Always looking for the "Edge," a new angle	Needs stimulus, attracted by new sights, sounds, people and opportunity
Energy level	Given to bursts of energy (impulsive)	Sharp intellect, articulate speech	Slow and steady; mulls things over before acting
Coping strategy	Experiences excess anxiety	Becomes angry and irritable under stress	Slow to anger
Medical tendency	Unexplained aches and pains	Workaholic "burnout"	Prone to weight gain
Performance flaws	Short attention span Can't keep a routine Light sleeper Learns fast, forgets just as fast	Sarcastic and critical Too demanding Lives by his watch Workaholic Never skips a meal Never "wastes" time	Seeks emotional comfort from overeating; needs more sleep and wakes slower than others; empathetic to a fault

Note: All people are combinations of these three, Vata, Pitta, and Kapha, but one of the three is always dominant in the body.

Figure 21.

Vietnamese Voodoo

> *"The wise Buddha once observed that our greatest weapon is in*
> *our enemy's mind, meaning an enemy's blinding anger, greed,*
> *hatred and other negative emotions can all be turned to our*
> *advantage, allowing us to 'get inside his head' in order to*
> *'throw him off his game.'"*
>
> —*Cao Dai Kung-Fu: Lost Fighting Arts of Vietnam* by
> Dr. Haha Lung, Loompanics, 2002

Vietnam lies halfway between India and China along one of Asia's ancient trade routes. This has been both boon and burden for the people of Vietnam.

The blessing in this is that Vietnamese culture has benefited by contact and contribution from so many diverse visitors from all over Asia—India, Thailand, Japan, China, and from as far away as Europe.

The curse part is that, inevitably, all of these visitors *overstayed* their welcome!

As a result, the Vietnamese have spent the last 2,000 years in constant warfare, fighting to expel one uninvited (invading) "guest" after another: Khmer, Chinese, French, Japanese, the French (again!) and, finally those overdressed and noisy Americans.

But not all pivotal battles are fought with blade and bullet on an open field. Indeed, many of the most important battles in Vietnam history took place behind what has been called "a black curtain" of subterfuge, espionage, and policies penned with poison-dipped poniard. In my earlier book, *Cao Dai Kung-Fu* (2002), I said:

Open battles are easy to record. All we need do is follow the noise and count the bodies. What isn't as easily seen are the many intrigues and hidden agendas playing out behind the black curtain, masterful schemes and intricate skulduggery just as important to the unfolding of history as are bullets and bayonets. Unfortunately, all we inevitably end up with when trying to decipher the comings and goings of crafty cabals, secret societies, and shadowy government agencies is always the same: a dancing tendril of smoke glimpsed behind us in a dark mirror, whispers and winks.

What can't be taken by force, can often be wrested away by skulduggery; what can't be defended openly, can often be supported via subterfuge.

In order to survive, the Vietnamese were forced to master, not just blade, bludgeon, and bomb but also the Black Science.

The Black Crows. One Vietnamese group that realized early on they might have to fight the French Foreign Legion one day and Freemasons the following day, bartering with European merchants today, getting the better of Japanese *Yakuza* tomorrow, was the *Cao Dai* religious sect.

Officially founded as a spiritualist movement in the 1920s, but with a spiritual/political blood-pulse going back centuries, the Cao Dai not only maintained a well-trained self-defense force but also fielded a wide ranging network of intelligence operatives. The most adept of these agents were (are?) a secretive cadre known as *O Nhm*, "Black Crows."

A Cao Dai Black Crow agent was part mystic and magician, part spy . . . and all *ninja*; adept at gathering intelligence and willing to use any method to accomplish his (or her) mission—from making spirits appear, to making enemies disappear.

Black Crows were masters of *Am thi tinh*, the "art of suggestibility," propaganda intended to sow doubt and harvest fear in an enemy's heart.

Like Viet Cong out in the bush, Black Crows were guerrilla-adepts at stringing *mental* trip-wires and planting passion-dipped *punji* across the path of their intended victim.

O Nhm knew that somewhere within the *That tinh*, the "Seven Passions," we all possess, could be found a weakness to successfully trip up any foe.

Thus, *joy* can be turned to *sorrow*, sorrow dissipated by joy.

Love made to doubt becomes jealousy and *hate*. In turn, hate can be dispelled or at least confused by the appearance of love.

Love and *lust* all too often come disguised as one another.

Lust can all too easily override *fear* (i.e. common sense).

What we fear we also hate. Yet people often use intense hate to hide secret lust . . . even from themselves.

And *anger* can be used to either open our eyes (e.g., "righteous anger" in response to injustice), or it can blind us by "feeding" emotions like hate and fear.

The Five Jewels. Black Crows called their overall strategy of assessing and assigning task to a situation *Giao Hoat*, which literally means "craft and cunning."

Giao Hoat consists of five complementing and overlapping stages, called "jewels," designed to aid an O Nhm agent in first assessing a situation (or individual) and then crafting an appropriate "approach strategy."

- *Can Nao* (lit. "War of Nerves"), consists of *alertness* (realizing that a problem exists, preferably while the problem is still small) and the *patience* (to gather necessary intelligence before acting).
- Dom do (lit. "to watch"). At this stage we "watch," i.e., gather intelligence either through direct experience or else through agents.
- *Coi Mach* ("to evaluate"). At this stage we sift the intelligence gathered, separating wheat from chaff.
- *Ngu Quan* ("Five Weaknesses"), similar to the *Wu Hsing Gojo-Goyoku* strategy of Japanese Ninja—itself derived from the Chinese Taoist *Wu Hsing*. (See Lung and Prowant, 2001:31.) At this stage, we look to see which of *the five senses* dominates our target. This corresponds to one (or more) of the emotional "warning FLAGS" (Fear, Lust, Anger, Greed, Sympathy) which dominates all of us at one time or another.
- *Choc* (lit. "to draw out"). At this stage we blend all the intelligence gathered in the previous four stages into a "jewel" so dazzling, it will literally "draw our enemy out" into the open. This stage is sometimes called *Lam me* (lit. "to bewitch").

"In war, you use whatever works, no matter if that tool, tactic, or technique was crafted by friend or foe. The finest weapon is the one you pry from your dead enemy's hand."
—Lung, *Cao Dai Kung-fu*

CHINESE FACE

"Those who use their mental powers for living rule others. Those who use their physical strength for living are ruled by others."
—Confucius

When it comes to strategy, East or West, China's Sun Tzu is the acknowledged master.

Sun Tzu's first book was *Prime Principles of Victory*, a treatise concentrating on deceit. But most students of Sun Tzu are more familiar with his masterpiece *Ping Fa*, "Art of War."

There were, of course, other strategists before Sun Tzu, most of whom he undoubtedly studied. But after Sun Tzu, all would be compared to him, and it would be—and still is—his ideal we shoot for.

Unfortunately, Sun Tzu is a lot like the weather: everybody talks about it, few actually do anything about it. It's the age-old problem of "appreciation" versus "application."

Appreciation in this instance doesn't simply mean admiring a piece of art, it means the practiced ability to expertly compare and critique a work of art. With a minimum of study, any one of us can learn to appreciate fine art. But how many of us have it in us to *apply* that appreciation towards becoming a Picasso?

Likewise, haven't we heard it argued time and again that learning to play the game of chess will somehow transform us into master battlefield strategists. Yet when pressed on the issue, no one seems able to explain—convincingly—how shuffling little plastic pieces back and forth can turn us into the next Alexander or Patton?

Some dismiss master strategists like Sun Tzu, myopically complaining "Why should I waste my time studying some decrepit Chinaman, when I'll never be put in command of 10,000 troops?"

Well, with an attitude like that, young man, of course you won't!

Philosophy, be it meditative or military, is easy to talk about, hard to apply practically. Revelations 10:9 warns: "Take this scroll and eat. It will be sweet in your mouth, but bitter in your belly."

"Sweet in your mouth," easy to talk about. "Bitter in your belly," difficult to apply.

Finding practical applications today for ancient wisdoms is what makes the masters of tomorrow.

For example, Sun Tzu warns: "When you have surrounded your enemy, you must leave him a way of escape. Never press an enemy at bay" (chapter VII: 31–32).

In combat, this means that desperate men, trapped with no way out, will fight to the death. Therefore, on the battlefield always give the enemy army a way out, a way to withdraw with honor.

In China this is referred to as saving face; "face" being a synonym in the East for honor, dignity, and status.

Though originally intended for use on a Chinese battlefield 2,500 years ago, this particular Sun Tzu principle can easily be applied to our one-on-one interactions today.

For example, in an argument even when a person knows they're 100 percent wrong, even when they realize you've trapped them in an indefensible position, they may still stubbornly hold their ground for fear of losing face, or, in today's jargon, fear of being "punked out."

Now, rather than browbeating and belittling them (unless this was your intent all along!), leave them a clear avenue of escape, one that allows them to retain their dignity, give them time to "double-check their source" (See *The Art of No-gotiation*, in chapter 5.)

They may be so relieved by your show of mercy that you will turn them into an ally. (At the very least, you will have demonstrated your ability to totally crush them at your leisure!)

An indolent student carries the masters under his arm. A wise student carries them in his heart. Keep the masters not to your shelf, but within yourself.

Thus, the goal is not just studying past masters but developing the ability to apply their knowledge to the "real" world.

Sticking to our methodology to "look for the similarities rather than the differences," we can easily recognize basic themes running through the teachings of all these past masters.

The Three Principles

When studying strategy in general and Chinese strategists like Sun Tzu in particular, we recognize three recurring principles:

System and setting. In any situation, circumstances must be viewed as a whole. We must see the big picture.

This means not only seeing how things are unfolding (system) but also the background (setting) against which events are playing out.

Seeing the big picture can also mean having to postpone immediate gratification in favor of long-term gain; waiting when we would rather attack, retreating rather than pressing forward with your assault—be it verbal or violent.

Conversely, anytime we can frivolously distract or otherwise bog down an enemy's resources with trivia, making him lose sight of the big picture by forcing him to deal with little irritating issues, we are well on our way to seizing the upper hand.

In other words, keep your eyes on the prize.

Balance. The universe is a naturally self-balancing system. It rushes to fill a vacuum. It mercilessly thins any species that underestimates or overpopulates.

In Chinese Taoism, this is yin-yang, balance.

Traditional Chinese medicine uses this principle, going on the assumption that (dah!) a sick person either has too much of something, or else too little of something else.

Simple addition or subtraction.

The doctor either adds what is needed or else subtracts what is too abundant in the patient's life; redirecting the patient's bodily energy (chi) to or away from an affected area.

This same principle can be applied to warfare—military or mental.

Too much of my enemy is concentrated over here (either his physical troops or simply his attention), so I distract him by making a noise over there, and he immediately sends part of his troops to check out the noise. Throwing a pebble over his shoulder . . . heh-heh-heh, the oldest trick in the book!

Judo is based on this very principle: He pushes, I pull. He pulls, I push. Either way, he fails.

> *"Dodge left, strike right. Dodge right, strike left. Fake an attack*
> *forward to cover your retreat. Pretend retreat . . . before springing*
> *forward with ferocity!"*
> **—Li Chung, eighth century**

Correspondence. Master Samurai Yagu Munenori (1571–1646) taught that winning a battle by commanding a great army is no different from winning a sword fight in one-on-one combat.

As above, so below. The rules governing the big also apply to the small and vice-versa. Go on the assumption that all things are connected.

While particular correspondences and connections might not immediately be apparent in all situations, they do exist, and discovering these hidden connections—a previously unknown weakness?—provides just the edge you need to overcome your foe. (See also Lung and Prowant, 2001.)

*"Steadfast as Earth, I await the enemy's movement. When he
moves, I flow into him like Water, I strike and consume him
like Fire!"*
—T'ai Li'ang, 374 BCE

K'ung Ming

Sun Tzu's strategy proved its worth during China's Warring States Period
(453–221 BCE). As the name implies, this was a time of chaos and cruelty,
ambition and atrocity, yet a time that nonetheless stimulated not only the
Chinese art of war, but Chinese culture as a whole.

Such is the nature of struggle and strife. Shades of Nietzsche: What
doesn't destroy me makes me stronger! The heavier the burden, the more
the muscle grows. The more unforgiving the whetstone, the better the blade
benefits. The harder the times, the more hardy the heroes have to be.

The fall of Rome, the Crusades (World War I), the War Between the
States, World Wars II (1914) and III (1940) . . . and 9/11. Tumultuous times
test our mettle . . . and our metal.

One such period in China's history followed the fall of the Han Dynasty
in 220 CE, when China was split into the warring kingdoms of *Shu*, *Wu*, and
Wei.

The daring darling of this age was *K'ung Ming*, of Shu. Also known as
Chuko Liang, K'ung Ming was a wily young warrior who outwitted and out-
lasted most of his rivals to become a great general and scholar in later years.

Part Robin Hood, part Rommel, an obvious student of Sun Tzu, K'ung
Ming's life was novelized in the 1400s in Kuan Chung's epic *A Tale of Three
Kingdoms* as part history, part teaching metaphor. For example:

One of K'ung Ming's earliest triumphs was against another notable
strategist, *Cao Cao* when Wei armies were sweeping over Shu. (More on *Cao
Cao* in a minute.)

In expectation of battle, the Shu and Wei armies were camped on opposite sides of a wide river.

When 10,000 arrows scheduled to be delivered to the Shu army failed
to arrive, the commander of Shu was ready to retreat until young warrior
K'ung Ming comes up with an audacious plan to collect the arrows needed.

That night, as a thick fog rolled in blanketing both sides of the river,
Wei sentries were suddenly alarmed by the sound of boats moving on the

river. Convinced Shu forces were attempting a surprise attack, Wei archers all began firing towards the sound of the approaching enemy boats, exhausting all their arrows before their commanders could stop them.

On the other side of the river, the Shu commander slapped K'ung Ming on the back as they watched Shu troops pulling back their unmanned boats, boats all linked together with rope, each boat piled high with bales of straw, all the bales of straw now bristling with 10,000 reusable arrows "donated" by their enemy!

This ploy was not a matter of chance on K'ung Ming's part, rather it was a matter of prior study. Remember: Chance favors the prepared mind.

In anticipation of fording, K'ung Ming had studied the river, marking its currents and—like any warrior worth his salt—was already an accomplished meteorologist, and so knew the night would belong to fog.

More important, though still young, K'ung Ming already knew human nature.

Listening to the boisterous enemy camp across the way, K'ung Ming had recalled Sun Tzu's observation: "When the enemy's night camp is noisy, it is because he is fearful" (*The Art of War*, IX:36).

Armed with this knowledge, K'ung Ming reasoned that Wei commanders would be unable to prevent their frightened soldiers from firing all their arrows—that is, even if Wei commanders realized the trick in time.

K'ung Ming's ploy also echoes another of Sun Tzu's commands, whether we interpret it figuratively or literally: "A wise general's troops feed on the enemy."

Promoted for his ingenuity, K'ung Ming was put in command of a small force sent to prepare the defense of the walled city of Hsi.

Yet no sooner did K'ung Ming arrive at Hsi than he learned that a large Wei force, commanded by General *Ssuma Yi* was on their way to take the city. Realizing there was no possibility Shu reinforcements would arrive in time, K'ung Ming inexplicably orders what few troops he has into the hills as he prepares to meet the enemy alone!

When Ssuma Yi arrives he is shocked to discover the gates of Hsi wide open. On closer examination, he spies K'ung Ming sitting atop the city's wide wall, dressed not in armor but in a comfortable robe, playing the lute for a pair of giggling girls.

Alarmed, suspecting a trap designed to lure him into an undefended city, Ssuma Yi immediately orders his force to bypass Hsi.

K'ung Ming smiles as he watches the Wei army head off into the hills, where he knows they will have to thin out their ranks in order to pass through a narrow canyon . . . where K'ung Ming's own smaller force waits in ambush*

Unfortunately for Shu, K'ung Ming was not commanding Shu forces when the commander of Wu tricked the commander of Shu by dressing condemned prisoners up in Wu uniforms, and making them cut their own throats in a successful bid to terrorize Shu troops (see Lung and Prowant, 2001:38).

The Martial King

"In war it is best to attack minds not cities. Psychological warfare is better than fighting with weapons."
—Mao Tse-tung

Cao Cao (also written Ts'ao Ts'ao), the most famous general of the Three Kingdoms Period, lived from 155 to 220 and was not only the contemporary of K'ung Ming, but his rival and equal as well.

First and foremost, like Sun Tzu before him, Cao Cao preferred to avoid bloodshed, declaring that one should, "Fight only as a last resort." But, when conflict was unavoidable, one must "Let your enemy create your victory."

To accomplish this Cao Cao's main maxim was clear: "Nothing is constant in war save deception and cunning. Herein lies the true Way."

Cao Cao is quick to point out that there is no one hard and fast rule for accomplishing victory, since the dynamics of war were constantly shifting: "Just as water has no constant form, so too war has no constant dynamic. As water adapts to each vase, so too those adept at war adopt an attitude of flexibility, thus adapting to flux and circumstance. So much of this cannot be known in advance but must be judged on the spot with a practiced eye."

The only constant in Cao Cao's world was getting to the party before your foe.

Cao Cao was famed (feared!) for how fast he could get the lead out, arriving at the scene of battle before his enemies ever suspected his army was on the move. His philosophy was simple: "Make a show of being far away . . . then march with all haste to arrive before the enemy even suspects you are

---

*A variation of following Sun Tzu's advice to "Always leave an enemy a way out" is that you can leave them a way out, straight into your ambush!

on the move! Choosing a circuitous route that gives the illusion it requires a great distance to travel, even when you start out after the enemy does, so long as you calculate correctly, you can still arrive before your enemy."

Cao Cao was renowned for this, so much so that a superstition sprang up among his (ever dwindling!) circle of enemies: "Never speak Cao Cao's name lest that old dragon appear!" This is similar to the Western adage-cum-susperstition: "Never speak a demon's name lest he appear!"

In this respect, Cao Cao shared the philosophy of Confederate General Nathan Bedford Forrest, who, when pressed for the "secret" of his winning battle after battle, snapped: "It's whoever arrives *first* with the *most!*"

When actual warfare was unavoidable, Cao Cao did his best to acquire as extensive intelligence on his enemies as possible, employing *Lin Kuei* spies to gather intelligence, while sending other spies to act as agents provocateur, to "split the enemy's forces" by sowing dissent and confusion.

And, while Cao Cao literally made the "rules" when it came to combat, when time and clime—circumstance and happenstance—demanded, he could just as quickly discard the rules in favor of some unorthodox and unexpected maneuver designed to bring him victory.

For example, although Cao Cao tells us, "Do not call up your army in bitter winter nor in blistering summer, since it is too much of a hardship on the common people," he himself successfully attacked the state of Wu in the dead of winter.

Another time however, Cao Cao literally signed his own death warrant after he inadvertently tramped down a farmer's crops, this after having given his men express orders to leave the farmer's land unmolested. Only after much pleading—and a near mutiny by his troops—Cao Cao finally gave in and instead cut off his hair as punishment.*

Cao Cao used his Black Science not only on his enemies but, when need be, on his own troops:

When it was reported to Cao Cao that the army's supply of grain had been allowed to run dangerously low, Cao Cao called for his chief supply officer, Wang Hou. "There is something I need from you," Cao Cao told the officer. "Something necessary to reassure the men what we have not neglected them." "Whatever my Lord needs, I will gladly give," Wang bowed.

---

*Cutting off one's hair in ancient China was a serious punishment since many Chinese wore their hair long in a queue in the belief that, upon their deaths, the gods, or the Celestial Buddha would lift them up to Heaven by their pigtail.

Without another word, Cao Cao drew his sword and decapitated the man! He then placed Wang's head on a pole to which he attached a sign which simply read, "Wang Hou, Granary Officer." In this way all Cao Cao troops saw that the officer they believed responsible for their hunger had been punished by their beloved General.

Like all craftsmen, Cao Cao knew the importance of respecting your tools of the trade. Cao Cao's craft and trade was war, his loyal troops, the tools of his trade. Still, he was also smart enough to have created the idea of need to know: "The troops can share in the joy of a successfully executed campaign, but not in the pain of its conception."

Of course, Cao Cao saved his best tricks for his enemies: playing on their weaknesses or, as he put it: "I let my enemies create my victories."

Once, finding his smaller force trapped in a narrow canyon, enemies at both ends, Cao Cao had his men dig holes into the side of the canyon walls then, leaving half his men hiding inside these holes, he boldly advanced to attack the enemy at the far end of the canyon. Seeing his advance, the enemy force behind quickly rushed into the canyon, intent on attacking Cao Cao's exposed rear.

But no sooner had they passed the men Cao Cao had hidden inside the canyon walls than those men fell in behind them and attacked the enemy's rear! Cao Cao then suddenly turned his own troops back, crushing the trapped enemy between the two halves of his forces.

The enemy at the far end of the canyon was so stunned by this turnabout that not only did they fail to rally to the aid of their trapped allies but, in panic, they fled!

According to Cao Cao, there are five virtues a general must possess: wisdom, integrity, compassion, courage, and severity. Compare these with Sun Tzu, chapter I, verse 7.

If these are the five *virtues*, then the negative attributes we want to look for (and eventually find a way to exploit!) in our enemies must be their *opposites*:

wisdom	ignorance
integrity	treachery
compassion	ruthlessness/hatred
courage	cowardice/fear (one of the five "FLAGS")
severity	sympathy (another one of the five "FLAGS")

In the end, Cao Cao's credits reach far beyond the battlefield.

Cao Cao stands accused of rewriting Sun Tzu's *Ping Fa*. Whether or not this is true, he does get the credit for breaking Sun Tzu's *Art of War* down into its present thirteen chapters. He also is credited with creating (or at least honing) a form of unarmed combat *wu shu*, which incorporated the practical lessons he'd learned on the battlefield. Nowadays this martial art is referred to as "Iron Wall Kung-fu."

Eventually Cao Cao became king of the Wei state and was dubbed the "martial King" for his undisputed mastery of the art of war. Later his son would one day become Emperor and declare his father to be *T'ai Tzu*, literally "respected founder" of the Wei Dynasty.

Chinese Face-Reading

> *"The human face contains a world of secrets."*
> —Henry Linn, *What Your Face Reveals*

By now there should be no doubt in your mind that developing an ability to read the intent and intrigue written in another's face often spells the difference between kissing Victory's lips or kissing your enemy's ass!

In wartime, anticipating the movement of 10,000 enemy troops often comes down to correctly reading the face of a single enemy commander, or reading the truthfulness on the face of a captured spy who's being vigorously . . . questioned. (See *Theatre of Hell: Dr. Lung's Complete Guide to Torture*, 2003.)

Whether trying to read the faces sitting around you at the Saturday night Texas Hold 'em table, or the face of the shyster across from you at the negotiation table, whether your goal is to get your blood enemy to drop his guard, or just getting some fine filly to lower her standards, by now you are literate enough in Black Science and mind control to be able to read the tells and twitches on another's face that all too often betray hidden anxiety or duplicity. (See Figure 18, p. 94.)

The Chinese, however, take the skill of face-reading to a whole new level, claiming to be able to tell not only a person's personality by the shape and features of the face, but also to be able to determine that person's past, present, and even their future.

As you can tell, this form of physiognomy goes far beyond just noticing that bead of sweat on another gambler's upper lip. According to the Chinese, one's face changes with one's mind. Good deeds and good intentions can bring about positive changes in your *joss* (luck, fate, karma) and this will be reflected in your face. Bad deeds and malicious intentions, on the other hand, cause correspondingly unfortunate changes that will also show up on your face. (Maybe someone should have told Dorian Gray!)

Siang Mien, the Chinese "art of face-reading," goes back thousands of years and is one of the oldest professions in China. In a culture that still places high values on precognitive insights, abilities, and arts (e.g., astrology, numerology), face-reading has always been popular, especially among the aristocracy. It's no secret that more than once Siang Mien has chosen the emperor of China.

Though banned along with other feudal superstitions, when the Communists came to power in China, face-reading has remained popular down to the present day. Despite the ban, it was common knowledge that high-ranking Communists, including Mao himself, remained firm believers in the art.

Gui Gu-Tze, from the Warring States Period, is considered the "Father of Chinese face-reading." Author of the classic face-reading text *Xiang Bian Wei Mang* (250 BCE), Gui Gu-Tze was also a great philosopher and educator. Coincidentally, one of his students was *Sun Bin*, author of *The Lost Art of War* and a direct descendent of Sun Tzu.

Gui Gu-Tze undoubtedly gleaned his information from both personal observation and calculation and from foreign sources like ancient texts on face-reading imported from places like Tibet and India. For example, the *Kama Sutra* instructs in the art of knowing the character of a man from his features. (Lung and Prowant, 2001:65).

Two respected Chinese pseudosciences are also known to have influenced Gui Gu-Tze: The first was the *I-Ching*, an ancient system of divination traced back to the twelfth century BCE, called possibly the oldest book in the world (Linn, 1999:9).

The second obvious Chinese influence on Gui Gu-Tze was the Taoist theory of *Wu-hsing*, the "Five Elements" (see Lung and Prowant, 2001:31).

According to *Wu-hsing*, all things and situations are constructed from five "elements": Fire, Water, Earth, Wood (also called Void), and Metal (also called Wind). In each instance, one of these elements is dominant. These elements either compliment or cancel out one another.

Like so many other superstitions, pseudosciences, and just down-right silliness in life, it doesn't matter whether you personally believe in the art of face-reading or not. So long as whomever you are dealing with believes in it, it will affect you. So it behooves us to at least familiarize ourselves with the art. Those believing in this system might use it to prejudge you, to stereotype you the minute you walk through the door from something so simple as the shape of your face.

Never forget that beliefs—no matter how bizarre and unproven—will always find adherents. And belief is more powerful than reality. (9/11.)

As to the future of face-reading, it remains alive and well throughout the East. According to Linn (1999): "Without a doubt, the fascinating art of face reading will continue to play a significant role in the political, social, cultural, and personal events in China for a promising future in the personnel and strategic decision-making processes of both private corporations and government agencies throughout the world" (page 8).

Any chance face-reading might fall out of favor in this technological age? No way. As popular as ever in the East, face-reading continues to grow in popularity in the West, where computer software has already been developed that blends the ancient art of face reading with modern high-tech Biometrics.

The following low-tech face-reading technique will help you determine if someone is lying to you: You already know you can spot a laughing liar when his eyes don't match his smiling lips. By using your thumb (or a playing card, etc.) to surreptitiously block out the lower part of his face—his smiling mouth—you can see if his eyes match his lips.

In the same way, according to Siang Mien, the left side of the human face is yang (male, conscious), while the right side is yin (female, subconscious). As a result, the two halves are not always in agreement. By obscuring one side of a person's face, you can see when the two sides are not in agreement (i.e., one side will actually look like it is slightly frowning), indicating that, at the very least, that person has doubts about what they are saying.

SAMURAI SLY

"When you cannot be deceived by men you will have realized the wisdom of strategy."
—Miyamoto Musashi

Everyone knows samurai have nothing in common with ninja. Samurai were guided by *Bushido*, a strict code of conduct and chivalry requiring them to meet other Samurai face-to-face on a brightly lit field of combat.

Ninja, on the other hand, are the ones who put the "dead" in "the dead of night." Their only code is "*Masakatsu!*" whatever works—fighting face-to-face, going toe-to-toe, with a foe only when left no choice.

The underhanded tactics of the Ninja were so anathema to the Samurai ideal of honorable comportment and confrontation that one samurai *shogun* banned even the speaking of the word *ninja* (lit. "one who sneaks in") under penalty of death. Yet it's common knowledge many medieval ninja clans were founded by *ronin* samurai. And, quiet as it's kept, even "respectable" samurai were not above using the occasional ninja trick or two.

When a samurai used ninja tactics and succeeded, he went down in history as a brilliant and unconventional martial genius. When he failed, even after resorting to ninja tactics in desperation, he not only went down, but was also declared despicable for daring to trespass the sanctity of Code Bushido.

This same warrior's ideal versus practical strategy is found among the Norse. Even Norse Gods like Odin and Thor who, while preferring a fierce battle guaranteed to give them bragging rights in *Vahall*, won as many battles with Black Science (mind control) as with battle axe.

As we will see, some of Japan's most celebrated samurai not only used ninja tactics and technique, but more than one of these respected heroes are even credited with founding ninja schools of their own.*

Yoritomo's Art of Influence

> *"To influence others! What a marvelous gift, and what assured*
> *success to him that possesses it!"*
> —B. Dangennes

Around 762 CE a specialized cadre of knights was commissioned in Japan. Drawn from well-to-do families and known as *Kondei* ("Stalwart youth"), they were the first *samurai*. Up till this time, the Japanese army had been made up mainly of spear-wielding foot soldiers but these new samurai preferred the sword, blatant symbol of both their rank and their willingness to do bodily harm at the least trespass. Their code was Bushido, "The Way (do) of the Warrior (*bushi*)."

---

*(Dis)honorable mention goes to Hideyoshi Toyotomi, a commoner—not even born a samurai!—who in the 1500s used his ninja technique to become the undisputed ruler of Japan (Lung and Prowant, 2000:8).

When not busy protecting the realm from real and imagined threats, Samurai clan leaders (*Daimyo*) entertained themselves by manufacturing reasons to go to war against rival samurai clans. Finally in 1192, Yoritomo, Daimyo of the *Minamoto* clan, succeeded in beating down his rivals to become Japan's first *shogun*. Where so many would-be warlords before him had failed, Yoritomo succeeded by employing a bellicose balance of blade and Black Science.

Yoritomo was aided in his conquest by his younger brother *Yoshitsune*, later credited with founding the *Karuma-hachi-ryu*, a martial arts school that specialized in teaching guerrilla (ninja) tactics to Minamoto troops.

Legend says Yoshitsune learned his unorthodox martial arts from half-human/half-crow forest demons known as *Tenqu*; a thinly disguised reference to the *Shinobi* ninja clans who lived in Japan's central forest and who lent their lethal expertise to the Minamoto cause.

Given Yoritomo's ruthlessness, it is hardly surprising he would stoop so low as to ally himself with hated ninja. In order to swell his ranks, Yoritomo even knighted samurai from the "barbarian" *Ainu* (lit. "Hairy ones"), the original Caucasian inhabitants of the Japanese islands (cf. "Samurai Anthropologist", in *Discover* magazine, September, 1989).

Despite his great accomplishments, Yoritomo has gone down in history as the Stalin of his day—a ruthless and paranoid dictator who no sooner seized power by crushing his present enemies, when he began settling scores with all past foes. He settled these scores all the while compiling a list of anyone he suspected might be a future threat—including his brother Yoshitsune, whom Yoritomo rightly or wrongly accused of plotting a coup.

Yoshitsune prudently escaped to become the stuff of legend, eventually becoming Japan's version of Robin Hood. And like Stalin, Yoritomo outlived his enemies. Ironically the warlord who finally succeeded in bridling Japan, died mundanely after a fall from his horse.

While moralists belittle Yoritomo's accomplishments by maintaining he slaughtered his way to power, and then hung on to that power by making regular—swift, sure, and sanguine!—examples of any who opposed him, the truth is Yoritomo used diplomacy just as often as he did decapitation.

Like many conquerors, Yoritomo discovered that conquest is easy, control is not. Early on he realized that the key to both conquest and control over individual and empire lay in one's ability to exert influence. Influence is simply when we succeed in substituting our will for that of others.

Yoritomo's thoughts and techniques for mastering the "art of influence" were rendered into English, via the voice of his "translator/interpreter" B. Dangennes, in 1916.

Yoritomo exposes twelve ways we can increase our "influence" and, thereby, our personal power:

Increasing our pyschic forces. Psychic forces is a synonym for "mental ability and agility" e.g., our powers of perception, concentration, and decision making. Yoritomo maintains that all individuals have an innate need for what he calls the "perpetual pursuit of the highest," a desire to strive to be the best we can be, to experience and express ourselves fully.

> *"The struggle for life becomes more and more arduous, and the*
> *power of our hidden faculties should expand in accordance with*
> *ever-growing necessities."*
> **—Dangennes, in Taishi Yoritomo, *Influence***

Seven hundred years later, on the other side of the world, Nietzsche called this same innate urge the "will to power."

Failing to live up to our potential, either because of our own indolence or because of deliberate interference from our enemies, is the cause of that vague feeling of dissatisfaction so many of us carry around in the back of our mind . . . feelings of dissatisfaction an alert and adroit enemy can all too easily encourage into more and even more self-destructive feelings of doubt, defeatism, and self-loathing. Of course, we can do the same to our enemy!

Thus, the first step to increasing our influence—if only to protect ourselves—is to develop and make full use of our mental abilities. Remember: It's a myth—and an excuse!—that we only use 10 percent of our brain. But it is true the average person only uses their brains 10 percent efficiently.

The "cure" for this? Simple: *Refuse to be "average"!*

Increase your psychic forces, your mental abilities, and thereby increase your power of influence over others. For what good is it to cultivate a fine vine if it bears no wine:

> *"Opinions are powerless so long as they only confuse the brain*
> *without arming the hand."*
> **—Joseph von Hammer, *History of the Assassins*,**

By persuasion. Exercising influence by persuasion entails subtlety, bringing ourselves more into synch with another person in order to nudge them in the direction and into the deeds we desire.

Yoritomo provides four guidelines for persuading others:

1. Banish suspicion by establishing trust with them. (See *The Art of Lying*, in chapter 5.)
2. Learn how to listen, both to what others are saying (consciously and unconsciously) and to what they aren't saying. Is this not the bread and butter of mind control?
3. Don't browbeat.
4. At least pretend to share their sympathies. Sympathy being one of the warning FLAGS.

By influence of the eyes. From that stern look of reproach from parents and teachers we're taught to cringe from as children, to alluring, wallet-draining looks cast by fashion models, to the will-sapping gaze of Rasputin and Charlie Manson, our eyes hold the power to scold, seduce, and stupefy.

In *Black Science* (Lung and Prowant, 2001), we learned the importance of making eye contact as well as how to read a person's eyes in order to tell when they're lying through their teeth (see page 70 of the book).

> *"Few persons escape the influence of the human eye. If its look is imperious, it subjugates; if it is tender, it moves; if it is sad it penetrates the heart with melancholy."*
> —**Dangennes, in Taishi Yoritomo,** *Influence*

Yoritomo says we can take this to the next level by enveloping the ability to influence (communicate) with our eyes; allowing our emotions—sincere or feigned—to freely flow from our eyes. This means not only developing a forceful, dominating stare guaranteed to stop someone in their tracks, but also mastering those sincere, compassionate, and caring looks that are the key to unlocking the heart of another.

That with a mere look we can influence another isn't in dispute:

- Eyes downcast tell people we're sub-servient . . . and no threat.
- Eyes demurely turned aside tells a person you're modest . . . and maybe a little bit shy. (Guys take note, gals *love* it when you do this!)

- Eyes wide means very interested.
- A surreptitious, single wink instantly makes someone our accomplice.
- A smiling wink can stir thoughts of passion.

Thus, with a single practiced glance we can show approval or sow confusion, incite passion or instill paranoia; a single look, influencing both friend and foe for thrill or ill.

By words and speech. Yoritomo advised us to keep it short and sweet, warning that "Too great wealth of words is hostile to conviction."

> *"The word is the most direct manifestation of thought; hence it is one of the most important agents of Influence when it clothes itself with precision and clearness, indispensable in cooperating in creating conviction in the minds of one's hearers."*
> —Dangennes, in Taishi Yoritomo, *Influence*

Yoritomo was not only ahead of his time in understanding the value of concise propaganda, but, if Dangennes can be taken at face value, Yoritomo (1916) may well have invented the idea of countering short attention span syndrome with a well-crafted sound byte: "Those that know how to present their thought in a few phrases, in a way that impresses itself on their listeners, may easily become leaders of the masses" (page 62).

Yoritomo's method for creating simple and effective messages is, first, *think deeply* on what we want to say beforehand, then *transform our thoughts into images*. When crafting these images, Yoritomo advises we (1) use incisive words that (2) draw mental pictures, we can easily implant, (3) images that will take root in our listeners' mind. We are then free to project these images into the minds of others using what Yoritomo calls "the form of lights and shades," that is, openness when appropriate, subterfuge when expedient, as suits situation and temperament.

Yoritomo's Rules of Speech:

- Speak with conciseness
- Speak with clearness
- Speak with moderation
- Speak with discretion Says Yoritomo: "From indiscretion to lying the step is short . . ."

Yoritomo also said: "Speech is the distributor of the thoughts that surround us, of which the reiterated suggestions, after impregnating certain groups of cells in our brain, travel by affinity to haunt the same group of brain-cells in other auditors" (page 65).

By Example. J. Paul Getty once said: "No psychological weapon is more potent than example." In other words, you're known by the company you keep.

> *"Our most frequent associations are never indifferent to our mentality, and we always submit, voluntarily or unconsciously, to the ascendancy of those that surrounds us, unless we have sufficient influence over their minds to compel them to submit themselves to us."*
> —Dangennes, in Taishi Yoritomo, *Influence*

We influence those around us, or they influence us. (And you thought you could stop worrying about peer pressure when you graduated from high school!) Sometimes those around us form a positive support network, one that strengthens us by stimulating our imagination and challenging our abilities—making us better people.

On the other hand, our association can be negative, we can find ourselves trapped in toxic relationships, surrounded by vampires who drain our life's blood while they ravage our precious resources (see *Shadow Warriors*, later).

It's been said you can't teach what you don't know, and you can't lead where you don't go . . . *Sure you can!* Political leaders no longer fight beside the troops they send to die in foreign lands, and high school coaches are often called to substitute for the algebra teacher. In a pinch, you "fake it till you can make it" . . . or at least until you can make it out the door!

Tell the truth, would you really be surprised to find out that, in most situations, most people don't have a clue what the Hell they're doing? That's why they're so relieved when some take-charge guy shows up that seems to know what's going on . . . someone willing to *take responsibility* off them (i.e., to take the weight of making decisions at the risk of later being blamed when it all goes horribly wrong!).

Chapter one/verse one from "*The Cult Leader's Bible*" reads: Relieve the sheep of any responsibility (i.e. fear of future guilt/blame), and make them *believe* you know what you're doing, and they'll follow you anywhere! (Did you notice you can't write *relieve* or *believe* without sticking a "lie" smack dab in the middle? heh-heh-heh.) We lead by example. We teach by example. And we learn by example—often without being consciously aware of it.

Nothing inspires the faint of heart so much as seeing the example of someone else stand up against impossible odds, boldly defying the merciless juggernaut (Gary Cooper in *High Noon*, 1952). And who can forget the image of that lone, June, 1989, prodemocracy demonstrator defiantly holding his ground in front of an advancing line of Chinese tanks?

Of course politicians and cult leaders are quite adept at manufacturing convenient enemies for them to take a stand against, inspiring their followers by their heroic example . . . inspiring those followers to dig deeper into their pockets.

> *"Ability and achievement are bonafides no one dares question, no matter how unconventional the man who presents them."*
> —J. Paul Getty

By psychic influences. Dangennes defined "psychic influences" thus: "It is the art of substituting for the want of resolution in others our own will, which they obey blindly, sometimes unconsciously, ever glad to feel themselves guided and directed by a moral power which they can not elicit in themselves" (in Yoritomo, 1916:82).

Yoritomo is careful to point out that this overpowering psychic influence is not some magical force, nor is it outright hypnosis—though, as a student of Black Science, you'll quickly spot elements of true hypnosis technique in it (Lung and Prowant, 2000:89). Yoritomo (1916) describes psychic influence as "an intensity of determination" that surges outward from us like a wave, to wash over and inundate the will of others:

> It is not necessary to have, as many pretend, recourse in magic in order to become past masters in the art of influencing our fellows; what is needed above all is to keep ourselves constantly in a condition of will-power sufficient to impose our commands on minds capable only of obedience. Intensity of determination, when it reaches a certain point, possesses a dazzling influence which few ordinary mortals can resist, for it envelops them before they are aware of it and thus before they have dreamt of endeavoring to withdraw themselves from it. (page 82)

By decision. Yoritomo continues: "You can thus instruct yourself in this art, so difficult and nevertheless so important, for the influence which he who is accustomed to wise and prompt decisions exerts over others is always considerable" (page 108).

We admire people who can make decisions. And we like others to see us as someone capable of making decisions. But studies show we also like others to make decisions for us, to take responsibility away from us. Sure, you are the exception. (Heh-heh-heh.)

The sorry fact is that most people are not very good at making decisions. The more things change . . . the more people stay the same.

Schools today teach regurgitation, not problem solving.

As a result, according to Yoritomo: "The majority of the irresolute love to deceive themselves by delusions which their imagination creates, and thus become only too often the architects of their own misfortune" (page 100).

That's why "Problem Solving 101" is a prerequisite for mind control:

- *Clearly define the problem.* Most people never get past this first step. When you fail to progress beyond this initial step, it's called "just bitching."
- *Brainstorm options.* Write down every possible solution no matter how seemingly farfetched. Don't stop until you come up with at least twelve options.
- *Prioritize options.* Cut your brainstormed options in half, keeping only those options with the most likelihood of success . . . now, cut them in half *again*.

Take the options you're left with (at least three) and put them in order of most likely, most do-able.

- *Implement your best option.* Just do it.
- *Adjust* to changing circumstance. If necessary, move on to your second option, and then your third, keeping those elements of options one and two that were at least viable in part.

Yoritomo adds that decisions should be made through use of:

- Reflection and concentration
- Presence of mind (awareness)
- Will (the determination to see a decision through)
- Energy (the strength to see a decision through)
- Impartiality (the ability to observe and decide objectively)

- A desire for justice, a quest for recompense, balance and completion (an idea expressed centuries after Yoritomo by the *Gestalt* school of psychology)
- Forethought, with an eye toward stopping problems before things get out of hand

(FYI: One man's desire for justice is another man's revenge!)

> *"The Master excels at resolving conflicts before they arise,*
> *conquering his enemies before they become threats."*
> —Tu Mu, 803–852 CE

To the indolent and the uninitiated, our foresight and forethought will make it look like we possess ESP. In less enlightened times, such free (*full*) thinkers were declared witches and blasphemers. How dare they challenge Court and Church by using more than 10 percent of their brain. Shame on you Galileo-Galilei, the pox upon you Giordano Bruno! Again, quoting Yoritomo (1916): "We should not confound forethought with the art of divination, although, in the eyes of the vulgar, it sometimes takes on the appearance of it" (page 101).

You've already figured how using your five senses to their fullest can easily be mistaken by some for your having a magical sixth sense. We are cautioned not to take advantage of this unforeseen consequence (or boon?).

According to E. B. Condillac (1715–1780):

He who would influence others should above all things know how to influence himself in order to acquire the faculty of self-concentration which will allow of his reaching the highest degree of discernment. Many soothsayers have owed their influence over the multitude only to that spirit of concentrations that passed for prophecies. It is wrong and delusive to give credence to magic which is trickery, but we bear within us a power equal to that of the sorcerers whose deeds are related; this is the magic of the influence which the prudent and self-possessed man always exercises over his fellows.

Of course, you would never personally be tempted to take advantage of such a misperception (naivety, stupidity) on the part of others. (Heh-heh-heh.)

On the other hand, it could work to your advantage if your mark/target/enemy believes you possess the power to read his thoughts, to anticipate his every move. One man's superstition is another man's salvation. A man's superstition is often the best—and easiest!—cross to nail him to. (See *Kyonin-No-Jutsu*, Lung and Prowant, 2001:76.)

By ambition. Joseph Von Hammer (1935) said: "It is nothing to the ambitious man what people may believe, but it is everything to know how he may turn them for the execution of his projects." It used to be a good thing to be called "a real go-getter." But nowadays, if you're caught trying to get ahead—to better yourself—you're all too often accused of trying to be better than the next guy (or gal). Furthermore, in today's politically correct circus, that means you're somehow inherently racist, sexist, or otherwise chauvinistic in some way.

Nowadays, *ambition* is quickly becoming a dirty word. But, back in his day, Yoritomo saw ambition as a good thing: "It is by believing steadfastly that we shall attain the highest power, that we shall acquire the qualities that make a man almost more than man, since they allow him to govern and subdue those by whom he is surrounded" (page 43).

Yoritomo goes on to give two examples how ambition helps produce influence:

First, ambition shows courage and boldness, making us an example to others. Second, ambition overcomes poverty. Says Yoritomo: "Poverty is only allowable if it is voluntary, that is to say, if it is the result of a decision which prefers that condition to another more brilliant but less independent . . . Nevertheless, riches are the key of many marvels and they are above all the key of many influences" (page 125).

While running after riches in and of itself is not an exalted ideal, being rich has several benefits beyond just being the concrete evidence of our ability to map out a campaign—be it military or monetary—and see it through to success. Riches give us power that can be used to help others, as well as a means of exciting interest and influencing the multitude. And, in the end, that's what it's all about: the power to influence.

Yoritomo has the last and lasting word when it comes to amassing wealth, stating a universal truth, as obvious in his day as it still is in ours: "the poor man exercises little influence over the multitude" (page 122).

Yoritomo also warns that our ambition should be without false modesty, without unworthy means, and without intrigue and illusion, as these are all flaws in character an alert enemy can all too easily exploit. While, ideally, our ambition should be free from intrigue, the success of one inevitably engenders the envy and enmity of the many.

How does "a man of Influence" deal with his enemies?

According to Dangennes, in Yoritomo (1916): "He lifts his eyes too high to recognize the vulgar herd of envious who swarm around his feet, he is content to spurn them with the tip of his shoe; unless, overmuch beset or tormented by their incessant attacks, he crushes them under foot, as we do with an importune insect, which we try at first to drive away and which we destroy, without ill feeling, simply to rid ourselves of its repeated and irritating stings" (page 121).

What was it Machiavelli said about enemies? Either leave them be . . . or else utterly crush them underfoot!

Having invested our time and effort into mastering this art of influence, should we then feel guilty when we find we can so easily exercise this power of influence over others, or for that matter when we employ any Black Science (mind-control) tactic to give us the edge needed to accomplish our goals? Should the patient and alert tiger feel guilty for snatching the distracted chimp who has strayed too far from the tree. Should a ditch digger sweating all week to provide for his family feel guilty when he picks up his paycheck? Should the graduate feel guilty when he is finally handed his scroll and key?

Two men offered equal blades, one whittles a whistle to amuse himself and annoy the rest of us, while the other adroitly wields that steel to carve himself a future. Yoritomo puts it this way: "As for those in whose minds we substitute our own will for that which they tend to manifest, they are generally dull or frankly vicious souls, who combine with their natural defects a kind of moral weakness, which renders them accessible to outside influence" (page 92).

Compare Yoritomo's ruthless (or is that refreshing?) attitude toward what he elsewhere refers to as "slow-moving minds" to what another Black Science adept wrote 600 years later. In 1795 Marquis de Sade wrote: "As to those susceptible souls who might be 'corrupted' by exposure to my writings, I say, so much the worse for them."

In the East they call this karma. In the West, they simply say you get what you got coming, you get what your hand calls for.

"It is not given to all to possess in themselves the aggressive spirit necessary to command the influences which must emanate from our brain in order to result in forming the convictions of others."
—Taishi Yoritomo

By perseverance. Yoritomo said: "For perseverance is the mother of many gifts; from her is born circumspection which clasps hands with application and patience" (page 129).

Dangennes, in Yoritomo (1916), defines perseverance as "the slow but sure accent toward a goal that assumes a more definite shape the nearer we approach it" (page 128).

Think of "perseverance" as synonymous with persistence, yet antonym to pest. Being persistent pays off. Being a pest just pisses people off. (See Types of No/The Art of No-gotiation, chapter 5.) By perseverance, we complete the quest undertaken. This success, in turn, breeds influence, not only in the form of concrete reward (wealth, etc.) but also in the awe and admiration and, yes, envy we receive from others.

When people view us as someone who perseveres until the job gets done, they see a dependable leader they'll gladly follow down any road . . . and a dangerous enemy whose path they are loathe to cross. In this tepid age, when we stay the course, when we doggedly persevere (or can hoodwink others into believing we do), we evoke more respect—we exercise more influence—than our "half-ass'n" competition. We persevere by simply going forward. Over obstacles, around obstacles, under them; using any and all means at our disposal to accomplish our goal. Step-by-step . . . Masakatsu!

To quote Yoritomo: "Every work is made up of a chain of acts more or less infinitesimal; the perfection of each of them contributes to that of the whole" (page 145). He also said (page 128): "Few persons are born with a silver spoon in their mouths, but everybody can aim at conquering fortune by a series of continual and rational efforts. . . . The man who would spring up thirty cubits at a single leap would spend his life in ridiculous attempts, but if he wishes steadily to mount the steps that lead him to that height, he will attain it, sooner or later, according to the dexterity, the agility, and the perseverance which he displays."

By concentration. According to Yoritomo (1916): "Without concentration, no success is possible" (page 141). *Concentration*, synonymous with *mindfulness*, is the next-to-last step on Buddha's "Noble Eight-fold Path" that leads us to enlightenment.

In Buddhism, mindfulness/concentration manifests in practice as mediation, and is the core of the Zen (Ch. Ch'an) branch of Buddhism that came to be favored by the samurai. Zen emphasis on developing powers of concentration fit perfectly with the samurai way of life, where the already thin line between life and death must be walked daily.

Even when only training in the *dojo*, the least lapse in a Samurai's concentration could mean serious injury, let alone what could happen on the open battlefield.

In any field of endeavor, from digging ditches to digging up dirt on our foe, lack of concentration is enemy number one:

> *"If we reflect well on it, we shall see that most of our troubles can*
> *be set down to carelessness."*
> —Taishi Yoritomo

Consequently, those who do not take the time to develop their powers of concentration, those who allow their concentration to waver, and those whose concentration *we* purposely and successfully break, are already lost. Quoting Yoritomo again: "[They] can only with difficulty concentrate themselves on a task that requires a little application; they are the slaves of the instability of their impressions; beginnings, however arduous, always find them full of enthusiasm, but this fervor soon grows cold, and if success does not present itself immediately they will hasten to give up their project and devote themselves to another which will soon have a like ending" (page 134).

By confidence. There are two types of confidence: Confidence we actually have and confidence we pretend to have. Any show of confidence, real or successfully acted can impress (influence) others.

> *"Confidence is the foundation of courage and the*
> *mainspring of action."*
> —Taishi Yoritomo

Confidence wins people over. That's why Dangennes calls *confidence* the "mother of conversion." Our show of confidence inspires others, either through their corresponding confidence (belief) in us, or the confidence we instill (plant) in them by convincing them they can succeed too. Proviso, Dangennes, in Yoritomo (1916): "In order to implant it in the heart of others, it is necessary to possess it—this splendid confidence in ourselves which works wonders" (page 170).

We gain confidence by simply trying. Not necessarily by succeeding. To muster up the courage to initially try an unknown takes more effort than continuing on after a failure. This is why our enemy's dreams must be discouraged (and when need be crushed!) before he can take that first—most frightening—step that, win or lose, will fill him with the confidence to take future steps . . . in our direction!

By sympathy. For Yoritomo, *sympathy* isn't a synonym for *pity.* Rather, he uses it to mean "getting in sync" with others, particularly with our target. This action begins with simple verbal and physical mirroring and progresses to psychological sync where we express the same attitude and beliefs as our mark does.

When people believe we feel as they do, that we identify with them, it gives them the confidence they need to open up to us, opening the door to what Dangennes calls "beneficent suggestion" (page 179).

Having established sympathy, we can then exercise our newfound influence to gently lead them in the direction we want. (See The Art of Seduction in chapter 5.)

> *"One of the secrets of dominating power lies in exciting similarity of feelings by adopting for the time being those which are within the compass of the person whom we wish to influence."*
> —Taishi Yoritomo

> *"Real influence over others is only acquired at the price of complete mastery of oneself."*
> —Dangennes, in Taishi Yoritomo, *Influence*

No-Sword, No-Mind

*"[Musashi's] Zen was godless. It was the Zen of the old
Samurai warriors who meditated to perfect their breathing and
most of all their sword stroke."*
—Bart Kosko, *Fuzzy Thinking*

During his violent life, Ben No Soke, better known as Miyamoto
Musashi (1594–1645) killed over a thousand men, over sixty of those during
personal duels, the rest while fighting in one of the six different wars he
fought in over the years. Though by the time of his death Musashi would be
universally acknowledged as *Kensai* "sword saint," the greatest swordsman
who ever lived in Japan, ironically Musashi defeated as many foes with his
brain as he did with his sword.

First, Musashi mastered the traditional single samurai long sword, before
then developing a style of fighting using two long swords, leading to the
founding of his Nitten-ruy, "Two Swords" school.

Not satisfied, Musashi continued to perfect his chosen *Do* ("way/path")
by mastering other samurai weapons—the bow, spear, and so on. Still not
satisfied, Musashi dared study forbidden ninja weapons.

Ever on guard against the unfamiliar, all too often we fall at the feet of
the familiar.

Musashi mastered *Kakushi-jutsu*, the ninja art of fighting with small, easily
concealed weapons while studying (and helping to found) the *Emmei-ryu*
"Clear Circle" school (cf. *Classical Budo* by Donn F. Draeger, Weatherhall
Press, 1973). Thus, Musashi killed men during full-scale battles, as well as his
scores of personal duels, using every conventional weapon of his day, as well
as using unconventional "environmental weapons" (e.g., his empty scabbard,
a dagger, a tree limb, an unstrung bow).

But always, no matter what the tool in Musashi's hand, he ultimately
defeated his foes first and foremost using Black Science (mind control), by
playing on their emotional weaknesses; bravado, anger, and confusion.

Two years before his death—from, believe it or not, old age!—Musashi
jotted down his thoughts, tactics, and techniques into his *Go Rin No Sho* "A
Book of Five Rings"; required reading for all serious students of the Black
Science. (And, yes, there will be a test on it . . . a test called life!)

The "five rings" part came from Musashi dividing his opus into "Ground"
(Earth), "Fire", "Wind" (aka Style), "Water", and "Void" (aka Wood), reflecting

each chapter's overall approach to strategy. (See Wu-Hsing in *Black Science*, Lung and Prowant, 2001.)

Though written 400 years ago, Musashi's *A Book of Five Rings* remains one of the greatest classics on warfare even written and is respectfully spoken of in the same breath as Sun Tzu's *Ping-fa*. Far from being an "outdated" manual on medieval sword fighting, *A Book of Five Rings* is recognized for its application to every realm of endeavor. Knowledgeable Japanese businessmen consult Musashi on a daily basis.

Musashi was one of the original "think outside the box" guys. Unfortunately not everyone takes the time to develop this skill. Thus, while many may appreciate Musashi, just as many run into the problem of how to practically apply Musashi; transferring his insights and instruction from battlefield blade combat to Black Science "mind control."

Musashi would say, "It's *all* brain combat!" All battles are first won in the mind.

Therefore, in developing our overall attitude, our strategy for life in general and special endeavors in particular, we must concentrate on developing what Musashi calls *Senki*, our "war-spirit." Senki includes, but it not confined to, our focus, our combination of concentration and determination.

Whatever the task at hand, we must focus on it with the same intensity as we would if facing a samurai in a life-and-death confrontation. As on the battlefield, so in the boardroom. On the battlefield, the least lapse in concentration—a faltering of our war-spirit—and we are treated to a quick death. As simple as that.

So, too, in the equally ruthless boardroom where a blink in our attention span at the wrong time and our fortune flies out the window—our world collapses and the next thing we know we're living in a cardboard box. Slow death. This is what Musashi means when he tells us that our "everyday stance" should be the same as our "martial stance."

Thus our war-spirit must be maintained at all times. Studying Musashi's teachings can help us develop this indomitable war-spirit.

Closely examining the *Go Rin No Sho* we notice five basic themes running through Musashi's strategy:

1. Become your enemy.
2. Upset your enemy's balance.
3. One equals 10,000,000.
4. Two swords are better than one.
5. No sword is better than two swords.

Become your enemy. Says Musashi, "To become the enemy means to think yourself in the enemy's position." This echoes Sun Tzu's dictum to "Know yourself and know your enemy, and in a thousand battles you'll never be defeated."

This is the number one principle, not just in battle, but in life as well. Likewise, this has echoes of Clauswitz's "No battle plan survives first contact with the enemy."

We whitewash over those parts of ourselves we don't want others to see, painting a grandiose portrait of ourselves and our motive (no matter how distorted and falsely colored!), a picture we proudly display to attract or intimidate others.

The enemy's job is to keep us from reading him like a comic book. All the while, we're trying to get a glimpse of our enemy's real face, knowing he too hides his true face behind the garishly painted and distracting fard and facade he displays to the world.

We want to discern his spirit and ". . . discover his resources. It is easy then to defeat him with a different method once you see his resources."

All the while following Musashi's admonition in his "Water" chapter: "Don't let the enemy see your spirit."

Upset your enemy's balance. I move my enemy. My enemy does not move me. Once we understand how our enemy thinks, we can take steps to unbalance him.

At the top of Musashi's list of ways to unbalance a foe are: danger, hardship, and surprise—all designed to induce what Kensei refers to as a "fluctuation of the enemy's spirit." In other words, throwing him off balance, preventing him from initiating or following through with his best laid plan.

In the chapter titled "Wind", Musashi tells us that, once we have succeeded in unbalancing our opponent we can then ". . . win by attacking the enemy when his spirit is warped." Musashi follows this up by pointing out how we can unbalance an opponent during one-on-one combat by frightening him with our body, our voice, and our sword.

It's not hard to see how these three can be applied to psychological combat as well: body language, ranging from the seductive to the intimidating; the right word dropped in the wrong ear at just the right time; that three feet of razor-edged steel we keep in the trunk of our car for cutting through . . . red tape (metaphorically speaking, of course).

Says Musashi: "Victory is certain when the enemy is caught up in a rhythm which confuses his spirit." That's our job.

Further along in this "Wind" chapter, Musashi gives us five ways of "moving an opponent's attitude" and unbalancing him:

1. Attack where his spirit is lax (e.g., exploit any sloth or lack of focus in your enemy). Create this condition when possible.
2. Throw him into confusion. Create this condition when possible.
3. Irritate him (through the use of anger and frustration). Create this condition when possible.
4. Terrify him. Fear is the first of the deadly warning FLAGS. Go out of your way to create this condition. Remember Machiavelli's advice that it is better (safer!) to be feared than loved.
5. Take advantage of the enemy's disrupted rhythm when he is unsettled.

One equals 10,000,000. For Musashi, the strategy of defeating one man in single combat is the same as defeating an army of men, and vice-versa: "The spirit of defeating a single man is the same for defeating ten million men."

Musashi is not alone in this assessment: "Winning a battle by commanding a great army should be no different from winning a sword fight in one-to-one combat" (Yagu Munenori, 1529–1646). This is an ancient concept: the idea that by studying some part of a thing, we can discern a larger pattern.

In Japan the saying goes, "The little Do leads to the big Do." *Do* in this case meaning "way," the path in life we follow. In other words, the essence and meaning of the universe at large can be apprehended through diligent attention to a little "do" (in this case *way* meaning a discipline such as a martial art or some other art or craft).

Whether a swordfight or a contest of wills, noticing minute flaws of movement and motivation, thought and action, is the key to finding that fatal chink in our foe's defenses—physical and psychological. The most armored of warriors can easily be brought low by the least unguarded emotion. Likewise, small success paves the way to bolder undertakings. The example Kensei gives for this is the way we can build a great statue of Buddha from a one-foot model.*

---

*There is a metaphor here waiting to happen, and perhaps a Zen koan: the one-foot model being each of us, destined (?) to become a great Buddha.

Two swords are better than one. Even those who remain in awe of Musashi's mastering the art of fighting with two swords still all too often miss the philosophical meaning behind Musashi's Two Swords school.

Two Swords means using all our resources, developing what Musashi called a twofold gaze of both sight and perception. According to Kensei, "Perception is strong, sight is weak."

If this sounds vaguely familiar, it's because it is mentioned in part I of this book . . . and on damn near every page since!

In other words, the eye (along with our other senses) can easily deceive us. To counter this, we must develop a deeper, more intuitive perception, one that uses the "twin swords" of both heart (instinct/intuition) and mind (thought and reason).

In samurai culture this was known as "Bunbu Itchi," literally "pen and sword," reminding Samurai to seek a balance in their studies of both the martial arts and the liberal arts. Musashi himself took time to master calligraphy and painting. Musashi's "Ground" chapter tells us: "Know the smallest things and the biggest things, the shallowest things and the deepest things." In today's vernacular it's "The more you know, the better you throw!" (i.e., the more experience and access to information we have at our disposal, the more the likelihood we will be able to take advantage of any opportunity or else counter any threat that comes knocking on—or kicking in!—our door.)

On still another level, *Two Swords* means using both sides of our brains, left and right hemispheres, concrete and abstract thinking, our full faculties. (See *Two Heads are Better than One* in part II.)

No-sword is better than two swords. The tale is told that when the *Shihan* of the first (of many) sword academies Musashi attended decided to retire he passed his most prized katana along to his eldest student . . . but that he gave the empty scabbard to Musashi.

Students of zen will be quick to grasp the significance of this. This gift foreshadowed Musashi's eventual creation of his "No-Sword" school.

In *Go Rin No Sho* Kensei expresses his disdain against what he calls "narrow spirit," a combination of closemindedness and predictability. In the same breath, Musashi also warns us against having a favored weapon or favoring one combat stance/attitude over another because it makes us predictable. Ergo, no matter how good you get with a sword—even two swords—you will still be limited to what a sword can do.

Never limit yourself. That's your enemy's job.

If you favor no specific weapon or strategy, then your enemy has no idea what you're going to bring to the party, so he has to try and prepare against all possibilities and against all possible angles of attack . . . an impossible task. Sun Tzu understood this: "If my enemy doesn't know where I am going to attack he is forced to prepare everywhere. Forced to prepare everywhere, he is strong nowhere."

Nothing better illustrates (and instructs us in) the Way of Musashi's "No-Sword" than the following tale:

One day Musashi is challenged by a belligerent samurai while the two are crossing between islands by ferry.

"What's your style of fighting," the samurai demands to know.

"No-Sword style," replied Musashi.

Fast forward: Despite Musashi's best efforts to ignore him, the Samurai picks a fight and Musashi finally agrees to duel the challenger. *But*, suggests Musashi, rather than fight on the cramped ferry, they should instead fight on that sandbar they're approaching.

The challenger quickly agrees and leaps overboard as the ferry passes the sandbar.

Landing on the sandbar, the samurai whirls, sword at the ready— only to watch the ferry continue on toward the far shore—a smiling, waving Musashi still on board!

Hours later, drenched in humiliation and dripping rage, the challenger finally wades ashore where he finds Musashi patiently fishing out of a small rowboat.

"You tricked me!" screams the samurai.

"Your eagerness to die tricked you," shrugs Musashi.

"Your No-Sword cannot defeat my sword!" declares the challenger, advancing menacingly.

"It already has," Musashi says smugly.

Confused by his intended victim's seeming lack of concern, the challenger hesitates, for the first time noticing that Musashi is unarmed.

"Where is your sword?" the samurai asks, on guard against more chicanery.

"The No-Swordsman keeps his sword where it will do the most good," Musashi replies cryptically.

"No more tricks! Where is your weapon?" demands the Samurai, his sword raised high.

"There," sighs Musashi, pointing to the water lapping at the side of the boat.

Still suspicious, the samurai cautiously bends over the gunwale . . .

"Bah! I see nothing but my own reflection?"

"And that is where the No-Swordsman keeps his weapon . . . *in the mind of his enemy!*" Musashi explains as he caves the samurai's skull in with the rowboat's heavy oak.

If this story sounds familiar, you may have seen the same lesson taught in Bruce Lee's *Enter the Dragon* (1973). The tale is perhaps anecdotal, although during what most consider to be Musashi's greatest challenge, in 1612, he succeeded in killing master duelist Sasaki Kojiro using a wooden sword he'd carved from his oar.

> *"When you cannot be deceived by men you will realize the wisdom of strategy."*
> —Miyamoto Musashi, 1645

Laughing with the Long-Nose

> *"Discard even the True Law, let alone the false ones."*
> —Takuan, 1573–1645

As part of their ongoing use of *Kyonin-no-jutsu* ploys, the Shinobi Ninja of medieval Japan encouraged the belief that they were descended from demon-spawn known as *Tengu* (lit. "long nose").

Musashi was not the only medieval samurai to be caught "laughing with the long-nose," augmenting his samurai skills with ninja tactics and technique.

Yagu Munenori was another. Munenori was the son of Yagu Muneyoshi (1529–1606) himself a respected Samurai strategist. As a young man, Munenori studied with the *Rinzai* school of *Zen* under Master Takuan, learning the five samurai virtues: humanity, loyalty, courtesy, wisdom, and trust.

Only because of the night do we appreciate the light.

To give himself the edge, literally, Munenori studied with the *Shinkage-ryu*, the "New Shade" school founded by sixteenth-century master Kamiizumi Hidetsuna.*

The *Shinkage-ryu* taught sword fighting and other tactics derived from Ninjutsu.

Like Musashi, like most independent thinkers (i.e., Black Science adepts!), Munenori knew enough to never be satisfied with yesterday's accomplishments.

Once he'd mastered the sword and numerous other martial arts weapons, Munenori had a revelation: What if he got caught *without* a weapon?

Taking the next logical step, Munenori devoted the rest of his life to developing the unarmed art of *Muto* (lit. "no sword", not to be confused with Musashi's "No-Sword"). The Mu in Munenori's Muto comes from the Chinese *Wu*, meaning "nothing," *To* is "sword," hence "Muto." Munenori's Muto specialized in disarming an armed opponent.

In a demonstration for the Tokugawa shogun, Munenori easily disarmed several samurai armed with various weapons.

When a mounted *Daimyo* dismissed Munenori's unarmed fighting style, snickering that Muto would be useless when faced with a mounted attacker, Munenori slapped the man's horse on the snout, making the horse rear up and throw the Samurai to the ground, where Munenori easily disarmed the dazed man. The shogun was so delighted by this display he gave Munenori the job of teaching Muto to Tokugawa troops.

Munenori is often depicted in Japanese fiction as a cross between Jack the Ripper and J. Edgar Hoover because of the way he recruited ninja into a network of secret police he ruthlessly used to spy on and "deal with" all enemies of the Tokugawa Shogunate.

Musashi and Munenori died a year apart. But whereas Musashi and his masterpiece *Go Rin No Sho* was world renowned, Munenori's equally insightful and instructional *Heiho Kaden Sho* are little appreciated outside Japan.

Munenori's text was written in 1632, thirteen years before Musashi's *A Book of Five Rings*, and we can only speculate how much influence Munenori's strategy may have had on the unfolding of Musashi's own developing strategy.

Munenori's ideal is to become a man of *daiki taiku*.

---

*You will remember Hidetsuna from the "rice cakes" incident in *Black Science*. (Lung and Prowant, 2001:162)

> "A man of *daiki taiku* does not at all concern himself either
> with things learned or with laws. In everything, there are
> things learned, laws, and proscriptions. Someone who has
> attained the ultimate state brushes them aside. He does
> things freely, at will. Someone who goes outside the laws
> and acts at will is called a man of *daiki taiku*."
> —Hiroaki Sato, *The Sword and the Mind*

This smacks of Nietzsche, and rightly so for it is a call to free up the free flow of our "will to power," to reach an impeccable point where we are no longer bound by laws of dependency and deportment. In Japan they call this *shibumi*—to live flawlessly.

This is not a blueprint for anarchy, to trespass laws merely for the juvenile joy of doing so. Rather, this is the concept at the core of Zen, that in order for us to truly master an art we must first learn proper form and technique . . . and then forget those techniques when we reach the point where our art and craft becomes second nature and can be done sans conscious thought. Thus, we transcend the laws that govern that particular art.

Within Munenori's overall strategy for getting—and keeping!—the upper hand we can spot several distinct tactics and techniques all of which were, by necessity, practical, applicable for both combat and equally deadly court intrigue.

Ken and Kan: seeing. To survive long enough to become a man of *daiki taiku* meant developing both *Ken* and *Kan*. *Ken* means to observe with the eyes. (Coincidentally, the archaic English word *Ken*, from the Scots, also means "to see," "perceive," and "to understand.")

Kan means "insight," a deeper level of perception (i.e., "seeing" with the mind). (Recall Musashi's admonishment that "Perception is strong, but sight is weak"?)

All Masters agree: To see with senses alone is not to "see".

Hyori: "Not being seen. Munenori maintains that a man of *daiki taiku* is justified in using any and all means (*masakatsu*) to accomplish his ends: "Even if you inwardly hide the truth and outwardly carry out your stratagem, when you succeed in the end in pulling your opponent into the truthful way, all deceptions become truths."

This includes using *Hyori*, a catch-all meaning "double-dealing," which Munenori defines as "the stratagem of obtaining truth through deception." "Truth through deception"? How very Orwellian! (Let's not forget Munenori ran the secret police for the Tokugawa regime.)

Hyori means we hide our intent using *kyoku* ("deception") techniques crafted to lure an opponent in by feigning weakness ("When strong, appear weak", Sun Tzu), and by such ploys as *suigetsu* (lit., "Moon on water"), getting close to an enemy (via disguise, by feigning friendship, etc.).

Munenori's techniques for psychologically outmaneuvering a foe were gleaned from actual physical confrontations after he realized the similarities between the physical battlefield and the battlefield of the mind.

War is war, it matters little whether your foe hides his true face behind a bulwark of pike, or a courtiers' fan, whether he thrusts at you with whetted weapons or with dry wit, let no trespass go unchallenged!

For example, the *Shin-myo* body language signs that telegraphed to Munenori another swordsman's intention to strike were little different from tells he noticed when a man was lying to him.

Munenori also borrowed much of his ultimate strategy—both for physical and for psychological combat—from his ninja studies. These he then distilled into eight "attitudes of attack," attacks common to both physical sword attacks and/or attacks with the mind-sword. (See Figure 22, below.)

Figure 22: HYORI "DOUBLE-DEALING" AKA "DANCE OF THE GOBLINS"

Name	AKA	English Meaning	Physical Strategy	Mental Strategy
Kasha	Korinbo	"Flower wheel"	Offer left side, strike right	False peace offering. Prentend to fear him.
Akemi	Fugenbo	"Open body"	Bait him in, draw him in	Make him your friend, make friends with his friends.

Name	AKA	English Meaning	Physical Strategy	Mental Strategy
Zentai	Tarobo	"Waiting fully"	Wait patiently, strike forward suddenly.	Make him paranoid. Make him prepare everywhere so he is strong nowhere (Sun Tzu)
Tebiki	Eiibo	"Entrap"	Fake sudden withdrawal, draw him into an ambush.	Pretend to listen, pretend friendship to draw him into ambush (à la *The Cask of the Amontillado*)
Ranken	Shu tokubo	"Wild sword"	Appear to strike blindly, fake a first deliberately ineffective attack, before launching real attack.	Make him overconfident, make him underestimate you.
Jo	Nigusoku	"Two weapons"	Fighting two opponents simultaneously, keep one foe in the other's path.	Divide and conquer by playing one foe off against the other. "Get a dog to eat a dog."
Ha	Uchimondo	"Development"	Use a two-pronged attack, distracting with your initial strike before making your coup de grace (similar to Ranken).	Divert his attention and energies away from your true target. Make him waste valuable resources.

| **Kyu** | Futarikake | "Final cut/ coup de grace" | Fighting two opponets simultaneously, push one into the other (similar to Nigusoku). | Drive a wedge of suspicion between allies. |

From political intrigue to assassination, so much of Munenori's medieval methodology is still relevant to today's study of Black Science and mind control:

War in the mind. "A man in the position of general must be able to set up camp and maneuver his army for battle not only on the actual battlefield where victory or defeat is decided, but also within the confines of his mind. The latter is the art of war in the mind."

Foresight. "Foreseeing a disturbance from the various developments in the state and stopping it before it breaks out."

Chance. "Seizing the chance ahead of time means carefully observing your opponent's mind and making an appropriate move just before he makes up his mind."

Intrigue. "Your Lord may be flanked by sycophants, who when facing him feign an air of morality, but who when looking down at the ruled give an angry glance. Such men, unless you lie low before them, will speak ill of you for something good you have done. As a result, the innocent suffer and the sinful thrive. Understanding this is more important than the ability to judge your opponent's stratagems in a sword fight."

Assassination. "At times, because of one man's evil, thousands of people suffer. So you kill that one man in order to let thousands live. Here truly, the blade that deals death could be the sword that gives life."

Practice. "An unpolished jewel attracts dirt and dust. A polished one doesn't become soiled even if put in the mud. Train hard and polish your mind so that it may remain."

Strategy. "The thing to do is to force your opponent to follow your changes and by following his resultant changes to win."

Experience. "To explain the mind with words, it exists in others as well as in yourself, and does good or evil things day and night, in accordance with its karma. The mind leaves the house or destroys a country, and depending on its owner, it may be good or evil. . . . Because, however, few explore and bring it to light what the mind is really like, everyone continues to be misled by the mind. . . . Those who happen to have brought its nature to light have a hard time putting what has been learned into practice. The ability to speak eloquently of the mind may not mean enlightenment on the subject. Even if you hold forth on water, your mouth does not become wet. Even if you speak eloquently of fire, your mouth doesn't become hot. You cannot know the real water and real fire without touching them; you cannot know them by explaining them from books. Likewise, even if you speak eloquently of food, hunger will not be cured. The ability to speak is not enough for knowing the subject at hand . . . as long as they do not behave as they preach, they have yet to know the mind. Until each person explores the mind in himself and knows it fully, the matter will remain unclear."

Humility? "I am not saying these things because I have mastered my own mind. I say these things even though it is difficult for me to conduct myself, move and stay still as if my mind were correct, as if I met the dictates of a correct mind. I note this because it is a state to strive for."

Shadow Warriors

> *"There are certain persons who when near you seem to draw something from you, to pump you, to absorb your force and your life; a species of vampire, without knowing it, they live at your expense."*
> —DePote De Sennevoy, *Magnetic Therapeutics*

In *The Secret Power Within: Zen Solutions to Real Problems* (1998), Chuck Norris devotes an entire chapter to what he calls "The Shadow Warrior," his term for troublemakers, gossip mongers, and backbiters:

Shadow warriors are no joke, especially when they take the form of lawyers, friends, and advisors to one or both of the parties who are having a problem. In that capacity, like the ninjas of legend, the shadow warrior is most often invisible, but the havoc he creates is very real indeed. . . . One of the problems in dealing with shadow warriors is that their presence may be unknown to you. (page 104)

According to Chuck, shadow warriors often first appear as friendly faces offering us free advice that we later pay through the nose for, after they've sown what Chuck calls "seeds of discord," turning friendly ground into hostile territory.

Examples of such shadow warriors abound:

Iago in Shakespeare's *Othello*, and Lady Macbeth are the consummate "shadow warriors" in fiction. Haman in the Old Testament book of Esther, Potiphar's wife (who screwed Joseph over because he wouldn't screw her), and Judas Iscariot are shining examples of biblical shadow warriors. And let's not forget how easily Satan—the ultimate shadow warrior!—manipulates God into rocking loyal servant Job's world.

In real life, Gregori Efimovich Rasputin (1871–1916) wins hands-down as the perfect example of how a single shadow warrior can bring down an empire.

Closer to home, your particular shadow warrior could be a coworker, subtly making you look bad in the eyes of the boss, or even a loved one who "out of concern" is always telling you how your latest venture is already doomed and how you're fated to fall flat on your face—again, "So why even bother trying?"

How can we avoid falling victim to the defeatism and/or deliberate manipulations of such shadow warriors? Chuck gives his advice: "First and foremost, be wary when dealing with someone who has a sudden change of attitude. It is then wise to create good perimeter defenses, and to prepare for an all-out battle because one can never overestimate the damage a shadow warrior can do" (page 107).

Of course Chuck, being the nice guy he is, doesn't consider that it sometimes works to our advantage to temporarily don the dark garb of the shadow warrior ourself. For example, to sow discord when we discover two of our enemies glancing our way in whispered negotiation. What's the odds anything good—for us—is going to come out of their comparing notes?

Sometimes the more practical (paranoid) Samurai Daimyo even resorted to hiring ninja . . . "gardeners" to help them weed their garden.

Honor is the most valued of commodities. Never waste yours on a dishonorable man.

Chinese vampires. Much of the lore, legerdemain, and lethality of Japanese Shinobi-ninja can be traced back to tactics, techniques (and training?) taken from Chinese *Moshuh Nanren* (Lung, 1997a, 1998; Lung and Prowant, 2000). Yet even among lions, there are always to be found lions with longer teeth.

Master strategists and interrogators for the various Moshuh Nanren cadre were called "T-zi-bu," which literally means "taking the other's essence to boost one's own," in other words, a "vampire"!

Moshuh Nanren (sometimes themselves referred to as *Lin Kuei*, "demons") employed T-zi-bu operatives for a variety of tasks, but they seem to have originated as female agents adept at stroking secrets from foes (paging Delilah!) since the name originally implied a form of sexual vampirism, similar to medieval Western legends of a succubus (demons appearing in the guise of beautiful women who suck the life out of sleeping men).

True T-zi-bu (pronounced T-zee-boo, sometimes spelled *Caibu*) were masters at getting information, not only by stealth and via the Moshuh Nanren's extensive spy network(s), but also by targeting individuals using what has been called *Dim Mak Hsing*.

You might recall from *Black Science* (Lung and Prowant, 2001) that Moshuh Nanren, and later the Shinobi, were believed to possess the secret of the dreaded death touch (Ch. Dim Mak).

Whereas the original death touch is said to have originated in India as a purely physical art known in Sanskrit as *Varma adi* ("striking at vital spots") or simply *Marman* "death spots," the Dim Mak of the Moshuh Nanren had both a physical component as well as a *psychological component*.

T-zi-bu psychological ploys are based in the *Pakua* "8-Trigrams" (see Lung and Prowant, 2001, and chart, opposite).

These "8-Trigrams" can be (and have been) applied to physical combat (e.g., Pakua Boxing created by Taoist alchemist Yu-hau Shan, employing circular movements and open hand strikes) and to Black Science ploys meant to undermine an interrogatee's resistance, sabotage a negotiator from getting the upper hand, or soften up an opponent by planting doubt in his mind.

Vampires do exist. Perhaps not the blood-sucking, albeit always impeccably dressed vampires on *Buffy the Vampire Slayer*, but vampires nonetheless.

These vampires also suck at your life's blood—often your *financial* life's blood—or else undermine your relationships. (Sounds a lot like Chuck's "shadow warriors," huh?)

T-ZI-BU 8-TRIGRAMS PLOYS

Chinese	Physical	Controls	Mind Ploy
Ch'ien	Head	Head	Attack his mind using the five FLAGS (Fear, Lust, Anger, Greed, and Sympathy)
Kan	Ears	Kidneys	Upset and undermine your foe with gossip & disinformation
Ken	Hands	Neck	Attack him through his job, co-workers, his boss. Uncover past deeds
Chen	Feet	Left side of the abdomen	Question his motivation, make him doubt his chosen path in life. Incite his *spleen* (i.e., ill will and malice)
Sun	Buttocks	Spine (from first segment of the coccyx up to the seventh vertebrae)	Excite his lusts, especially his sexual desire.
Li	Eyes	Head (again) The senses	Dazzle him with illusion, confuse him with the play of white world grey. (see *ninja Shadowhand*, Lung and Prowant, Citadel, 2004)
K'un	Abdomen	Midsection abdomen	Attack his appetites (both physical (addictions) and psychological (lusts, fetishes and phobias). Unbalance him (Tan Tien)
Tui	Mouth	Right side of the abdomen	Incite his ill temper (gall) by putting words in his mouth. Make him choke on his own words.

Dawn of the Dons. Hebrews 13:2 says: "Do not neglect to show hospitality to strangers, for thereby some have entertained angels unawares."

The Japanese were never an "overly" superstitious lot, but they did know a devil when they saw one. They knew the *tengu*, those half-man, half-crow demons who materialized out of thin air dressed all in black, with their pointed hats and capes made of feathers. Some argued that these were merely men—*ninja*! it was whispered—but men nonetheless. Thankfully most of these sons of Susano the Storm god kept to their own clans in the great forest.

Occasionally an *Oni* demon would cross your path, fierce-faced dressed in pelts, who could alter their size at will, giants one minute, tiny mischief makers the next.

But the worst by far were the Marebito, "spiritual guests," mysterious visitors who would show up on your doorstep unexpected. In the north they call them *Namahage*, but in the south they call them simply *Dons*, brutes and devils.

They arrived looking like young men wearing horned demon masks and straw capes. It was bad luck to forbid them entrance into your home. Those that came at New Years were called *Toshidon*.

These are spirits that must be placated with food and drink and by never daring to refuse whatever burden or obligation they ask of you. Not that one could resist, for it was widely known that these visitors possessed kotadama, the ability to command "the spirit of the word," the power to entrance with just a word, to freeze a victim in their tracks. Such was the power of their words.

> *"The notion of kotodama has in the twentieth century been elevated to a pseudo-science by some popular writers who view the entire Japanese language as uniquely endowed with spiritual power."*
> **—Bocking, 1997**

Japanese in general and practitioners of the Shinto religion in particular understood the power of the spoken word, believing a spirit resides within each word. To speak the word, sometimes even to merely write the word, invokes the spirit within that word. Some of these spirits are good. Some not. For not all words are created equal.

(Review Shadow-Talkers in chapter 5.)

Imi-kotoba ("taboo words") included words that should not be spoken during sacred ritual, nor in the vicinity of shrines, negative words such as *blood*, *sweat*, *meat*, *grave*, and *cry*. Due to the rivalry between religions, words specific to Buddhist practice are also forbidden to be spoken at Shinto shrines. Should this occur, an often elaborate ritual is required to cleanse the site.

Other words were more mundane, but no less forbidden. For example, at one time the word *ninja* (lit. "to enter by stealth") merited the death penalty since it was considered an insult to the Japanese people in general and to the Code Bushido of the Samurai in particular that any Japanese would even think of engaging in such underhanded acts.

Tatari are curses, powerful spells that spell certain doom. Dons were thought to possess this power, having the power to curse—or bless—with a single word, and with a single whisper to literally spellbind a person to performing a specific task. (See The Control of Candy Jones in *Black Science* [Lung and Prowant, 2001].)

The power of words wielded by word wizards are well documented: Rasputin, Charles Manson, Rush Limbaugh. From words that incite riots ("Burn, Baby Burn!") to words designed to quell riots ("Can't we all just get along?"), words have the power not just to move people but to raze cities.

Coming out the mouth of an accomplished politician, the right words all too often lead us into the wrong war. Out of the mouth of an unscrupulous hypnotist and, despite what they tell us, you can be convinced to do acts you wouldn't normally think of doing, up to and including murder.

Case in point: On March 29, 1951, a thirty-three-year-old man named Hardrupp shot and killed two people in Copenhagen during a botched robbery. When arrested his defense was he had been repeatedly hypnotized into committing the robbery by a man named Nielsen. After a sensational trial, Hardrupp was found guilty but was only sentenced to a mental asylum with possible release in two years. Nielsen the hypnotist, on the other hand, was tried and convicted and received a life sentence for committing murder by hypnotism!

Predictably, prosecutors had argued the common held belief that it's impossible to make someone do something while under hypnosis they wouldn't normally do. However, the defense's expert witnesses, including Paul Reiter, former governor of the Denmark insane asylum and later head of the psychiatric department at the Copenhagen City Hospital, testified that when Hardrupp had committed the crime he was clinically insane since he was in "a semi-conscious state while deprived of his free will by repeated hypnotic suggestion."

According to Dr. Reiter, any person is capable of committing any act while under hypnosis so long as the hypnotist presents the crime as being for a worthy purpose. In this instance Nielsen had convinced Hardrupp that the money from the robbery would be used to combat communism!

During *Shogatsu*, the Japanese New Year's period, young men do indeed don straw capes and horned devil masks and visit (harass!) the homes of honest Japanese folk. This is almost Japan's version of Halloween, since tradition demands that these Toshidon be invited into your home, where they will be fed fish and sake. In return, they will give a blessing to the household or threaten unruly children.

This custom is rooted in darker times past, when households were visited by true *Don* devils. At the very least these were ninja armed not only with hidden dirks but with sinister agenda. No one dared refuse their "requests." If you were lucky they only wanted food or nightly shelter. Other times though, they would recruit your son's strong arm or your daughter's ready smile to their cause.

Of course some superstitious hosts still suspected these Dons were not true men; recognizing them for the shapeshifting devils they were, demons, who only took on the shape of men when they passed through the *kuro-torji* "dark gate" that joined our world to theirs.

There are few accounts of Dons using physical force to accomplish their aims, more often it was the power of persuasion inherent in their words alone that crumbled any hope of resistance. Sometimes these words were recognizable to their hosts, othertimes Dons spoke in foreign tongues, commands with the power to paralyze, or else sing-song chants that seemed to lull the listener into calm acquiescence.

Some of the "foreign" words employed by the Dons were *majinai*, "magic words," probably derived from ancient *mantras*, perhaps from as far away as India. Other Don spells and chants were passed down from ancient shamanistic times, from the *Ainu*, the original peoples of the Japanese archipelago.

"Fuku wa uchi! Oni wa soto!"

("Good luck in! Demons out!" Shinto chant)

The Three Diamonds' Way

I know what you're thinking. How does all this ancient Asian warrior philosophy affect me? I don't carry a samurai sword and ninja aren't dropping out of the trees on top of me.

What about that plotting piss-ant shadow warrior in the computer cubicle next to you, the one even now scheming on how to get your job for his brother-in-law? Oh well, worst-case scenario: He succeeds and you and your whole family end up living in a cardboard box . . . at least you're still living.

That's a ninja sitting in the seat next to you on the plane . . . 9/11.

So maybe ninja *are* dropping out of the trees—and out of the sky—all around you . . . And maybe you do carry a sword, the sword of the mind; hopefully two; Musashi's twin blades of sight and insight.

Dirk Skinner in his *Street Ninja: Ancient Secrets for Mastering Today's Mean Streets* (Barricade Books/NY 1995) convincingly argues that, despite what we might think, the pressures and dangers of current times are not that far removed from similar threats faced by the beleaguered Shinobi ninja clans of medieval Japan. Consequently, says Skinner, many of their tried-and-true tactics and techniques, both physical and psychological, will still work for us today. Says Skinner, "The old ways still work. There are no new answers, only new questions."

Still think names like "Musashi" and "Munenori" mean nothing to you? What about "Mitsubishi"? You may have a samurai to thank for that automobile you're driving.

In 1870, Samurai Yataro Iwasaki founded the Mitsubishi ("Three Diamonds") corporation and, because of nine insightful guiding principles he put down in writing early on, his company has survived—and *prospered*—down to the present day; making civilian vehicles during peacetime, jumping to war material, up to and including World War II fighter planes, to supply Japan's dreams of empire.

All agree Iwasaki possessed rare insight into human nature. A student of Sun Tzu? Musashi? All of the above. But all the philosophical insight in the world means nothing, unless it can be translated into practical action.

Iwasaki's method has stood the test of time and is as easily applicable to our lives today. Following are Iwasoki's nine guiding principles:

1. *Do not be preoccupied with small matters but aim at the management of large enterprises.* Translation: "Think big!" . . . and then *do big*! Note

that Iwasaki doesn't say we should ignore small matters, only that we must not be preoccupied with small matters—squandering precious resources on trivial concerns. That's what they make lackeys for!

Hence we follow the advice of every Black Science master from Sun Tzu on down: Deal with little matters before they become big matters.

2. *Once you start an enterprise be sure to succeed in it.* Translation: Finish the job or the job'll finish you.

3. *Do not engage in speculative enterprises.* Get the facts and then act on the facts.

4. *Operate all enterprises with the national interest in mind.* Translation: See the "big picture." No enterprise operates in a vacuum.

5. *Never forget the pure spirit of public service and makoto ("sincerity").* Translation: Do what you say, say what you do. Someone is always watching.

6. *Be hardworking, frugal, and thoughtful to others.* Translation: Set the bar for subordinates . . . and set it *high*!

7. *Utilize proper personnel.* Translation: Don't send a boy to do a man's job. Breasts can't type. And no matter how much your wife bitches, don't hire your brother-in-law.

8. *Treat your employees well.* Translation: Take care of your people and they'll take care of you. And, take care of your enemies, before they take care of you!

9. *Be bold in starting an enterprise but meticulous in its prosecution.* Translation: *Do it now!* And do it well.

"Step by step walk the thousand-mile road . . . Study strategy over the years and achieve the spirit of the warrior. Today is victory over your self of yesterday, tomorrow is your victory over lesser men."
—Myamoto Musashi

CONCLUSION: *THE SLOTH, THE QUEST, AND BECOMING A BETTER WALKER*

Evolution or revolution? One way or another, life moves ahead. New technologies replace ancient techniques. The same God of Lightning whom we once cowered in terror from when he hurled his flashing and crashing wrath down on us is now securely bound within our microcircuitry and now it is we who make him dance with just a flick of our finger, to light our homes and animate our machines. Some things do change.

Ah, but people, they haven't changed much down through the ages. They'll still buy a pig in a poke and have enough left over to put a down payment on the Brooklyn Bridge. And when you point out this shortcoming to them, most will just grin and try to wax philosophic—though most of them couldn't spell *philosophic* if their life depended on it! "That's just the way it's always been," they shrug, as if this startling insight somehow relieves them of any responsibility to better themselves and their world.

That's just the way it's always been . . . ? But that doesn't mean it has to be that way *tomorrow*, does it?

Ray Bradbury (1953) understood tomorrow:

I hate a Roman named Status Quo! Stuff your eyes with wonder, live as if you'd drop dead in ten seconds. See the world. It's more fantastic than any dream made or paid for in factories. Ask no guarantees, ask for no security, there never was such an animal. And if there were, it would be related to the great sloth which hangs upside down in a tree all day every day, sleeping its life away. To hell with it, shake the tree and knock the great sloth down on his ass.

But you must not tempt the gods, they warn. Cower and cover your eyes when the Lord of Lightning passes, lest you anger the gods by trying to spy out their secrets. Ah, but what kind of "gods" can they truly be if even I can spy out their secrets? If even I can steal their thunder?

That we must be ever watchful—true. That we must tread cautious—prudent advice. But that we must not dare Olympus. Nay, we must! We must set our eye steadfast to study the prize, and seek out—and surpass—those successful steps taken by those who have dared before us: the seeker, the sage, and the shogun:

> *"Do not wait for the desired object to come to you, but rise up and set out to look for it; when you have found it you will undertake its conquest, and when it becomes your possession you will gather together your friends to make them share in your good fortune and to tell them by what means it has befallen you."*
> —Taishi Yoritomo, *Influence*

And as surely as bolts from the blue may fell you, so too there will always be those of your fellows who try to dissuade you from success—your daily progress only making their daily regress all the more apparent. And should you stumble during your quest to ride the lightning, they will instantly shrill about you like a murder of crow, "We told you not to tempt the gods!"

Has it ever occurred to them the gods might appreciate a little entertainment from time to time? Lucifer's eyes were never as open-wide as when he was falling. So, too, we learn so much more from falling than we ever do from never rising to the task in the first place.

Thus, though we may fall, we will not have failed, for we will have learned more than those who never tried. For even in falling, we will benefit those few like ourselves who come after, seizing up our muddied banner to carry it further—forward! What matters if only a single step at a time?—for a single step is one more step than a man can take sitting on his fat ass bemoaning his lean existence.

One small step for man . . .

Sometimes it's enough just knowing we are not him, that we're not them—all those who never fail, who never fall flat on their faces . . . because they fear to even make the attempt. One foot in front of the other, step-by-step, we walk the way of past Masters. And if that path is rock-strewn and rough, the road less traveled, so much the better, for we are so much the stronger for having to raise our boot so much the higher:

"It is necessary that, in continuing what you have begun, your will, your intelligence, your sensibilities be ever on the alert. It is this unceasing activity in yourself that is the reward of your effort. The road on which you walk may, perhaps not lead you where you wished to go. But probably it will lead you to a better place. And for your walk you will become a better walker."
—G. A. Mann

GLOSSARY

aces-n-eights: A two-pair poker hand superstitiously believed to bring bad luck. Generically used to indicate that a scheme/operation has gone horribly wrong.

assassins: Medieval Middle Eastern secret society noted for its terror, treachery and mind-manipulation techniques.

banking: Holding back valuable information (indiscretion, faux pas, etc.) you've discovered about a person, information you can use to your advantage at a more opportune time.

bio-resources: People whose talents you utilize to accomplish your goals.

Black Science, the: Generic, any strategy, tactic or technique used to undermine a person's ability to reason and respond for themselves. (See "mind control.")

cheng and chi: Chinese, "direct" and "indirect" (i.e., sneaky) actions.

cognitive dissonance: Mental anxiety created when a person must reconcile their contradictory ideas and/or actions.

dead dog ploy: Giving up superfluous information in order to keep more important information hidden.

dropping lugs: Using innuendo and rumor to plant suspicion.

dyshemism: Words used as weapons.

fakir: Hindu mystic. (See *Siddhas.*) Also used generically to mean a swindler or charlatan.

false humility: To demur to another or pass up an opportunity to advance ourselves only because society and "good manners" say we should.

fard: "To paint the face with cosmetics." To wear a false face.

gray talk: Words and phrases deliberately crafted to confuse the listener.

half-assin': Hesitation and second-guessing.

hiracarrah: East Indian secret society of professional spies, agents provocateur, and assassins. Influential on the development of European espionage techniques.

hyori: Jp. "deception."

killer "b's", the: Techniques for infiltrating an enemy's mind: Blind, Bribery and Blackmail, Bloodties, Brainwashing, Bully, and Bury.

koan: Riddles used in Zen Buddhism, designed to "short-circuit" a student's rational mind in order to bring it to an insightful "breakthrough." Often used as a synonym for an unanswerable riddle.

kyonin-no-jutsu: Jp. Using an enemy's superstitions against him.

long-con: Involved and intricate confidence scheme. Big setup = big payoff.

"make your bones": To prove worth by accomplishing a difficult task.

mark, the: The victim/target of a confidence scheme.

masakatsu: Jp. "by any means necessary." Strategy that allows for the use of any tactic or technique in order to achieve your goal, i.e., the end justifies the means.

mushroom treatment, the: Overall strategy for dealing with enemies (i.e., "Keep 'em in the dark and feed 'em plenty of bullshit!").

nightside: The "dark side" of your personality. What Freud called the "ID". The secrets you bury and the ones your enemies dig up.

ninja: (Jp. "to sneak in"). Mysterious assassin-spies of medieval Japan known for their stealth and skulduggery. Generic, anyone who employs stealth and secrecy to accomplish their ends.

psychotronics: Any electronic device used to enhance or entrance the mind.

satsujin: Jp. "insight." (See *tells*.)

shinjiraren!" Jp. "It boggles the mind!" Exclamation used when amazed and/or confused by something. Generically, techniques designed to amaze and confuse.

short-con: Simple confidence schemes quickly executed. Small risk, usually small gain.

shuhari: Jp. "circle." Your circle of family and friends, and acquaintances.

siddhas: Skt. "powers." Enhanced powers of mind and body developed by Hindu mystics. (See *Fakir*.)

tantric: Skt. "forbidden." Taboo mystical practices (drugs, sex, etc.) used by Hindu mystics as a fast-track to gaining enlightenment and *siddhas*. Also spelled Tantrik.

tells: Twitches, itches, and bitches that reveal what one is really thinking.

warning flags, the: The five weaknesses: Fear, Lust, Anger, Greed, Sympathy.

SOURCES AND
SUGGESTED READING

Barash, David. *Beloved Enemies: Our Need for Opponents*. New York: Prometheus Books, 1994.

Bearden, Keith. "100 Mighty Sex Facts." *FHM* magazine, Sept. 2001:122.

Bhagavad-Gita. (misc. trans.)

Blass, Thomas. "The Man Who Shocked the World." *Psychology Today*, Jan./Feb. 2002:26.

Bocking, Brian. A Popular Dictionary of Shinto. NTC Publishing Group, 1997.

Bradbury, Ray. *Fahrenheit 451*. 1953.

Dees, Morris, with James Corcoran. *Gathering Storm: America's Militia Threat*. New York: HarperCollins, 1996.

De Shipper, Simone. "Blame the Name." *Popular Science*, Aug., 2002:36.

Dhammapada (Sayings of The Buddha). (misc. trans.)

The Economist. "The Future of Mind Control." 2002A.

Freud, Sigmund. *The Future of an Illusion*. Tr. W. D. Robson-Scott. Originally pub. 1927. Doubleday/Anchor Books edition, 1964.

Funk, Wilfred, Litt. D. *Word Origins and Their Romantic*

Hausman, Carl. *Lies We Live By: Defeating Double-Talk and Deception*. London: Routledge, 2000.

Hayden, Thomas. "Gotcha! Strange but True: This is the Golden Age of Hoaxes." *U.S. News and World Report*, Aug. 26–Sept. 2, 2002.

Hentoff, Nat. "How the FCC Saves You from Indecency." *Village Voice*, May 25, 1993.

Holzer, Robert D. *ESP and You*. New York: Hawthorne Books, 1966.

Jung, Carl G., editor/introduction. *Man and His Symbols*. Dell, 1964.

Keegan, John. *The Mask of Command*. Penguin Books, 1987.

Kosko, Bart. *Fuzzy Thinking: The New Science of Fuzzy Logic*. New York: Hyperion, 1993.

Levinson, David, and Karen Cistensen, eds. *Encyclopedia of World Sport: From Ancient Times to the Present*. ABC-CLIO, 1996.

Lieberman, David J. *Never Be Lied to Again*. New York: St. Martin's Press, 1998.

————. *Get Anyone to Do Anything and Never Feel Powerless Again*. New York: St. Martin's Press, 2000.

Linn, Denise. *The Secret Language of Signs*. New York: Ballantine Books, 1996.

Linn, Henry B. *What Your Face Reveals: Chinese Secrets of Face Reading*. Llwellyn Publications, 1999.

Lozoff, Bo. *"We're All Doing Time*. 1985

Lung, Haha. *The Ancient Art of Strangulation*. Boulder, Colorado: Paladin Press, 1995.

————. *Ninja Craft*. Ohio: Alpha Publications, 1997a.

————. *Assassin! Secrets of the Cult of Assassins*. Boulder, Colorado: Paladin Press, 1997b.

————. *Knights of Darkness*. Boulder Colorado: Paladin Press, 1998.

————. *Lost Fighting Arts of Vietnam*. New York: Citadel Press, 2006.

Lung, Haha, and Christopher B. Prowant. *Black Science: Ancient and Modern Techniques of Ninja Mind Manipulation*. Boulder, Colorado: Paladin Press, 2001.

————. *Mind-Manipulation: Ancient and Modern Ninja Techniques*. New York: Citadel Press, 2002a.

————. *Shadowhand: History and Secrets of Ninja Taisavaki*. Boulder, Colorado: Paladin Press, 2002b.

————. *Theatre of Hell*. Port Townsend, Washington: Loompanics Unlimited, 2003.

————. *Ninja Shadowhand: The Art of Invisibility*. New York: Citadel Press, 2004.

MacGregor Ministries. "News and Views in the World of Cults." Pamphlet. Canada: 1998.

Machiavelli, Niccolò. *The Prince*. 1513. (misc. trans.)

————. *Discourses*. 1531. (misc. trans.)

Miller, William A. *Make Friends with Your Shadow: How to Accept and Use Positively the Negative Side of Your Personality*. Augsburg Publishing House, Minnesota, 1981.

Musashi, Miyamoto. *Go Rin No Sho (A Book of Five Rings)*. (misc. trans.)

Norris, Chuck. *The Secret Power Within: Zen Solutions to Real Problems*. New York: Little, Brown and Company, 1998.

Omar, Ralf Dean. "Ninja Death Touch: The Fact and the Fiction." *Black Belt*, Sept. 1989.

————. *Death on Your Doorstep*. Ohio: Alpha Publications, 1993.

————. *Prison Killing Techniques: Blade, Bludgeon, and Bomb*. Port Townsend, Washington: Loompanics Unlimited, 2001.

Pearsall, Paul. *Superimmunity: Master Your Emotions and Improve Your Health*. New York: McGraw-Hill, 1987.

Piaget, Gerald W. *Control Freaks: Who They Are and How to Stop Them from Running Your Life*. New York: Doubleday, 1991.

Poundstone, William. *Biggest Secrets*. New York: William Morrow and Company, 1993.

Price, Robert M. "Of Myth and Men." *Free Inquiry*, Winter 1999. Vol. 20, No. 1.

Protocols of the Wisemen of Zion. (misc. trans.)

Ringer, Robert J. *Winning Through Intimidation*. Crest/Fawcett, 1993.

Ripley's Believe It or Not! Special Edition, by Mary Packard. Scholastic, Inc. 2001.

Sato, Hiroaki, tr. *The Sword and the Mind*. New York: Overlook Press, 1985.

Shapiro, Ronald M. "How to Negotiate So Everybody Wins." *Bottom Line/Personal*, Oct. 1, 2001.

Shulman, Dan. "The Biology of Benevolence." *Psychology Today*, Dec. 2002.

Shulman, Polly. "Liar Liar Pants on Fire." *Popular Science*, Aug. 2002. 54–60.

Skinner, Dirk. *Street Ninja*. New York: Barricade Books, 1995.

Sun Tzu. *Ping Fa (Art of War)*. (misc. trans.)

Temes, Roberta. *The Complete Idiot's Guide to Hypnosis*. Indiana: Alpha Books, 2000.

Vankin, Jonathan. *Conspiracies, Cover-ups and Crimes: Political Manipulation and Mind Control in America*. New York: Paragon House, 1992.

Von Hammer, Joseph. *The History of the Assassins*. 1935.

Whitlock, Chuck. *Chuck Whitlock's Scam School*. New York: MacMillan, 1997.

Young, Lailan. *Secrets of the Face*. New York: Little, Brown and Company, 1986.

Yoritomo, Taishi. *Influence: How to Exert It*. 1916. Translation by B. Dangennes. Kessinger Publications Company.

About the Author

Dr. Haha Lung is the author of more than a dozen books on mysterious cults of the East, including *The Ancient Art of Strangulation* (1995), *Assassin!* (1997), *Knights of Darkness* (1998), and *Cao Dai Kung-fu* (2002).